DATE			

MEDICAL CARE
IN THE UNITED STATES

The Debate Before 1940
A documentary series, reproducing
in facsimile the most important
primary sources on medical care
in the United States to 1940

EDITED BY
Charles E. Rosenberg
UNIVERSITY OF PENNSYLVANIA

A GARLAND SERIES

Germs Have No Color Line

BLACKS AND AMERICAN MEDICINE   1900–1940

Vanessa Northington Gamble, M.D.

Garland Publishing, Inc.
NEW YORK & LONDON 1989

IIntroduction copyright © 1989 by Vanessa Northington Gamble

Library of Congress Cataloging-in-Publication Data

Germs have no color line : blacks and American medicine, 1900-1945 / edited with an introduction by Vanessa Northington Gamble.
p. cm. — (Medical care in the United States)
Collection of articles reprinted from various sources, originally published, 1900-1945.
Includes bibliographies..
ISBN 0-8240-8333-4 (alk. paper)
1. Afro-Americans—Health and hygiene.   2. Afro-Americans—Medical care.   I. Gamble, Vanessa Northington. II. Series.
[DNLM: 1. Blacks—collected works. 2. Public Health—United States—collected works. 3. Tuberculosis—ethnology—United States—collected works. WA 300 G375]
RA 448.5.N4G47   1988
362.1'08996073—dc19
DNLM/DLC
for Library of Congress   88-37413

Printed on acid-free, 250-year-life paper

Manufactured in the United States of America

CONTENTS

INTRODUCTION

In the Fall of 1929, supporters of Provident Hospital, a black hospital in Chicago, launched a campaign to raise funds to create a center of black medical education at the institution. The slogan of the campaign, "Germs Have No Color Line," was well chosen. It served to remind potential white donors that, if not for humanitarian reasons, then at least for self-protection, the improvement of black health care deserved their financial support. It also echoed concerns voiced by many white physicians, especially those in the South, that the diseases of black Americans posed a threat to white Americans. By 1900, medical and public health authorities, both black and white, agreed that the health status of blacks was much poorer than that of whites. They disagreed, however, on causes and solutions.

This volume examines the "Negro health problem" as it was detailed and debated within the pages of medical, public health, and social science journals from 1900 to 1940. It contains documents that focus on three questions: What was the nature of the black health problem? What were thought to be its causes? And what strategies were proposed to improve black health within a segregated society? The volume concentrates on tuberculosis, also known as consumption. The extraordinarily high incidence of tuberculosis in black people led to many public health efforts to contain the disease in this population. It also resulted in much medical writing on the subject. This disease, more than any other, illuminates the issues and controversies that surrounded the improvement of black health care during the first four decades of the twentieth century.

The Negro Health Problem: What Was It?

In the years before World War II, medical and public health commentators painted a bleak picture of the health of black people.[1] They reported that blacks succumbed to several diseases at a much greater rate than whites. These diseases included tuberculosis, cardiovascular disease, pneumonia, syphilis, and pellagra. In 1920, the tuberculosis rate per 100,000 was 85.7 for whites and 202 for blacks; the pneumonia rate per 100,000 was 97.1 for whites and 145.9 for blacks; and the heart disease rate per 100,000 was 93.1 for whites and 126.4 for blacks.[2] During the period 1929–1931, the life expectancy for black males was 47.5 years and for black females 49.5, as compared to 59.3 years for white males and 62.8 for white females.[3] In 1930, the black death rate was 82 percent higher than the white.[4] Difficulties with diagnosis and the reporting of disease make the accuracy of some of these data questionable. Nonetheless, the central point remains valid: medical and public health experts firmly believed that black Americans were less healthy than white Americans.

This discrepancy in the health of blacks and whites prompted attention from medical and public health authorities, especially those in the South. In writings published during Reconstruction, white Southern physicians maintained that emancipation had led to a widening of this gap. Slaves, they argued, had led idyllic lives. Moreover, the increased disease and death rates that followed the Civil War demonstrated that the race could not take care of itself without the strict supervision of white people. This argument maintained that the inferior constitutions of blacks led them to lead lives of self-indulgence and dissipation. Freedom revealed their proclivity for sexual promiscuity and alcohol and their ignorance of the rules of cleanliness and personal hygiene. Consequently blacks were less healthy than they had been during slavery and died in far greater numbers. The physicians further suggested that the increased mortality rates would solve the race problem because blacks were headed for extinction.[5]

By the turn of the century, this pessimistic view of the future of blacks found fewer adherents within the medical and public health communities. It had become clearer that, although the percentage of the American population that was black had declined, the absolute number of blacks had increased.[6] The fatalistic predictions were replaced by the belief that blacks, no matter how diseased, would be permanent members of American society. And with this change in opinion, the poor health status of black people was seen, not as a solution, but as a problem. Furthermore, the increased black migration from the South to the cities of the North and Midwest made the black health problem a national, not just regional, dilemma.

Self-interest mandated that whites not totally neglect the health problems of blacks. Dr. Seale Harris, a physician and public health officer from Bullock County, Alabama, warned his colleagues:

> If for no other reason than that of self-protection, it is high time that the whites
> of the South, . . . should take steps to prevent the continued spread of
> tuberculosis among negroes.[7]

At the 1914 meeting of the American Public Health Association, Georgia physician, L.C. Allen, called the black health problem "the white man's burden." He noted that the health statuses of the black and white citizens were inextricably linked because "disease germs are the most democratic creatures in the world; they know no distinction of 'race, color, or previous condition of servitude.'"[8]

Calls to improve the health status of blacks were not limited to Southern physicians. Philadelphia physician, H. R. M. Landis, observed that blacks had excessively high rates of tuberculosis and that their employment as cooks, nurses, maids, laundresses, made them a menace to the white community. Measures to control the disease among whites, therefore, had to include programs aimed at blacks.[9] Edwin Embree, President of the Julius Rosenwald Fund, a Chicago-based foundation that maintained an extensive Negro Health Program, reiterated the servant connection. He noted that even whites who adamantly refused any social contact with blacks were at risk because of their close personal relationships with nannies and maids. "Bacteria have a disconcerting fashion of ignoring segregation edicts." he warned. "Jim Crow laws have never successfully been set up for the germs of tuberculosis, pneumonia, typhoid or malaria."[10]

The image of hordes of diseased blacks with "death-dealing micro-organisms at their hands"[11] and the threat they posed was overexaggerated. But it served a purpose. Fear forced whites not to totally ignore the health care needs of black people. At the same time, however, this approach defined the black health problem in terms of the needs and interests of whites. Blacks were depicted more as public health pests than as the hapless victims of disease.[12]

Black physicians took a different stance. Dr. Edward Mayfield Boyle, of Washington, D.C., assailed the literature that promoted the dogma that the black race was "like the fly, the mosquito, the rats, and mice, an arch-carrier of disease germs to white people."[13] Black physicians agreed that members of their race had higher morbidity and mortality rates for certain diseases, but criticized the inferences made from such data. They did not believe that these rates reflected physiological inferiority, but rather social pathology. The ill health of the race was due to poverty and discrimination. In addition, black physicians harshly criticized theories that were promulgated under the objective guise of science, but were influenced by racial prejudice. If higher morbidity and mortality rates indicated inferiority, they questioned, why were conditions that affected whites disproportionately—for example polio and suicide—not considered signs of white inferiority?[14]

Black physicians, social scientists, and activists considered this high incidence of disease to be one of the most serious dilemmas faced by the black community. They realized that efforts to improve the plight of black Americans would prove fruitless unless the community's health problems were addressed. In a speech before the John A. Andrew Clinical Society, a black medical association, Dr. G.N. Woodward reminded his colleagues of the importance of public health activities. He argued that racial progress was impossible in a race handicapped by disease and by impaired health.[15] On a similar note, Dr. Algernon B. Jackson, Director of the School of Public Health at Howard University School of Medicine, observed that "the economic and social progress of any people shall always be measured in terms of its health and physical well-being."[16] The black community viewed its health problems as a social dilemma of monumental proportions that jeopardized the race's social, political, and economic advancement.

Black Susceptibility to Tuberculosis: Race or Environment?

In 1920, the tuberculosis death rates for blacks was 2.7 times the white in South Carolina and 2.3 times the white in North Carolina.[17] These excessive rates were not limited to the South. Between 1910 and 1920 the proportion of blacks in Philadelphia who contracted the disease was four to six times that of whites.[18] These statistics led one white observer to call the disease "the principal agent which threatened the extinction of our 'brother in black.'"[19] The black community also recognized the danger posed by tuberculosis. W.E.B. DuBois, the noted black social scientist, observed that "the greatest enemy of the black race is consumption."[20]

Physicians and public health experts sought to explain these high morbidity and mortality rates of black Americans. However, they did not agree on causation. Some observers held genetic and racial characteristics responsible, while others pointed to environmental factors. A third group viewed an interplay of racial characteristics and environmental factors as the basis. An examination of this debate illuminates the divergent, and sometimes conflicting, explanations and solutions to the black health problem.[21]

Robert Koch isolated the tubercle bacillus as the causative agent of tuberculosis in 1882. By the turn of the century, most physicians had accepted the germ theory. They did not, however, believe that it adequately explained the increased morbidity and mortality from tuberculosis in black populations. They sought alternative hypotheses that did not refute the germ theory, but would identify contributory factors that either lowered the body's resistance or increased its exposure to the bacillus.

Medical and public health authorities were especially concerned about the apparent increase in tuberculosis in blacks that followed emancipation. Some southern physicians went so far as to say that they had never seen a case of the disease in blacks before the Civil War.[22] It was generally accepted, even by black observers, that tuberculosis had increased in blacks after the War. Although it is difficult to determine accurately, the incidence of the disease probably did increase because of the migration of blacks from isolated plantations to congested cities.

Hereditarians pointed to anatomical and physiological differences or to innate mental characteristics to explain the differences in racial mortality. The work of Frederick L. Hoffman, a statistician at the Prudential Insurance Company of America, formed the basis of much of the hereditarian ideology. Hoffman, in his influential 1896 monograph, *Race Traits and Tendencies of the American Negro,* asserted that blacks were inherently susceptible to certain diseases, including tuberculosis.[23] Dr. Seale Harris, for example, quoting Hoffman, alleged that blacks had less developed lung tissue and accessory muscles of respiration. "This physiological difference," he wrote, "no doubt accounts for, in a measure, the inordinate mortality from consumption, pneumonia, and the other pulmonary diseases among the negro."[24] Dr. Thomas J. Mays also believed that the inheritance of innate physical characteristics was key. In a 1904 article, "Human Slavery as a Prevention of Pulmonary Consumption," he contended that the former slaves lacked "the organized constitutional or mental strength" to cope with the demands of independence.[25] He noted that an impaired nervous system had resulted not only in an increase of tuberculosis but also of insanity.[26]

In a February 1915 address before a black church group, Dr. J. Madison Taylor, a white physician, also expressed hereditarian views.[27] He asserted that racial traits determined the health of black people. Taylor, assistant professor of nonpharmaceutical therapeutics at Temple University Medical School, stated that blacks and whites had totally different racial characteristics and conformations. Blacks, the physician informed his audience, were susceptible to tuberculosis because they were structurally maladapted to live in northern cities. He concluded, "In order that the Afro-American . . . survive or even . . . maintain a fair measure of health, it is imperative that he shall keep out of the big cities and live in the open country."[28] Taylor asserted that his arguments were based on the latest scientific knowledge, but the increased migration of blacks to Philadelphia no doubt played a role in his statements. It is also important to note that Taylors remarks appeared in the *Journal of the National Medical Association,* a publication of the black medical society. In an editorial that accompanied the article, the journal's editors refuted his claims that blacks were in danger of becoming extinct.[29] However, they defended their publication of the controversial article because it provided "food for thought."[30]

Most observers of the black health problem did not think that the inheritance of anatomical and physiological characteristics were principal factors in explaining the black tuberculosis rates. They focused instead on lifestyle and environmental considerations. The explanations were not always straightforward. Even some hereditarians included environmental factors in their arguments. For example, Dr. Seale Harris, offered contradictory explanations. Not only did he believe that racial characteristics were important, he also asserted that "the great prevalence of tuberculosis is not so much due to any inherited tendency to the disease as to their [blacks] habits and environment, which render their tissues less resistant to the tubercle bacilli."[31]

Proponents of environmental causation argued that the increase in the black tuberculosis rate after the Civil War confirmed their theory. The War had not changed any inherent physical characteristics of slaves; it had only altered their environment and mode of living. However, environmental explanations were not homogeneous. They ranged from narrow interpretations that found moral deficiencies and individual actions responsible for the excessive death rates to broader interpretations that attributed the rates to social and economic factors.

Many white observers contended that the living conditions of freedmen were more harsh than those of slaves and that this had led to the increase in tuberculosis. Slaves, the argument went, had been well cared for on the plantations and had been provided with adequate food, housing, and medical care. It was in the master's best interest to do so because "a sickly negro was of very little value—a dead negro none."[32] According to these authors, the healthy mode of living found in slavery had made blacks resistant to the ravages of the tubercle bacillus.

The comments of Dr. H.J. Achard of Chicago were representative of these sentiments. He reported that after years of "enforced work," freedmen took an unaccustomed rest that drastically changed their existences from the idyllic ones that they had had as slaves. Their lives now included "dirt, irregular living, alternating between stuffing and starving, excesses of various kinds, often indulgence in alcohol, crowded, unventilated quarters and insufficient clothing."[33] Achard claimed that this mode of living had enabled blacks to become "tuberculized" or establish contact with the disease.

Many white authors who supported environmental causation also held blacks responsible for their poor health. Consistent with traditional views of public health, they argued that immorality was a principal factor that influenced the health of a people. Debauchery and ignorance, they argued, made the body less resistant to disease. They criticized blacks for living in ignorance of the rules of personal and community hygiene and looked upon their deplorable living conditions with disdain. These writers maintained that the "excessive and corrupt immorality"[34] of blacks made apparent by emancipation was responsible for the increase in tuberculosis and other diseases such as syphilis and pneumonia. They made little mention of the hostile social and racial climate in which the former slaves found themselves.

Black physicians, public health experts, and social activists challenged these theories of black predisposition to disease and espoused broader interpretations. They considered external social and economic factors to be the primary determinants. A 1906 monograph, *The Health and Physique of the Negro American*, presented the viewpoint of the black intellectual community. W.E.B. DuBois edited the volume as part of the Atlanta University studies of the social status of black Americans. He examined, in detail, the Negro health problem and argued that the differences in morbidity and mortality between blacks and whites were caused not by racial traits, but by social conditions. DuBois emphatically refuted theories of inherent susceptibility and black inferiority. He concluded:

> With improved sanitary conditions, improved education, and better economic opportunities, the mortality of the race may and probably will steadily decrease until it becomes normal.[35]

Other black authors echoed DuBois' conclusions. Dr. Charles A. Lewis of Philadelphia asserted that the health problems of blacks had been caused, in large part, by "an economic set-up that failed to net them a living wage, which in turn fostered improper nourishment." In a 1905 address, Dr. John E. Hunter of the National Association of Colored Physicians and Surgeons reiterated this relationship between economic class and health status.[36] He informed the

American Anti-Tuberculosis League that those blacks who," by reason of industry, education, and morality," had been able to move from the tenements had very low rates of tuberculosis.[37]

Other black observers pointed to white oppression and neglect. Dr. Edward Mayfield Boyle, in a rebuttal to the previously noted remarks of Dr. H. J. Achard, observed:

> Those who once exercised the right of tutelage over 'body and soul' have . . .
> become, in a large measure, the freedmen's oppressors. Whereas during slavery
> Negroes were engaged in all manner of physical endeavors and counted
> efficient as workmen, as freedmen they are vigorously opposed in many a line
> of industry and labor wherein their employent was once indispensable.[38]

Black social critics also noted that although blacks had higher morbidity and mortality rates, and consequently a greater need for health care, they had more restricted access to hospital and sanatorium beds. Dr. Peter Marshall Murray, a prominent black physician, reported in 1930 that one bed existed for every 139 white Americans, but that only one bed existed for every 1,941 black Americans.[39] Many of the beds for black patients were located in separate facilities. Black medical and hospital leaders acknowledged, however, that much of the care offered in these institutions was of inferior quality. The hospitals were hampered not only by the lack of financial resources, but by the exclusion of black physicians from approved postgraduate training programs. Such actions, of course, adversely affected the health of black people.

By defining black susceptibility to tuberculosis in terms of socioeconomic factors, black medical and public health professionals hoped to repudiate medical theories that portrayed their race as inherently "tuberculous." They feared that the acceptance of such beliefs would result in less aggressive intervention on the part of whites, if they thought that blacks were doomed by their heredity. They also believed that it was crucial for social uplift efforts that blacks not view tuberculosis simply as a racial or genetic disease. The remarks of Dr. John P. Turner, secretary of the Philadelphia Academy of Medicine, a black medical society, illustrate this conviction. He wrote:

> The Academy is making him [the Negro] realize . . . that consumption is to a
> large extent, especially in his case, a result of poor housing facilities and poor
> economic conditions. We feel that to give the Negro a new vision, a new hope,
> is to aid him to reduce his mortality through the consciousness that he must
> not have consumption just because he is a Negro.[40]

Black professionals provided an optimistic message: the health problems of black Americans could and should be corrected and prevented. Their work served to remind the black masses that "when the American Negro has attained . . . excellences of living he will be just as healthy as the white man."[41]

As the century progressed, experts, black and white, acknowledged that a multiplicity of medical and environmental factors caused the increased rates of tuberculosis and other diseases in blacks. Increasing numbers of white experts accepted the theory that social and economic factors played primary roles in the disease rates of black Americans. One of the most prominent advocates of this position was Philadelphia physician, Dr. Henry Robert Murray Landis. Landis, a nationally recognized authority on tuberculosis and a founder of the National Tuberculosis Association, established a medical clinic in 1914 to treat blacks at the Henry Phipps

Institute. This clinic pioneered the use of black physicians and nurses, under white supervision, to treat black patients and to conduct educational outreach programs.[42] Landis considered "tuberculosis, more than any other disease a social problem" and included "better housing, a knowledge of dietetics, [and] occupation problems" as part of the armamentarium to battle it.[43]

In 1937, the *Journal of Negro Education* dedicated an entire volume to an examination of the black health problem. The authors, many of them white public health experts and statisticians, underscored the growing acceptance of socioeconomic theories. Dr. Michael M. Davis, a prominent medical economist, reported that poverty was correlated with poor health and inadequate medical care for both low income blacks and whites. However, he noted, "race accentuates the economic problem."[44] Blacks, even with sufficient means, were often denied access to hospitals and sanitoria. S.J. Holmes, a professor of zoology at the University of California, contended that blacks were not constitutionally inferior. Their increased morbidity and mortality were due to an unfavorable economic and educational status. But, "inherited racial peculiarities" still played a role.[45] Racial characteristics determined which diseases most affected blacks. In the same volume, Louis I. Dublin, a statistician at Metropolitan Life Insurance Company, reported on a study of black health conducted by the company.[46] The study demonstrated that the health status of blacks continued to lag behind that of whites. Dublin attributed the health problems of blacks primarily to socioeconomic factors: poverty, ignorance, and lack of proper medical care. However, he too acknowledged that racial susceptibility to particular diseases could not be totally discounted. Dublin's study also offered reason for optimism. He noted that the death rates for black policyholders declined 35 percent between 1911 and 1935. Dublin hypothesized that this decline resulted from the establishment of successful public health campaigns. By the late 1930s, theories of racial susceptibility had not vanished, but they were no longer viewed by the mainstream medical and public health community as evidence of black inferiority and as the primary determinants of black health status.

Medical and Public Health Solutions in a Segregated Society

Proposals to decrease the disease rates of black people during the first four decades of the twentieth century focused on environmental solutions. The appropriate response to the problem from the hereditarian perspective might have been to do nothing. The race was inherently diseased and was doomed. However, this resolution to the black health problem found few advocates. As Dr. Lawrence Lee reminded his audience at the 1914 convention of the American Public Health Association:

> Every dollar spent in improving the conditions of the negro race benefits the
> whites as well. If the whites and negroes live in the same community the health
> of the whites cannot improve unless the health of the colored also improves.[47]

Medical and public health officials, increasingly cognizant that "germs have no color line," realized that some action had to be taken.

Efforts concentrated on measures to increase the resistance of the black population and to prevent the spread of bacteria. As with causation, remedies varied. Southern extremists even mentioned the reinstitution of slavery. Dr. J.H. Stanley of Beardstown, Tennessee, commented: "I do not know what to suggest for the prophylaxis of tuberculosis in the negroes unless we put them back into slavery, and I do not suppose they would like that very much."[48] Most Southern physicians did not go as far as Dr. Stanley, but they did advocate strong state action as a substitute for slavery. The state, they argued, could isolate those infected with infectious disease and force blacks to leave cities in order to prevent overcrowding. The state could also provide "systematic, *disciplinary* training of his [blacks'] physical, mental, and moral powers."[49]

Most white commentators supported less radical measures. They urged the enforcement of sanitation laws to clean up the tenement housing in which many urban blacks lived. They hoped that white landlords would realize that it was in their self-interest to do so. Since many whites viewed the high rate of tuberculosis and other diseases simply as a result of immorality and ignorance, they urged the development of educational programs to teach blacks moral values: hygiene, thrift, sobriety, and chastity. They made very clear that they were advocating industrial and moral education, not classical education.

White authors also turned their attention to making changes in health care. One suggestion was that more hospitals and sanitaria be made available for black patients. They did not advocate the abolishment of racial barriers. Rather, they urged an increase in the number of beds and an improvement of the quality of care in segregated facilities and separate wards in mixed hospitals. Other proposals focused on the recruitment and training of black physicians and nurses for public health work. These medical personnel would be expected to work under white supervision. Dr. Henry R.M. Landis extolled the benefits of this approach and pointed to the accomplishments of the Henry Phipps Clinic. He maintained

> that those Institutions that make use of Negro doctors and nurses for the
> care of patients of the same race are, from the standpoint of number of patients
> and regularity of their attendance, most successful in the treatment of
> Negro patients.[50]

Black physicians agreed that their involvement was key to the solution of the negro health problem. "The best anti-tuberculosis remedy for the negro," declared Dr. John E. Hunter, "is the negro doctor."[51] But racial discrimination restricted the medical world of black physicians to separate, though never equal institutions—medical societies, medical schools, and hospitals. By the 1920s, the future of this world looked bleak. The growing importance of hospital standardization and accreditation threatened to eliminate the black hospital, and with it, the black physician's professional existence. In response, a group of black medical leaders associated primarily with the National Medical Association or NMA, a black medical society, and the National Hospital Association or NHA, an organization of black hospitals, launched a black hospital reform movement.[52] They hoped to achieve a "Negro Hospital Renaissance" by improving the educational and medical programs at black hospitals and by increasing the quality and quantity of hospital beds for black patients.[53]

Black physicians contended that their efforts to increase their professional opportunities would improve the health and social status of their people. Dr. Algernon B. Jackson, a professor of public health at Howard University, observed:

> The successful operation of hospitals among our people is doing much to bring
> about a higher degree of racial respect and goodwill, all of which breed a
> confidence and faith in the profession which is destined to lead our race to a
> higher level, socially and economically.[54]

Thus, the physicians' efforts throughout the 1920s and 1930s to improve the quality of black hospitals, nurse training schools, and medical schools, represented not only an attempt to promote the interests of the blacks masses, but their own professional interests.

Black observers also encouraged the development of black self-help activities.[55] The foremost example of such an endeavor was National Negro Health Week. The annual event had been established in 1914 by the National Negro Business League whose president was Booker T. Washington. The goal of the National Negro Health Week was to teach blacks about the principles of public health and hygiene in order to help them become stronger and more effective citizens. Its activities included lectures in churches and schools and the formation of brigades to clean neighborhoods.

Black commentators proposed strategies that were similar to those offered by moderate whites. They focused on educational programs, enforcement of sanitation laws, the strengthening of the black medical profession and institutions, and improvement in the access of black patients to hospitals and sanitoria. Black authors acknowledged that white support was indispensable for any efforts to improve black health care. However, they urged their white colleagues to be more sophisticated in their approaches to black patients. In a 1933 speech at the annual meeting of the American Public Health Association, Dr. Midian O. Bousfield, first vice-president and medical director of Supreme Liberty Life Insurance Company, one of America's most prosperous black businesses, offered some suggestions on improving public health activities in the black population.[56] He emphasized that any campaign had to demonstrate respect for the community and its goals. He urged that black community organizations be consulted before the initiation of any programs. He further instructed:

> It is well in speech making to make no reference to the race question. Leave
> out former experiences with colored people, forego any expression of your own
> lack of prejudice and omit the 'darky' story in dialect.[57]

Although black physicians and activists recognized the adverse effects of a segregated medical care system, most did not call for its dismantlement as a solution to the health problems of Afro-Americans. They advocated programs and activities that accepted the existence of separate facilities. This accommodationist position, exemplified by the National Medical Association and the National Hospital Association, emphasized black self-reliance, the development of black social institutions, and the avoidance of political activism on the issue of social equality. These physicians claimed that their programs represented a practical response to the racial realities of American life in the 1920s and 1930s. They agreed that separate institutions were necessary because integration was a slow process and the ill health of the race demanded immediate solutions.

The black medical community was not unified on this political ideology. A small, but uncompromising, group of integrationists rejected the existence of segregated medical facilities and programs. They advocated instead the complete equality of blacks into American society. Dr. Louis T. Wright, one of the first black physicians on the staff of Harlem Hospital and chairman of the board of trustees of the National Association for the Advancement of Colored People, was one of the most vocal proponents of integrationism.[58] At a 1938 hearing on national health insurance, he decried the existence of segregation in medical care.

It is hoped at this time that the American people will begin to realize that the

health of the American Negro is not a separate racial problem to be met by
separate segregated set-ups or dealt with on a dual standard basis, but that
it is an American problem that should be adequately and equitably handled
by the identical agencies and met with identical methods as the health of the
remainder of the population.[59]

Despite the vigorous campaign waged by Wright and his supporters, the accommodationists position prevailed within the black medical community until after World War II.

In the postwar years, the energies of black medical associations, even those that had previously espoused accommodationism, shifted toward the dismantlement of the "Negro medical ghetto." The organizations now recognized that segregated health care facilities contributed to the poor health status of black Americans. These institutions, they insisted, could not adequately meet the health and professional needs of black people. Ultimately the efforts of the medical civil rights activists led to legislative and judicial prohibitions against racial discrimination in medical facilities.

The civil rights movement, despite its many achievements, did not completely solve the health problems of black Americans. In 1985, a report issued by the Secretary of the Department of Health and Human Services, Margaret M. Heckler, documented that although gains had been made, the health status of blacks continued to lag behind that of whites.[60] The reasons behind these disparities varied and included genetic predisposition, socioeconomic status, and inadequate access to care. It is clear that these contemporary explanations have their historical roots from an earlier period when the "Negro health problem" was at the forefront of the national public health agenda.

Vanessa Northington Gamble, M.D., Ph.D.

Notes

1. Extensive discussions about the health status of black Americans before World War II can be found in Edward H. Beardsley, *A History of Neglect: Health Care for Blacks and Mill Workers in the Twentieth Century South* (Knoxville: University of Tennessee Press, 1987) and Douglas C. Ewbank, "History of Black Mortality and Health Before 1940," *Milbank Quarterly* 65 supplement 1(1987):100–28.

2. Charles S. Johnson, "Negro Health in the Light of Vital Statistics," *Proceedings of the National Conference of Social Work* 55 (1928):174.

3. Louis I. Dublin, "The Problem of Negro Health as Revealed by Vital Statistics," *Journal of Negro Education* 6 (1937): 269.

4. Ibid., p. 269.

5. John S. Haller, Jr., "The Physician Versus the Negro," in his *Outcasts from Evolution: Scientific Attitudes of Racial Inferiority, 1859--900* (New York: McGraw-Hill, 1971): 40–68.

6. Edwin R. Embree, "Negro Health and Its Effect Upon the Nation's Health," *Modern Hospital* 30 (April 1928): 52.

7. Seale Harris, "Tuberculosis in the Negro," *Journal of the American Medical Association* 41 (1903): 827.

8. L. C. Allen, "The Negro Health Problem," *American Journal of Public Health*, 5 (1915): 194.

9. H.R.M. Landis, "The Tuberculosis Problem and the Negro," *Virginia Medical Monthly*, 49 (1923): 561–66.

10. Embree, "Negro Health," p. 345.

11. E. H.Jones, "Tuberculosis in the Negro," *Transactions of the Tennessee State Medical Association* (1907): 175.

12. For example see C.E. Terry, "The Negro, a Public Health Problem," *Southern Medical Journal* 7 (1914): 458–67.

13. Edward Mayfield Boyle, "A Comparative Physical Study of the Negro," *Journal of the National Medical Association* 4 (1912): 125.

14. Edward Mayfield Boyle, "The Negro and Tuberculosis," *Journal of the National Medical Association* 4 (1912): 345.

15. G.N. Woodward, "Racial Health," *Journal of the National Medical Association* 16 (1924): 178.

16. Algernon Brashear Jackson, "Public Health and the Negro," *Journal of the National Medical Association* 15 (1923): 258.

17. Beardsley, *A History of Neglect*, p. 13.

18. David McBride, "The Henry Phipps Institute, 1903–1937: Pioneering Tuberculosis Work with an Urban Minority," *Bulletin of the History of Medicine* 61 (Spring 1981): 78.

19. Harris, "Tuberculosis in the Negro" p. 438.

20. W.E. Burghardt DuBois, ed., *The Health and Physique of the Negro American* (Atlanta: Atlanta University Press, 1906), p.73.

21. For detailed discussions of race and tuberculosis see Marion M. Torchia, "The Tuberculosis Movement and the Race Question, 1890–1950," *Bulletin of the History of Medicine* 49 (1975): 152–68 and Marion M. Torchia, "Tuberculosis Among American Negroes: Medical Research on a Racial Disease, 1830–1950," 32 (1977): 252–79.

22. For example see Allen, "The Negro Health Problem"; Harris, "Tuberculosis in the Negro"; and Thomas J. Mays, "Human Slavery as a Prevention of Pulmonary Consumption," *Transactions of the American Climatological Association* 20 (1904): 192–7.

23. Frederick L. Hoffman, *Race Traits and Tendencies of the American Negro* (New York: American Economic Association, 1896).

24. Harris, "Tuberculosis in the Negro," p. 835.

25. Mays, "Human Slavery," p. 194.

26. Ibid., pp. 193–94.

27. J. Madison Taylor, "Remarks on the Health of Colored People," *Journal of the National Medical Association* 7 (1915): 160–63.

28. Ibid., p. 162.

29. "Editorial: On Dr. Taylor of Philadelphia," *Journal of the National Medical Association* 7 (1915):

30. Ibid., p. 206.

31. Harris, "Tuberculosis in the Negro," p. 835.

32. Allen, "The Negro Health Problem," p. 195.

33. H.J. Achard, "Tuberculization of the Negro," *Journal of the National Medical Association* 4 (1912): 225.

34. Northern, "Tuberculosis Among Negroes," *Journal of the Southern Medical Association* 6 (1909): 412.

35. DuBois, *The Health and Physique of the Negro American,* p. 90. When DuBois became editor of *Crisis,* a publication of the National Association for the Advancement of Colored People, he continued his interest in health care. For example, see his "The Health of Black Folk," *Crisis* 40 (1933): 31.

36. John E. Hunter, "Tuberculosis in the Negro: Causes and Treatment," *Colorado Medical Journal* 11 (1905): 250–57.

37. Ibid., p. 251.

38. Boyle, "The Negro and Tuberculosis," p. 347.

39. Peter Marshall Murray, "Hospital Provision for the Negro Race," *Bulletin of the American Hospital Association* 4 (1930): 37.

40. Henry M. Minton, "The Part the Negro Is Playing in the Reduction of Mortality," *Hospital Social Service* 10 (1924): 13.

41. Boyle, "The Negro and Tuberculosis," p. 348.

42. For a history of this clinic see David McBride, "The Henry Phipps Institute, 1903–1937: Pioneering Tuberculosis Work with an Urban Minority," *Bulletin of the History of Medicine* 61 (Spring 1987): 78–97. For an earlier account of the work at the Phipps Clinic see Henry M. Minton, "The Part the Negro Is Playing in the Reduction of Mortality," pp. 10–16. Minton, in 1914, became the first black physician at the clinic.

43. McBride, "Henry Phipps Institute," p. 93.

44. Michael M. Davis, "Problems of Health Services for Negroes," *Journal of Negro Education* 6 (1937):441.

45. S.J. Holmes, "The Principal Causes of Death Among Negroes: A General Comparative Statement," *Journal of Negro Education* 6 (1937): 302.

46. Dublin, "The Problem of Negro Health as Revealed by Vital Statistics," p. 268–75.

47. Lawrence Lee, "The Negro as a Problem in Public Health Charity," *American Journal of Public Health* 5 (1915): 210–11.

48. "Discussion on the Paper of Dr. Jones," *Transactions of the Tennessee State Medical Association* (1907): 179.

49. Allen, "The Negro Health Problem," p. 203.

50. Landis, "The Tuberculosis Problem and the Negro," p. 566.

51. Hunter, "Tuberculosis in the Negro," p. 255.

52. For a comprehensive overview of the black hospital reform movement see Vanessa Northington Gamble, "The Negro Hospital Renaissance: The Black Hospital Movement: 1920–1940" (Ph.D. thesis, University of Pennsylvania, 1987). For a contemporary account of the movement see Murray, "Hospital Provision for the Negro Race," pp. 37–46.

53. John A. Kenney, "The Negro Hospital Renaissance," *Journal of the National Medical Association* 22 (1930): 109–12.

54. Jackson, "Public Health and the Negro," p. 258.

55. For examples see Dennis A. Bethea, "Some Significant Negro Movements to Lower Their Mortality," *Journal of the National Medical Association* 22 (1930): 85–88; M. O. Bousfield, "Reaching the Negro Community," *American Journal of Public Health* 24 (1934): 209–215; and Minton, "The Part the Negro Is Playing in the Reduction of Mortality," pp. 10–6.

56. Bousfield, "Reaching The Negro Community," pp. 209-15.

57. Ibid., p. 211.

58. For example see Louis T. Wright, "Health Problems of the Negro," *Interracial Review* 8 (January 1935): 6–8.

59. Interdepartmental Committee to Coordinate Health and Welfare Activities, *Proceedings of the National Health Conference,* July 18, 19, 20, 1938, p. 87.

60. United States Department of Health and Human Services, *Report of the Secretary's Task Force on Black and Minority Health, Volume I: Executive Summary,* (Washington: Government Printing Office, 1985).

TUBERCULOSIS IN THE NEGRO.*

SEALE HARRIS, M.D.

Health Officer of Bullock County from 1895 to 1903; President of the Southeastern Alabama Medical League; Councilor of the Alabama State Medical Association.

UNION SPRINGS, ALA.

Tuberculosis was a rare disease among the slaves in the southern states, yet, after a little more than a quarter of a century, it causes more deaths among the emancipated negroes than all the other infectious diseases. The negro death rate from tuberculosis is more than three times that of the whites from the same disease.

These statements, as startling to some as they are true, announce the motive which induced me to select for my theme on this occasion, "Tuberculosis in the Negro"; and if I can be the means of inciting any of you to consider the causes of this enormous mortality from that disease in the negro race and the measures to be taken for their relief, the objects of this paper will have been attained.

From the best information which I can gather, tuberculosis is unknown among the savage tribes in the interior of Africa. It is also unquestionably true that the negroes along the west coast of Africa were not affected by tuberculosis until the infection was carried there by the slave traders and colonists. However, since their exposure to the infection, the negroes in their native clime are not only more susceptible to tuberculosis than the white colonists who reside there, but the disease is more fatal among them. This is shown by the following table (Dr. Rudolph Matas, "The Surgical Peculiarities of the Negro"), which gives the mortality from tuberculosis in the English colonies for the negroes and whites on a basis of each 1,000 deaths:

	English.	Negroes.
Jamaica	7.5	10.3
Dominica	8.3	16.8
Guiana	6.4	17.9
Ceylon	4.9	10.5
Gibraltar	5.3	43.0

Tuberculosis was so rare among the slaves in the southern states that some physicians contended that the negro was immune to tuberculosis. I have heard large slave owners, and several physicians who had large

* Read at the Fifty-fourth Annual Session of the American Medical Association, in the Section on Practice of Medicine, and approved for publication by the Executive Committee: Drs. J. M. Anders, Frank A. Jones and W. S. Thayer.

practices among the slaves in Georgia and Alabama, say that they never knew of a case of consumption among the negroes prior to the war. The disease was so rare that in 1830 a Cincinnati physician reported a case of a negro with "undoubted consumption," in which the autopsy showed "unmistakable evidences of the disease." There were no doubt a few cases among the slaves, but the disease was rare and confined almost entirely to the slaves in the cities, where they were overcrowded and the sanitary conditions were bad. The fact that there were so few cases of tuberculosis among the negroes while they were slaves was a great triumph of intelligent, though enforced, hygiene, and it also proves that tuberculosis is a preventable disease, because prior to the war it was not of infrequent occurrence among the whites of the South. That consumption is almost a scourge to the emancipated negro we all know, and the only reason why it was not so with the slaves was that their habits and sanitary surroundings were better than those of many of their masters.

Because of their indolence and improvidence, I am sure that the majority of negroes in the South do not get a sufficient amount of the proper nourishing food and the other necessities of life on which to maintain health and vitality up to the normal, and such lack of nutrition, added to the worst possible ignorance and carelessness pertaining to personal hygiene, renders his tissues less resistant to bacterial infection of all kinds. In other words, it makes the tissues of the negro a suitable pabulum or soil for the invasion and propagation of the bacillus of tuberculosis. We also know that unless the tuberculous subject is well nourished he has but little hopes of recovery, and I am sure that one of the reasons why there are so few recoveries from tuberculosis in the negro race is that, as a rule, they are not provided with a sufficient quantity of palatable and nutritious food.

The following statistics of Charleston, S. C., which have been accurately kept for many years, show the increase in tuberculosis among the negroes since their emancipation: In 1860 the negro death rate was the same as for the whites, i. e., 12.00 per 1,000. The last census gives the white death rate in that city as 21.4, and the negro death rate of 43.1 per 1,000 of population. The deaths from "consumption," calculated at ten-year intervals, were in 1865, whites 57, negroes 74; 1875, whites, 54, negroes, 132; 1885, whites 57, negroes 209; and in 1895, whites 39, negroes 194. Estimated population in 1895 was, whites, 28,870; negroes, 36,295.

The census returns for the year 1900 show, in the "registration area," in which the statistics may be regarded as fairly accurate, that for every 100,000 of population there died from "consumption" 126.5 native whites and 485.0 of negroes.

I regret that I am unable to give any statistics regarding the mortality from tuberculosis in Alabama and the other southern states. I studied the census returns carefully and found but little that I thought would be of interest or value. The following letter came to my relief, and caused me to destroy most of the data which I had compiled from the census report, and I quote from it to show the fallacy of deductions based on mortality statistics of the United States Census Report, except those for the "registration area":

CENSUS OFFICE, WASHINGTON, D. C., Sept. 20, 1902.
Dr. Seale Harris, Union Springs, Ala.

Dear Sir:—I regret to state that this office can not furnish you any data that are of any value concerning either the general death-rate of the white and colored in the United States as a whole, the southern states, or for South Carolina and Alabama individually, or the mortality of these classes from tuberculosis.

The return of deaths in all of the southern states and in most of the other states was secured by inquiry of the enumerators, and falls very far short of being complete. In fact, the return is absolutely worthless for the purpose of computing death rates and any conclusions based on them would be erroneous. It is only in those states and cities that have efficient systems of registering deaths that we are able to secure anything like a correct return of the deaths that actually occur which can be utilized for determining the death rates. Unfortunately, there are no southern states, and very few cities which have a complete system of registration, and prior to 1890 this source of information was not utilized in any way in census statistics. Very respectfully,

W. A. KING, Chief Statistician.

The statistics for some of the southern cities are regarded as being as accurate as those for the registration area, and below I give reports of five representative southern cities:

	RATES PER 1,000 OF POPULATION.							
	All Causes.				Tubercular Diseases.			
	1890.		1900.		1890.		1900.	
	Wh.	N.	Wh.	N.	Wh.	N.	Wh.	N.
New Orleans	24.8	39.4	20.7	39.7	2.50	5.87	2.38	6.13
Mobile, Ala.	21.5	34.5	21.0	32.5	3.04	6.08	3.08	6.09
Charleston, S. C.	21.4	42.2	21.4	43.1	3.55	6.86	1.65	6.21
Savannah, Ga.	24.7	37.8	22.6	42.2	3.71	5.44	2.64	4.91
Richmond, Va.	22.3	37.6	18.1	32.8	2.30	4.11	2.05	3.94

The statistics which I have collected for Union Springs, with an equal population of whites and negroes, and which I think are reliable, show that in the past eight years there have died from tuberculosis fourteen whites and thirty-nine blacks; and of the considerable number of negro deaths reported with the cause of death unknown, I am sure that several died of tuberculosis. I do not know of any other statistics of any value for the small towns or rural districts of the South, for the reasons that the majority of deaths occur without the attendance of a physician, and are reported by midwives and undertakers, who know nothing of the causes of death.

The great prevalence of tuberculosis is not so much due to any inherent tendency to the disease as to their habits and environments, which render their tissues less resistant to the tubercle bacilli, and for the same reasons they fall easy victims to its ravages. However, it is no doubt true that there is a less development of lung tissue and the accessory muscles of respiration among the negroes than for the whites. Dr. McDowell, a surgeon in the United States Army, made frequent autopsies on white and colored troops during the Civil War, from 1861 to 1865. He found that their chest measurements were full (up to the army standard), but their lungs were always lighter and smaller than those contained in the same sized chest among the white troops. The statistics of Otis and Woodward for the same period are interesting. They found a less lung capacity and smaller brain for the negro troops than for the whites. They also found that of whites who contracted tuberculosis during the war, one out of two and one-half died, while of negroes twelve out of thirteen died. Dr. Russell, another army surgeon, states that the average weight of the negro was four ounces less than that of the white.

F. L. Hoffman[1] gives the following interesting table, which he compiled from the report of the Provost-General I), and the reports of the Surgeon-General,

U. S. A., 1893-94-95, which shows the difference in chest expansion of the slaves who entered the army, and of the emancipated negro of thirty years later:

COMPARATIVE CHEST MOBILITY OF U. S. RECRUITS, 1861-65 AND 1892-94.

Age Periods.	U. S. Army, 1861-65.		U. S. Army, 1892-94.	
	White.	Colored.	White.	Colored.
Under 20 years	3.26	3.17*	2.82	2.56*
20 to 24 years	3.25	3.28†	2.86	2.52*
25 to 29 years	3.22	3.25†	2.93	2.62*
30 to 34 years	3.22	3.19*	2.96	2.64*
35 to 39 years	3.26	3.18*	2.94	2.57*
40 to 49 years	3.18	3.34†	2.84	2.52*
All ages	3.24	3.23*	2.93	2.58*

* Excess in favor of white. † Excess in favor of colored.

This table clearly proves that there has been a diminution in the chest expansion of the negro since his release from slavery.

Gould has proven that the average lung capacity of the negro is considerably less than that of the white. Thus, for the average height of 5 feet 8 inches, the pulmonary capacity was for the whites 188.5 cubic inches, for the negro, 167.5 cubic inches—giving a mean difference in favor of the whites of 15.0 cubic inches. The pulmonary capacity of the average chest measuring thirty-six inches in circumference was for the whites 186.5, for the negro, 170.5—thus showing a mean difference of 16 cubic inches in favor of the whites.[2] Dr. R. M. Cunningham[3] has called attention to the "more or less encroachment of the abdominal organs on the thoracic viscera, and for that reason the perpendicular diameter of the chest of the negro is less than that of the same sized white." My observations, carried out on the line of Dr. Cunningham's ideas, from the examination of many healthy chests among the negroes, show that the normal liver dulness on the right side, sometimes extending as high as the fifth rib, and the tympanitic note over the stomach on the left side (Traube's semilunar space) of the negro are higher than that of the whites. I have also noted that Litten's diaphragm phenomenon is less marked in the normal negro than in the white.

Thus all observers agree that there is less development of the lungs of the negro than for the whites, and this physiologic difference no doubt accounts for, in a measure, the inordinate mortality from consumption, pneumonia, and the other pulmonary diseases among the negroes.

Dr. M. L. Perry, pathologist of the State Sanitarium of Georgia, examined the brains of 100 whites and the brains of 100 negroes. He found that the average weight of the brain of the negro was 100 grams, or 3½ ounces less than that of the whites. It is also well known that in the brain of the negro the convolutions are less complex, and the sulci are shallower than that of the Caucasian, which, added to the fact that his brain is smaller, gives the negro considerable less gray matter than for the white. Thus the negro's brain approaches nearer the Simian type than that of the Caucasian, which, according to our ideas of evolution, would place him on a slightly lower scale as a man than his white brother. Probably for this reason they are lacking in the inherent vital nerve forces which in serious illness is sufficient to make them succumb to all diseases, particularly those of a wasting nature like tuberculosis, than does his white brother, who is endowed with a better developed brain structure. I am sure that even under the most favorable circumstances, which I am sorry to say is given to but few of their

2. Gould. Military Statistics. pp. 480 and 493.
3. The Negro as a Convict. Transactions of the Alabama State Medical Association, 1893, p. 321.

Traits and Tendencies of the American Negro, page 161.

sick, the negro dies more readily from all forms of disease. I have known of many whites who have recovered from consumption when the treatment was begun early, but of the large number of cases which I have treated among the negroes I have seen but a few who showed even temporary improvement, and only one who recovered from the disease.

I would not be understood as meaning that there are any inherent differences in structure of the tissues of the whites and blacks—only a difference in development. The whites have many centuries of enlightenment and civilization under such varied conditions that there has been the psychical and physical development, which fits him to endure the manifold dangers of disease which beset us in our struggle for existence in this complex age, while the negro, a century or two ago, was a savage, perhaps a cannibal, who needed only to provide himself with food, of which nature so lavishes both animal and vegetable in the forest of the tropics of Africa. The heat of that climate made it unnecessary for him to have clothing to protect his body, and with the low altitude and the warm, humid atmosphere, less oxygen was required to maintain body temperature, so there was a corresponding lack of development of the lungs of the native African. This, the hygienic life which he was compelled to lead as a slave, was overcome to a great extent, as is shown by the table compiled by Hoffman, which makes it clear that the chest expansion of the negro was nearly, if not quite, equal to that of the whites in 1861-5, while in 1892-4 it was considerably less. However, the life of a slave did not fit the negro to provide for himself in a climate entirely different in environment to that which his ancestors had lived for ages, and the utter incapacity of the majority of negroes to take care of themselves and families in this climate is the great underlying reason why tuberculosis, which finds its victims in those of a lowered state of vitality, has increased so rapidly, and almost always proves fatal among the members of this unfortunate race.

The filthy habit of spitting shows its highest development among the colored population. Nearly all the men chew tobacco and their women use snuff, and the healthy and the tuberculous alike spit on the floors of many of their homes and churches. The best of their churches are provided with boxes filled with dry sand or sawdust into which they expectorate. The sputum, either on the floors or in the boxes, becomes dry and gets into the dust of the atmosphere, and the bacilli are inhaled in large numbers, and, lodging on lung tissue already weakened from the causes of which I have spoken, they find a favorable soil for their development. When we remember that the consumptive, with a cavity in his lungs, expectorates from 2,500,000,000 to 4,000,000,000 germs in twenty-four hours (Nuttall), and that tuberculosis is so prevalent among the negroes, we can see that this is no chimerical idea that their churches are among the great disseminators of tuberculosis.

Syphilis is not in the least allied to tuberculosis, but it is a well-known fact that syphilitics die from tuberculous diseases. Syphilis is certainly one of the great predisposing causes of tuberculosis, and the great increase in syphilis in the past thirty years has been *pari passu* with that of tuberculosis.

Gonorrhea, on account of their habits of licentiousness, is one of the most frequent diseases among negro men, and every physician who has examined many negro women knows how frequently they are afflicted with "pus tubes." Osler says: "Tuberculous peritonitis in America is a more common disease in the negro than in the white race, and recently collected statistics show that females predominate." Kelly has shown that a very considerable proportion of all cases is secondary to tuberculosis of the fallopian tubes. It is also well known that in man tuberculosis of the seminal vesicles often precedes the development of the disease in the peritoneum. My own observation has been that tuberculous peritonitis is a very much more frequent disease in the negro than in the white race, and that it is several times more frequent in women than in men. For this reason I am inclined to the opinion that gonorrheal salpingitis, prostatitis and seminal vesiculitis prepare the soil for the bacilli of tuberculosis, and from these loci minoris resistentiæ the disease originates and extends to the peritoneum. Therefore, it seems that the gonococcus is the indirect cause of a considerable proportion of negro deaths from tuberculosis.

A great many negro children die from tuberculous peritonitis, which is frequently secondary to the disease in the intestines, and I have no doubt but that the causes of death in many cases reported as gastroenteritis are really enteritis and peritonitis of tuberculous origin.

Nasal catarrhs, tonsillitis, bronchitis and other troubles which are commonly called colds, which are frequent precursors of phthisis pulmonalis, are very prevalent among the negroes, and are rarely ever treated. They are exposed to all kinds of weather, and in winter many of them do not have sufficient clothing to keep the surface of the body warm. Their lack of personal cleanliness, as is demonstrated by their proverbially characteristic odor, which, by the way, is not so noticeable in those who bathe frequently and regularly, prevents the skin from acting freely, therefore, predisposing factors in the development of so much consumption among the negroes, and for the same reasons they are prone to the most virulent types, i. e., acute pneumonia phthisis, phthisis florida or "galloping consumption." Those of us who have treated many cases of tuberculosis among the negroes have seen them die from the acute pneumonic type in a few days or weeks. I am quite sure that many of the deaths reported as due to pneumonia really result from acute pneumonic or bronchopneumonic phthisis.

While the lungs of the negro are the organs most frequently attacked by tuberculosis, he is subject to all its protean forms. Tuberculous pleurisy and meningitis and tuberculous disease of bones and joints are of frequent occurrence among them. Indeed, there is hardly a tuberculous condition which I have seen described that I have not seen in the negro. Lupus seems to be less prevalent among them than any other form of tuberculosis. Lupus, however, seems to be a rare disease in the South.

That tuberculosis is so prevalent among the negroes everyone admits, yet every year goes by and almost nothing is done to stay the hand of this fearful disease, which, with the other diseases to which the emancipated negro is especially prone, threatens the extinction of the negro race and, indeed, greatly endangers the happiness and lives of the whites of the South. This is no new theory with me. Hundreds of other physicians in the South hold to the same opinion, but the whites generally and the negroes do not seem to realize the danger which threatens to almost exterminate the "ward of the nation."

F. L. Hoffman[4] says: "It can be proven at the present time that the colored race is subject to an inordinate

4. Race Traits and Tendencies of the American Negro. p. 82.

mortality from consumption and respiratory diseases, which will menace the very existence of the race in the not far distant future."

Dr. Cunningham says in his paper on the "Negro as Convict": "In conclusion, I will submit that the race problem will be largely settled in the event of public works being established throughout the South, which means ready money for the negro; that means the profitable practice of prostitution; that means gonorrhea and consequent sterility; tuberculosis will do the rest."

Dr. Rudolph Matas,[5] in his splendid and comprehensive paper on "The Surgical Peculiarities of the American Negro," makes the following statement: "Tuberculosis has been called the "great white plague"; but if we look at this matter statistically and through the eyes of all experienced observers we would with greater propriety call it the black plague, as it is unquestionably the dominant cause of the increasing death rate of the negro in this country."

Dr. P. B. Barringer, Chairman of the Faculty of the University of Virginia, in his masterly address before the Montgomery (Ala.) "Race Congress," placed tuberculosis as the principal factor in "that grand but ghastly tragedy—the sacrifice of a race."

I am not an alarmist, and this paper, which calls particular attention to the weak points of the negro, is written for no other purpose than to call attention to the alarming increase of tuberculosis in that race, with the hope that something may be done which will lessen the frightful mortality of the disease in this generally kind-hearted people. The South is doing a noble part by the negro in the line of education, and I am glad that it is so, because without the guiding and protecting hand of a master, the African and his descendants in this climate and this strenuous age can only hope to survive the struggle for an existence through the education of their minds and the training and development of their bodies. If for no other reason than that of self-protection, it is high time that the whites of the South, on whom must fall all the cares and responsibilities of managing the affairs of state for the public good, should take steps to prevent the continued spread of tuberculosis among the negroes. If our cooks, nurses and other servants have the disease there is danger of our families becoming infected. Incidentally, I will mention that I do not believe that tuberculosis is decreasing among the whites of the South, and whatever steps are taken to lessen the prevalence of the disease should apply equally to the whites and negroes.

The methods to pursue in limiting an infectious disease like tuberculosis should be directed toward (a) increasing the strength and vitality of the individuals of the race, thereby rendering their tissues an unsuitable soil for the invasion and propagation of the specific germs of the disease, and in (b) preventing his exposure to the infective agent, as by the isolation of those already afflicted, and by destroying the organisms causing the disease.

The first proposition presented is the development and upbuilding of the minds, morals and bodies of a "child race," an alien people, placed under conditions and environments which would seem to be unfavorable to the growth and stability of the race, and wholly unlike those under which his ancestors had lived for centuries. In a paper like this I can only discuss this phase of the question briefly, but those who are interested I would

strongly urge to read "The Race Tendencies and Traits of the American Negro," by F. L. Hoffman, the able statistician of the Prudential Insurance Co. of America. He has collected and published in this book, at an enormous expenditure of time and energy, the largest and most valuable statistics bearing on all phases of the negro question that I know of in all the literature on the subject. He has applied statistical methods in forming his deductions, and, being a German by birth, and, therefore, free from the so-called race prejudice, his conclusions are of great value, and the facts and figures which he has presented can hardly be questioned.

Much may be done to develop the negro through education applied on the right lines. He has every opportunity in the South that the whites have of obtaining both a common-school and collegiate education, but the moral, physical and hygienic education of the race is almost wholly neglected. By educating the children in these matters they would instruct their parents on the hygiene of their persons and their homes. Their school buildings should be inspected by the health officers in every county and should be kept in a sanitary condition. Regular physical exercises, directed especially toward developing their lungs and the accessory muscles of respiration, should be a part of the daily routine of school duties. The children should be taught the importance of taking frequent and regular baths; that filth means disease, and cleanliness should be required of them. They should be shown the direful effects of immorality on their bodies as well as their souls. A higher standard of morals and education in their ministry and among their teachers would help much in this direction.

Regular daily lessons and talks on practical hygiene should be a part of the curriculum of every school. They should be taught how to live in their homes; that there "cleanliness is next to godliness"; that fresh air and sunlight are among the great boons to humanity, and if they would have health they must have plenty of both in their homes. They should be shown the dangers of overcrowding; that health can not be maintained when more than two or three sleep in the average-sized room; that there is danger in sleeping in the room with any sick person, especially one with a cough. They should be doubly impressed with the danger of spitting on the floors, walls, or any place where the sputum can dry and dust particles get into the atmosphere; that the germs of consumption, which disease, the youngest of them know, is the cause of many deaths of their relatives and friends, is carried through the atmosphere and breathed into their lungs, and that the dried sputum is practically the only source of infection. They should be instructed in the hygienic management of a case of tuberculosis; that there is danger in even a casual association with a consumptive who is careless in his habits of spitting, but that there is little danger of contracting the disease even by close association with a person who has consumption, and who is cleanly in his person and at his home, and who is careful to expectorate into vessels containing dilute solutions of an antiseptic fluid, or into spit cups, which are burned before the sputum has time to dry.

They should also be taught that health and happiness come from regularity of habits and work, diet, recreation and sleep, and that a liberal quantity of all are required to keep in perfect health. Above all, they should be taught the manliness and honor of physical labor, and that their education fits them for their life's work, and not for a life of ease and luxury; that there is as much honor in farming as in teaching or preaching

Transactions of the American Surgical Association, vol. 14.

Industrial education is, therefore, a movement capable of doing great good for the race. They should be taught to economize, to save their money and put it in homes and farms. That for their race the dangers of Sodom lie in the towns and cities; that there lurk consumption and death.

These things, and much more, should be taught to the negroes, not only for the sake of right, but to make them stronger physically, so that they may resist the infection of tuberculosis.

The isolation of those infected with tuberculosis would unquestionably limit the disease in a great measure, but the difficulties of enforcing or carrying into effect in any way the isolation of the thousands of indigent tuberculous negroes in every state in the South are so great as to make the suggestion impracticable, though something may be done on that line.

The state could enforce the isolation of the tuberculous patients in their convict camps and penitentiaries, which are often great harbingers of the infection of tuberculosis.

The establishment of sanatoria for the isolation of the tuberculous should receive more attention from philanthropists and the civil authorities. In Massachusetts and other states they have been successfully conducted by the state for several years. Such establishments need not call for expensive buildings, but rather the cottage system, or even on the plans of the plantation quarters for slaves, where the negroes enjoyed such immunity to tuberculosis. They should be located in the country, where the inmates can get plenty of outdoor exercise and when able do farm work, and assist in paying the expenses of such institutions. Very few negroes would be able to pay their expenses at these sanatoria, and they would necessarily have to be charitable institutions, but they could be maintained at a probably less per capita expense than those at the hospitals for the colored insane, and I am sure that the same number of tuberculous negroes are a source of greater danger to their families and to their friends than the same number of their insane, if left in the care of their families. Aside from the isolation feature of sanatorium treatment for consumptives, the hygienic education that it gives to the patient and through him to his relatives and friends will materially aid in protecting many who are exposed to the disease.

There should be several such sanatoria in every state. Even if they should entail a great expense to the state, in the end it will be economy, because in a few years, perhaps a quarter of a century, when tuberculosis will have a chance at the weakened offspring of this and the coming generation of negroes, the havoc will be so great among that race and the danger to the whites so clear that enormous expenditures will have to be made in order to relieve the acuteness of the situation. The state and municipal authorities will spend thousands to prevent an epidemic of smallpox or yellow fever, yet spend almost nothing to prevent the spread of a disease which destroys a hundred times as many of our citizens, and which entails far greater and more prolonged suffering than both of those diseases, besides the direful effects on the offspring of its unfortunate victims.

Unquestionably, tuberculosis should be managed by the health authorities, as are the other infectious diseases. In some of the cities every case of tuberculosis is required to be reported to the health officers, who instruct the patient and his family as to the methods to use to prevent the spread of the disease. The patient is not interfered with in any way, except that he is expected to employ the usual methods of destroying the sputa, and to follow the simple rules of hygiene to protect those with whom he comes in contact. After the removal or death of the patient the patient's room, or house, is disinfected just as for other infectious diseases.

The health officer of every city and county should be required to understand the use of a microscope, and it should be a part of his duty to examine, without charge, every specimen of sputum sent to him. He should also be skilled in physical diagnosis, so that the physician or patient could call him in to clear up the diagnosis in cases of doubt, as is required of him in the other infectious diseases. We all know that tuberculosis is one of the curable diseases if the diagnosis is made early and intelligent treatment is applied. If the public could be educated to call in the health officer in the early stages of tuberculosis and thereby become certain of the diagnosis, not only would many of the patients be saved, but it would aid in lessening the infection, because it would give the health officer the opportunity of instructing the patient and his family on the hygienic measures necessary to prevent the spread of the disease before the home had become infected.

Since the tuberculous patient is dangerous to his friends and the community only from his ejected sputa and directly in proportion to his habits of spitting, the antispitting ordinances, which are already in force in all cities for their public buildings, cars and streets, are doing great good by lessening the chances of breathing the infection from the atmosphere. The states should adopt such ordinances for public buildings of all kinds, including schools, churches and depots. Of course, they would not always be enforced, but a placard announcing the ordinances and stating the reason for their adoption, would call attention to the dangers of spitting, and would aid in molding public opinion against the spitting evil.

Physicians who come in contact with negroes at their homes should, more than any other class of whites, consider it a duty to instruct them in the simple methods of hygiene, particularly when one of the family is afflicted with tuberculosis. The whites should be educated along the same lines, and when the laity, both among the whites and blacks, properly understand the nature of tuberculosis, the life history of its germs, and the methods to employ to prevent its spread, then, and not until then, may we hope to limit the ravages of this disease, the greatest enemy to mankind, and which is the principal agent that threatens the extinction of our "brother in black."

5

HUMAN SLAVERY AS A PREVENTION OF PULMONARY CONSUMPTION.

By THOMAS J. MAYS, M.D.,
PHILADELPHIA.

IN the arduous research for new measures to stamp out pulmonary consumption it is astonishing to find that one of the most interesting episodes in the history of our country, which clearly points out the true and only rational path for the extermination of this disease, is entirely overlooked, viz., that pulmonary consumption was comparatively unknown among the plantation slaves of the South before the war, while in the large cities of the South during that period it was no more prevalent among them than it was among the whites. This rarity was so obvious and is verified by so many lay and medical authorities that it does not call for any extended statistical support. Thus, according to the health statistics of Charleston, S. C., of which I was not able to obtain an uninterrupted report up to the present time, the negro death rate of consumption in that city in 1860 was the same as among the whites, viz., 1.75 per thousand living. In 1867, whites 2.00, negroes 3.40; in 1876, whites 2.00, negroes 6.95; in 1881, whites 2.60, negroes 7.03; in 1890, whites 3.55, negroes 6.86; in 1900, whites 1.23, negroes 6.15; in 1901, whites 1.89, negroes 5.04; in 1902, whites 1.43, negroes 5.74. This shows that the disease was 228 per cent. more prevalent among the negroes in 1902 than it was in 1860, and that its death rate was 300 per cent. greater among the negroes than among the whites in 1902. A similar vulnerability of the negro race to consumption is shown in other sections of the South.

Thus in New Orleans its annual average death rate from 1897 to 1901—a period of five years—is 123 per cent. greater among the negroes than among the whites; in Atlanta, Georgia, from 1899 to 1901—a period of three years—it is 141 per cent. greater, and in Augusta, Georgia, from 1898 to 1902—a period of four years—it is 424 per cent. greater among the negroes than among the whites.

Now, on what score can we account for the enormous increase of consumption among the former slaves of the South since 1860 ? Why should the death rate from consumption be from 200 per cent. to 400 per cent. larger among the negroes than among the whites of the South at the present time, and this in spite of the fact that they were on an even basis in this respect in 1860 ? What destructive change has occurred in the environment of the Southern negroes since 1860 that has left the white race practically untouched ? Why should the negroes in the course of thirty-five years be transformed from the least to the most consumptive race in this country ? This came to them neither through a change of climate nor through the influence of migration, but in the land of their unwilling adoption in which they had continually lived for more than two hundred years, and without a single visible sign of warning. It is this : Since they obtained their freedom their entire social, economic, and political being has been revolutionized. In place of being dependent on their owners for their food, clothing, shelter, medical care, and nursing, as they were in the days of slavery, they are thrown on their own resources and are forced into a struggle for existence that is as unequal as it is tragic. They are thus brought into the most intense competition for existence with a people whose civilization is thousands of years ahead of their own development.

Their condition may be fitly compared to that of an animal which is confronted by a new geological epoch to which it must adjust itself or perish. It is not surprising, therefore, that in this task of readjustment many of them fall a prey to diseases of the brain and nervous system—the very organs which bear the brunt of the battle in adapting this race to its changed environ-

Clim Soc   13

7

ment, and for this and no other reason do they become consumptive.

That the brain and nervous system endure the strain of this
great contest is amply attested by the fact that before the Civil
War insanity, like consumption, was comparatively rare among
the negro slaves.

According to Dr. T. O. Powell,[1] this disease has increased
705 per cent. among these people from 1870 to 1890 in the
State of Georgia. This high authority also states : "I am forced
to believe that insanity and tuberculosis are first cousins, or at
least closely allied. The sudden outburst of insanity with the
colored race of the South came associated with tuberculosis, hand-
in-hand, keeping pace one with the other."

The same is true of North Carolina, for Dr. J. F. Miller,
Superintendent of the Eastern Insane Hospital of that State,
declares[2] that from 1885 to 1896 insanity increased 256 per
cent. among the colored people in that State, and that in 1884
consumption caused 14 per cent., and in 1895, 27 per cent. of
the total number of deaths in his hospital, and this in spite of a
reduction of the general mortality rate.

Dr. James D. Moncure,[3] Superintendent of the Eastern Hospital for the Insane in Virginia, states that whereas before emancipation there were about 60 insane negroes in that hospital,
now (1896) there are over 1000, an increase of over 1600 per
cent., and that they readily contract consumption.

It is obvious, therefore, that the tremendous increase of consumption and insanity among the Southern negroes is, in the first
place, due to the heavy economic and industrial burdens which
were suddenly placed on their shoulders, and which they had
neither the wisdom nor the organized constitutional or mental
strength to discharge; and in the second place, to improvidence
of living, to poor and improperly prepared food, to ignorance of
the laws of physiology, to bad hygienic surroundings, to over-

[1] Dr. T. O. Powell, Superintendent of the Georgia Asylum for the Insane, Report on the
Increase of Insanity and its Supposed Causes.
[2] The Effects of Emancipation upon the Mental and Physical Health of the Negro of the
South, North Carolina Medical Journal, November 20, 1896.
[3] Private communication.

crowding, laziness, and the lack of persistent employment, to improper care and nursing when ill, to dissipation of all sorts, to lack of self-restraint, to alcoholism, and other vices. On this point the testimony of Dr. Miller, who has been quoted, is very emphatic and applicable. He says : " The negro in slavery had no thought for the morrow, but he spent his quiet, humble life in his little cabin, with his master to care for every want of self and family. He lived under the best hygienic restraint. His habits of life were regular, food and clothing substantial and sufficient, and the edict of his master kept him in-doors at night and restrained him from promiscuous indulgence and the baneful influence of the liquor saloon. In sickness he was promptly and properly cared for by physician and nurse. Freedom came to him, and a change came over his entire life. Under his former manner of living he enjoyed wonderful immunity from brain and lung trouble ; and I confidently assert that the germs of these troubles came to the same man and race in consequence of his changed environment and the manner of life which followed."

That the same influence which gave immunity to the Southern slaves from consumption will produce the same effects elsewhere is shown on a somewhat less extensive scale by the event of the importation of Chinese labor into Cuba.[1] Thus from 1860 to 1870 Spain brought 250,000 coolies under contract to the island of Cuba. Their ages ranged from eighteen to thirty years, and they consisted of the scum and off-scourings, principally of the cities of Canton and Macao, and, in spite of the most careful selection, they brought with them consumption and other diseases and vices for which China is noted. The vast majority of them were placed on plantations, and being under contract and under the supervision of overseers who ministered to all their physical necessities, their conditions were identical to those which surrounded the negro slave in the South before the war. The result was that within the first few years consumption was eliminated, either through death or cure, and never reappeared in them or in their offspring.

[1] Dr. H. McHaton, Georgia Journal of Medicine and Surgery, June, 1902, p. 258.

From all that has been said, the prevention of pulmonary consumption resolves itself into such efforts of education as will impress the masses with the importance of leading a life similar to that (excepting slavery) which made the slave population of the South practically immune from this disease before the Civil War.

What was done once may be done again, for the laws of health which held true then are equally applicable now. Such efforts of prevention mean the inculcation of sound principles of hygiene ; the eating of wholesome and properly prepared food ; the wearing of suitable and seasonable clothing ; the avoidance of damp, unsanitary, and overcrowded dwellings ; the abstinence from nerve strain and overwork ; the shunning of strong drink and other vices; the teaching of the value of useful labor; the encouragement of agricultural and mechanical pursuits ; the training in physical development ; the supervision of proper convalescence from what to them seems a trivial cold or cough, or from acute illness or injury ; the procurement of effective medical attendance, and nursing in sickness or accident, etc.

Now a large hospital and dispensary practice among consumptives, extending over a period of eighteen years, has convinced me that the practical solution of the prevention of this disease is one of reaching the masses. People who are predisposed to or are suffering from this disease do not come to such institutions until the malady has gained a strong foothold and the stage of prevention has been passed ; not because they would not eagerly do so, for they possess as strong a share of the instinct of self-preservation as the common run of mankind, but they fail to realize the true significance of their condition until it is too late. Hence the only effective measure is to bring yourself in contact with the people by inaugurating a campaign of education. To bring this about is for a charitable organization to divide a city or some of its wards into convenient sized sections, allot each section to a competent physician, whose duty it will be to make a general canvass of his section once a month, or as often as is necessary, among all willing residents who show or possess a family taint, or who for any reasons are believed to be in danger of consumption, to take condensed histories of all such individuals and families, to impart advice in regard to food, clothing, shelter, habits, etc., to give medical counsel and treatment whenever needed, and to send all cases which need active supervision to an institution which is well supplied with all the paraphernalia necessary for the treatment of every defect in such individuals.

Tuberculosis in the Negro: Causes and Treatment.*

By JOHN E. HUNTER, M. D., Lexington, Ky.

Gentlemen of the American Anti-Tuberculosis League:

We bring to you the greetings of the National Association of Colored Physicians and Surgeons, and assure you that we are greatly interested in this work and gladly join in the battle against the "white plague."

I do not attempt to bring to you on this occasion a volume of statistics and theories on the subject of tuberculosis, for Koch and some of our own bacte-riologists in this country have taken this matter out of the uncertainty of theories, and placed it upon the plane of facts.

The history of the American negro before the war shows that he was comparatively free from tubercular infection, although no special statistics were very accurately kept along that line, as it concerned mostly his master. It is reasonable, however, to suppose that it was a very rare thing for him to fall a

*Read before the American Anti-Tuberculosis League, Atlanta, Ga., April 19, 1905.

12

victim of that disease, or his commercial value would have been depreciated in those days.

The official statistics, as compiled, and that, doubtless, somewhat imperfectly, show that the death rate from tuberculosis is much greater at present in the negro than in the white race; and that increase has taken place since he became a free man. In stating this fact, I want to thank Dr. Seale Harris, of Union Springs, Ala., for his very excellent and fair paper which he prepared on the subject of "Tuberculosis in the Negro," and read at the fifty-fourth annual meeting of the American Medical Association. It was explicit, systematic, scientific, and reasonable, and given in the spirit of sympathy for the weaker brother; and, in view of my appreciation of his fairmindedness, I wish to add this part of his paper to mine. He says: "I am not an alarmist, and this paper, which calls particular attention to the weak points of the negro, is written for no other purpose than to call attention to the alarming increase of tuberculosis in that race, in the hope that something may be done that will lessen the frightful mortality of the disease in this generally kind-hearted people."

Digressing somewhat, since we have to admit the fact that the pendulum of mortality from tuberculosis has swung too far to our side, we can only content ourselves in this sad hour with the boasts of our fathers, that in the days of slavery they could eat with impunity and grow fat on the bacilli of yellow fever, while their beautiful young mistresses and athletic young masters would either have to take to the woods or suffer the ravages of the disease. We can say, however, that our birth rate is still at par, if not a little above. So, in view of the fact that we have kept out of the way of this monster since we have been free, by reason of the inexperience and vicissitudes that naturally follow a new birth of people, we come to you, gentlemen, whose race has never known the yoke of bondage, and whose civilization, education, and ruling power of the world are as old as the birth of Christ, that you may teach and help us to improve our environments, so that we may lower this very undesirable mortality, and thereby help all mankind.

The study of the classes of the colored race reveals the same facts that such a study would reveal in any other race. Those who, by reason of industry, education, and morality, have lived above the environments that are conducive to tubercular tendencies, have a very low death rate from tuberculosis. The same is true, not only of classes of individuals of the same race, but also of nations. The death rate of the American Indian from tuberculosis exceeds that of any other race in the United States. This is due to his environments, lack of ability for self-government and of knowledge of hygiene and the laws of health. The same is true of the Chinese, whose death rate from tuberculosis exceeds that of any other civilized race of the world.

Tuberculosis in the negro is caused by the same tubercle bacilli that infect other races. The growth and development of these bacilli are influenced by the soil in which they find lodgment. Hence the cause and treatment of tuberculosis in the negro are the same as in other races.

Heredity does not balance the scale of environments. The consideration of tuberculosis would probably come under the heads of predisposing causes, preventive treatment, and the treatment of the disease itself.

While in bondage, the negro was not subjected to the crowded, unsanitary quarters of city life, for the reason that most large slaveholders lived in the rural districts, and had them engaged in outdoor work, reasonably well fed, and with such habits of life, together with fresh air, God's greatest blessing; hence he developed good chest expansion, robust and strong bodies. Along with the environments that confronted him when he became free, came the predisposing causes that brought about the increased mortality from pulmonary tuberculosis. Being turned loose from his former master in total ignorance of what was required in self-government, or of the laws of health, and likewise being a victim of many circumstances over which he had no control, he was made a subject of surroundings, habits, habitations and vices that were altogether different from his former life. And these vices into which he fell were not created by him, as they were already existing before he was made free, and indulged in by other races. Just out of bondage, without experience as a free man, and without any education at all, what an easy victim was he for these vices, such as drinking, gambling, and others equally as bad, and especially so when those examples were set before him, and held up to him by that race whom he had

been taught to respect and fear for over two hundred years. These allurements were not held out to him by his former owner either. My best authority for this statement comes from my own parents and others who served in those days, as slaves.

The great majority of our people are greatly exposed in their daily work, that of hard labor and toil. The life of the negro as a roustabout on the Mississippi river, exposed to all kinds of weather, without beds and proper food as well, is an example of the kinds of work; living on bad streets without drainage, deep in mud in winter, and equally as deep in dust during the summer. This is especially true in colored settlements. Illy ventilated dwelling places, too many in one room, many tenement houses in alleys and other places cut off from sunshine and pure air, air that is polluted by cesspools and stables of the houses on the front streets, the one-room cabin, badly ventilated places where large bodies of people congregate, low wages, poverty, and all that goes with it, are eminent predisposing causes.

The feeding period in poor children, with a large number of our race, is the time when the tubercular foundation is laid. Working mothers leaving their babes at home to be cared for by other children only a step higher in the family, depending for nourishment on a crust of bread dipped in "pot liquor" and coated with the dust of the floor, bad milk, if any at all, that has passed through a warm bottle of germs, likewise open the way for an enemy. Thus the children often have diarrhea, which is only Nature's flush to clear the alimentary track; then the whole constitution is dethroned, and the way paved for the reception of tubercular infection, and nothing left to resist its onward and powerful invasion.

In the poor and uneducated, often unnoticed obstructions in the naso-pharynx, as adenoids, diseased tonsils, and also tubercular glands, are weakening and unsanitary to the air passages. When such conditions exist, these children become mouth-breathers, thus their chances for inhaling greater quantities of disease germs are augmented. These are only a few of the legacies of environments and defects that strongly beget tubercular tendencies, and, in my mind, will carry more down to the grave prematurely than heredity.

In order to show some of the fruits of unsanitary tenement houses, permit me to call attention to one family that moved from one of the beautiful "blue grass" farms of Kentucky to town. This was a family of five healthy children, ranging in age from four to twelve years; parents of a good, healthful history and present good health, both of whom were hard working people, and of excellent habits as well. Coming to town, they rented the back part of an old building, two rooms only, cut off from sunshine and fresh air; in fact, a very sultry place indeed as compared with their former surroundings of country life. Soon after locating in this place, all the children fell victims of measles which ran a long and very depressing course. Following the convalescence from the acute part of the measles, each child developed pulmonary tuberculosis, four of

them dying within two years, notwithstanding they moved from these quarters after the death of one child. The oldest child, doubtless being stronger, is still living, although he will die in the near future. One interesting feature of this elder child, fourteen years old, was that the infection first manifested itself in the ankle joint, and I am quite sure it entered through an abrasion at this point. The bones soon became involved, and a resection was advised, and promptly refused on the grounds, as they put it, that they had already lost four of their children, and would not have this one killed by an operation. Hence the condition grew worse, and finally the foot became gangrenous. In the meantime small cavities developed in one lung. Now, the weather being very warm, the odor of the foot, in spite of deodorants and disinfectants in abundance, made the lives of the parents almost unbearable and I am sure quite uncertain, and then they consented and insisted on my amputating the diseased member. A foot to amputate on a fourteen-year-old boy, almost a living skeleton, with all the chances of death from shock, no chance whatever to take a general anesthetic. So, as the boy just would not die, the parents urged me to do something, in order that their lives might be prolonged to care for him until his end came. The stench of the foot was awful.

I decided upon my own plan of amputation. The boy was stimulated with small doses of the sulphate of strychnia, given hypodermically for twenty-four hours, and during that time the limb was wrapped in wet bichloride cloths. At the junction of the lower and middle third of the leg a circle of the parts was well injected with a normal saline solution containing one per cent. of cocaine. This gave a very satisfactory anesthetic. The foot was amputated, the flaps brought together with silkworm gut sutures. The time occupied was ten minutes. The boy rallied quickly from his fear of pain, looked and saw the stump dressed and expressed his gratification thus: "I am glad that old rotten foot is off me". Perfect union followed, the cough was improved, the hectic sweating stopped, the fever went down promptly, and the boy was out on his crutches in three weeks. He now left for the country, and did well for seven or eight months, and then began to cough and show signs of breaking down of the lungs. In the meantime, aside from plenty of fresh air and nutritious diet, I was giving the boy full doses of guaiacol. This was the best treatment that I could give this case under the circumstances, as the parents would not permit me to do anything for the infected joint, until they themselves felt the personal unpleasantness of camping around a gangrenous foot in the hot weather of August.

PREVENTIVE TREATMENT.

The preventive treatment of pulmonary tuberculosis in the negro consists in eliminating all of those predisposing causes that render the body suitable ground for the reception, growth, and development of the tubercle bacilli. One great preventive treatment of this disease in the negro in lowly life would be the requirement and enforcement of

property owners to make tenement houses more sanitary, both in construction and in location, prohibiting the building of so many houses in alleys that are cut off from sunshine and fresh air, and doing away with the one-room cabin in the country; demand the more frequent painting and whitewashing of tenement houses, and the disinfection of houses that have been occupied by people that have had any and all kinds of infectious diseases, compelling tenants to keep their homes clean, and also teaching them the knowledge and the proper use of some antiseptic, such as lime, carbolic acid, formaldehyde, etc.

In placing these antiseptics in bottles, be sure that the bottles are black. Do you know that the majority of the less informed negroes are afraid of anything contained in black bottles? Yes; if you are treating one of the illiterate class, do not put the first medicine in a black bottle, and especially not if it be in the hospital ward; or else the patient will get well immediately, and, instead of taking up his bed and walking, he will invariably prefer leaving it and running. Up in Kentucky, it is said that the whisky is so good that most people like to taste it; and, in view of this fact, any clear bottle, not black, that holds more than six ounces, is looked upon with an eye of very pleasant expectations. One old lady with whom I have practiced for a long time was housecleaning, and that required the use of some ammonia, which she had in a clear quart bottle. When she was through with it, she put the bottle in some obscure place out of the way, in order that her little grandchild would not get hold of it. The next morning, while she was in the kitchen getting the "old man" a "snack," he awoke from his slumbers, and, for some reason, his eyes fell into "this very obscure place" and beheld that clear bottle, and with one eye watching the "old lady" and the other on the bottle, he said "good mo'nin'," and that to the extent of about four ounces. This made a very unusual impression on the gentleman of the "old school," and the next impression he had was of his wife holding his nose and the writer of this paper pouring down his œsophagus a teacupful of vinegar to neutralize the ammonia, which brought him around in short order. Then the "old lady" with a sigh of relief said: "I was afraid when I put that clear bottle of hartshorn there, that the 'old man' would get mixed up with it, thinking it was something else". "Yes," said the patient, "you ought to put such dangerous stuff in a black bottle anyhow".

More attention should be given to the proper care of streets in colored settlements as a means of preventing disease; and instead of permitting the corners to be ornamented with cheap groceries and poison whisky in the rear parts of them, for a small license, it would pay better to have free city bath houses on said corners, for filth and bad whisky beget disease and crime, whereas cleanliness begets health and godliness. Such would bring better returns. Practical hygiene should be taught in the schools, teaching that tuberculosis is infectious, indirectly contagious, preventable and curable. Practical education along

this line will prevent many of the diseases that tear down the system and open the doors to tuberculosis.

Every high official who advocates education for the negro as a means of bettering his condition is an anti-tuberculosis league in himself; and those who advise the withholding of it as a remedy for making him better are sowing the germs that may infect their own families.

If the master, the mule, and the cotton field saved the negro from tuberculosis before the war, protecting him by law in rural districts, giving him living wages, and education for his children, will keep him, to a great extent, a tiller of the soil in the fresh air of the country; and, therefore, he will not run to the miserable hovels of disease in the cities for protection, and thus create hotbeds for the germination of the various germs of the most loathsome of diseases.

The best anti-tuberculosis remedy for the negro discovered in recent years, although somewhat osseous and plastic just now, is the negro doctor. Right here I wish to say that, when the colored physician made his advent in this new field of work in the South, his greatest encouragement came from the professional friendship, helping hands and wise counsel extended him by the white brother doctors. This we cherish, and hope for its continuance.

We have not only entered the homes of our people as bedside advisers in cases of sickness, but have gone, and continue to go, and should go, into the homes of all classes with explanatory teaching of the laws of hygiene and health. We go into the meeting places, the schools, the churches of our people, and preach the gospel of pure air. We know the masses, their habits and needs as well. We have endeavored to decrease the death rate from this disease in our race, and, by the help of God, we expect to do more in the future. We have not only tried to check the spread of disease in the unsanitary places, where many are forced to live by reason of low wages, and others because of their bad habits and other curcumstances over which they have not entire control; but we have been just as faithful in keeping its spread from the white families for whom these unfortunates work, as our fathers were faithful to their masters' families while they were in the battle-fields fighting for the Confederate cause. We do our whole duty!

In view of these facts, do you not think that, where there are competent colored physicians, valuable help could come to a community by some of them being on the Boards of Health? They are on the Pension Boards, and are paid for it, and why should they not be on the boards that seek for the betterment of the health of all?

THE TREATMENT OF TUBERCULOSIS IN THE NEGRO.

The treatment of this disease in the negro consists of fresh air and plenty of it, proper food and clothing and enough of them, and at the same time preventing the patient from infecting others and reinfecting himself. The question of travel for the negro of some means and intelligence, seeking health in sanatoria, is not worthy of consideration at this time; for a sick man traveling without civil rights, not knowing where he will be permitted to shelter his weakened body and quench his parching tongue, had better, yes, far better, remain at home with his family, and trust God for the rest. But with the brain and aid of such men in the front as constitute this organization, and that of municipalities, states, and federal government, together with our own greatest efforts, we may look up, with hope.

I hail from one of the greatest states in the union, the home of Henry Clay, the brainy and fearless Breckenridges, Ephraim McDowell, the father of abdominal surgery, the birthplace of Jefferson Davis and Abraham Lincoln, and the home of the now living and very active Mayor Thomas A. Combs —"Old Kentucky"—representing the fairest, the greatest and most pretentious city of its size in all of the world, Lexington, Kentucky.

When I moved into the home I now occupy, I was the only man and property owner of my race living in that square. As the city had not water pipes along that street, it became necessary for the property holders to build a private line. We came together, collected the money, and constructed the line. When completed, we all had water, and enjoyed all the benefits of its proper use. This was a common need of us all, and, as a business proposition, we united and got it. In the same home, I have had parties, and it has always been my choice to invite colored people, and all the people that have attended these parties have likewise been colored people. My white neighbors have also had their parties, and, as far as I know, all of their guests that were invited and attended were white people. I have never felt slighted, neither has my family, by not being invited to their social functions, and I do not believe they have felt slighted in the least by not being invited to ours, as they treat me and my family very neighborly still. This was a matter of choice, a social affair, one that always has and always will adjust itself if let alone. Socially, we are just as distinct and separate as the taps which lead the water into our different yards; but when it comes to the general good of the neighborhood, the best interests of the property holders, we are as the main pipe we all laid—united. Tuberculosis is a deadly scourge in the land, emitting its deadly germs seeking those they may devour, entering your home and my home, placing crape on our doors, causing tears and sorrow within. We must fight together and destroy this enemy, or else we ourselves will be destroyed, separately, by it.

It is stated that the Prussian ministry for railways has placed at every important railway center throughout the kingdom a magnificently built and appointed car for the transport of sick persons. These cars have been specially fitted up from plans supplied by sanitary authorities. Spring beds and every medical device for the alleviation of suffering during transit have been utilized. There are ice safes, gas stoves for cooking, rooms for attendants, and ingenious devices for muffling the sound caused by the motion of the train. It is not intended to make these carriages pay; they have been instituted chiefly on the ground of humanity.

Precautions for the prevention of contagious diseases epidemic among the school children of Kansas City are already being considered by the school board. The city medical department has offered to work in conjunction with the board in keeping down diseases of a contagious nature among the pupils. The school board will instruct the principals of the various schools to notice especially the pupils coming from the districts in which there are contagious diseases, and, should any of the pupils show symptoms of illness, to send them to their homes at once. During last year there were a number of cases of typhoid fever. Especially was this prevalent in the high schools. The fatalities from this malady during the year were eight students and one teacher. In the city physician's report, however, no cases of typhoid fever are mentioned.

Tuberculosis in the Negro

BY E. H. JONES, OF MURFREESBORO.

THIS is one of the vital problems of vast import that confronts the very threshold of our efforts regarding tuberculosis, owing to the fact that they are the most tuberculous race upon the globe. Therefore drawing the analogy this fact and their condition only forty years since, when they were slaves, well cared for, clothed and housed, leading an active, out-door life, well fed and cared for in every detail regarding health and comfort, supplied with the best physicians, restrained from dissipation, and made to observe personal and domestic hygiene. Then they were almost immune from this insidious and treacherous disease or malady. This should direct our attention and efforts to a most potent channel of danger. They daily traverse our every pathway, enter every department of our homes as servants, directly, if you please, from the contaminated and polluted huts, cabins, hovels, slums, and dives, handling every vestige of linen, clothing, furniture, bric-a-brac, books, etc., in our living apartments, dining-rooms, pantries, kitchens, and dairies. So you see we are ever subject to the death-dealing micro-organism at their hands. The children, in their tender and unsuspecting years, are cared for in the nursery by them, as well as in close contact every day until the school age is reached. Often our families and ourselves are in close touch in vehicles with the drivers, direct from some contaminated cabin, loaded with bacilli ready for propagation when the fertile soil is found. This is, most assuredly, an appalling fact that we, as guardians of health, should give our best effort and thought. It would not be interesting data to collate statistical reports to show the rapidly advancing progress of tuberculosis in the negro to this body of medical workers.

The spirit of the modern medical age is preventive medicine. We all are well aware of the many sacrifices that have been made along this line in the past few decades. Many brilliant and useful lives have gone to their reward for the cause they deemed para-

(175)

mount in the field of duty and honor. Now, gentlemen of this honorable body, shall we, as soldiers of this great cause, allow the blood-stained banner to trail at our feet? or shall we meet the issues courageously, storm the fort assiduously until capitulation is inevitable?

My suggestions along the line of action should necessarily be limited, as it would not be expected within the scope of this paper to enter an exhaustive detail of what had best be done. I feel sure, in the main, we are agreed that enactment and enforcement of personal, domestic, municipal, state, and national hygienic laws, pressing to effectual execution the knowledge you already possess. I think I can safely assert that with the proper laws and enforcement, tuberculosis, with many other maladies, could be almost wiped out in a generation did not ignorance and politics intercept our efforts. In the enactment of proper laws to combat this invading foe we should throw out the life-lines about the fountain head of this monstrous, death-dealing enemy of the human organism.

Tenement houses, residences, hotels, boarding houses, factories, public buildings of every character, and public carriers of every description, should have our guardianship in construction and management, in order that devitalizing surroundings and agents to germ life might not abound. This is no fancy or theory, but well-demonstrated and authenticated facts.

To effectually prosecute this crusade is largely a matter of educating the lay members of our vast domain, so rich with incalculable advantages in all the walks of life. The opportunity now dawns upon our much-favored profession to immortalize its name and prestige. One feature regarding tuberculosis in the negro race is that a large proportion of the victims are of the acute phthisic variety, running a rapid and fatal course, yielding little to measures usually instituted. We who are familiar with the habits of this race know their exceedingly morbid proclivities for crowding around their sick and attending the funerals in crowded houses, illy ventilated, and not in the best of sanitary condition. Couple their habits and environments with the virulent fecundity of this bacteriological giant and we have the situation well in mind.

21

I have not the temerity, the inclination, nor am I warranted in an effort to impress the idea that this race alone is our source of danger and contamination. If so, our struggle would be short and victory more sure. But too true, danger confronts us in every avenue of life. Palaces and mansions are frequent harbingers of this deadly germ. Spit laws, already being enacted by some municipalities and corporations, are minor measures and but small strokes in the proper direction. Laws governing the construction of residences, tenement houses, public buildings, public carriers, and resorts of every character, should be in line of as perfect hygiene and sanitation as compatible with circumstances, looking largely to ventilation, sunshine, and hydrotherapy.

The mortality has been greatly lessened already in many sections of our commonwealth, showing conclusively that we have not been asleep at the post of duty. In formulating our laws in this gigantic crusade of labor and love against the great white plague that is claiming so many victims from our ranks yearly, we should make it compulsory that every house, tent, or apartment for dwelling purposes, when vacated, be thoroughly disinfected before being again occupied. From observation, this is one of the most dangerous sources of contamination. This applies to public carriers, hotels, passenger trains, day coaches, sleepers, passenger boats and steamers, railroad stations, street cars, stores, in fact every place where germs might be deposited. The above mentioned means and places do not approximate consummation of this great warfare just begun, but may rest with unborn generations to triumph in the victory so nobly begun in the past few years.

Yet under the light of this progressive age and the developing resources, we are led to hope for the welcome refrain, resounding praises to the noble efforts of untiring workers for this cause. Take the charitable institutions of our country and we often find tuberculosis developing with the inmates. Seventy-eight per cent. of all deaths in the Tennessee State Prison is from this source, and seventy per cent. of that number are negroes. Certainly we can but recommend separate apartments for all infected persons in prisons, asylums, blind schools, almshouses, boarding-schools, etc.; also no one infected be allowed to enter schools of any char-

12

acter whatever or to work or board in any place or institution where others are at work or living. To meet this great end the medical profession should be made inspectors and compelled by law to report every case that develops to their respective boards of health, and cases at all questionable and not well defined from physical examination and history, the sputa or other secretions be at once subjected to microscopical test.

Now, my fellow practicians and scientists, there are volumes to be spoken, legislated, and executed. Who in the galaxy of this satellitic body will wear the brightest star and erect for himself that monumental estate that will never fade, but illuminate and memorialize himself to coming ages and pave the way to that ce lestial seat of honor divine?

Discussion on the Paper of Dr. Jones

Dr. J. H. Stanley, of Beardstown: *Mr. President.*—If I understood Dr. Jones' paper rightly, it was on the prophylaxis of phthisis pulmonalis in the negro race.

I happened to be born a few years previous to the war, consequently I was raised among the negro race, and I do not recall that we had any such disease as tuberculosis in the negro race during or previous to the war. I remember one case of scrofula close to my father's house, but I do not recall any case of what we call consumption in the negro race. Since the war, however, we encounter many cases of it.

As to the etiology, we know very little about it. Personally, I am ignorant of it, and would like to know, for I have noticed since the war negroes have this disease like the white people. I have noticed, too, that they die as frequently as white people since the war, and, if possible, I would like to find out why.

I do not know what to suggest for the prophylaxis of tuberculosis in the negroes unless we put them back into slavery, and I do not suppose they would like that very much.

I would like to hear from some one else, who can tell us something regarding how the disease may be prevented in the negro race.

Dr. J. S. Nowlin, of Shelbyville: I would like to say a few words in regard to consumption in negroes, as I have observed it. Prior to the war, I seldom ever saw a case of tuberculosis among negroes. In those days they had plenty of open air; they wore clothing sufficiently warm; they partook of plain, simple bread, and had a sufficient amount of exercise. These things speak for the manner in which they were considered largely immune from the effects of tubercle bacilli. Since the war it has been different. Now and then a case of tuberculosis developed in a negro family. They were kept in small cabins; they slept in the same room, many of them, and were not very careful in that particular direction. The great principle that is being taught now is that tuberculosis is not very contagious except in the house. In the open air and in the sunshine, and especially where the sputa is wet with dew or water; in my opinion it will seldom convey or produce the disease. But in the house where it is kept dry and everything is favorable for its development, as in a negro cabin, I have seen a whole family of negroes die. If the disease should attack a negro quarter, whole families of them may contract the disease and invariably die from it. This is conclusive proof of the effects of tuberculosis on the negro before and since the war. The great principles which should govern us in the treatment, as well as prophylaxis, of tuberculosis are plain, simple meat and bread, plenty of air at

(179)

24

night and during the day. I am satisfied that the negro was far more immune from consumption prior to the war than he is to-day. There is not a disease having any contagium — either strong or weak, which finds so great resistance or immunity in the human body as tuberculosis. The stubborn resistance increases from youth to old age.

DR. LOUIS LEROY, of Memphis: The paper before the Association is one of a good deal of interest to me because I have been working in that line for some time, and have had considerable opportunity to look into the subject.

Fundamentally, we have one point to consider, the others being almost side issues, that is, as we find tuberculosis to-day among the negroes, we find a disease affecting a hybrid race, and that is one of the keynotes. It is principally the yellow negro that shows the enormous death-rate from tuberculosis to-day. In all cases, wherever we find a hybrid race, we find a race which has not the stamina, physical, moral, or mental, of either of the races in the mixture. Then, again, we must remember that in the hybridization, as a rule, we add a vicious tendency to what might be expressed as the lowest strata of the upper race, mixed with the vicious tendency of the lower race. That carries with it to begin with a poor hereditary foundation, one lacking in natural resistant qualities. Again, we are in the attitude in regard to the negro question of attempting to force in one or two generations a civilization upon an inferior race which it has taken the Caucasian race centuries to attain. He staggers under the burden and falls, as you would naturally expect, even though you had no data on which to base your judgment. Then, his other vices add to the list of predisposing causes. Syphilis is almost universal among negroes in the cities, so that in our dispensary work we do not say, Have you got syphilis? but we say to them, When did you get it? (Laughter.) We take it for granted that he has it. Sometimes he does not know he has it, but he has got it just the same in most cases. That helps to lay the foundation for tuberculosis.

Again, in the antebellum days the negro got a drink now and then, when it was good for him possibly. Now, he gets a drink every time he gets paid off, and in between if he can. As has been said by one of the French writers, alcoholism makes a bed for tuberculosis. You gentlemen, who are familiar with the conditions in the larger cities, know to what extent the addiction to drugs, especially cocaine, has reached among negroes. Besides that, you also know the extent to which abortion is practiced among negro women. These things in the older days were not known, and yet every one of the factors I have mentioned is of stupendous moment as a predisposing cause in any infectious disease. Possibly no one cause mentioned would of itself suffice to insure the contracting of the disease, but taken collectively they leave an outlook for the race which is hopeless, if help from without is not forthcoming.

DR. G. M. BURDETTE, of Lenoir City: In antebellum days such a thing as tuberculosis upon a plantation was unknown. I never saw a case of tuberculosis among the negroes of the South. I was born and raised in Georgia and never saw a single case of tuberculosis in a negro. I think one of the prime factors to be considered is the food they have. If they were put upon the same regimen and same food now as they had then, tuberculosis in a great measure would be eliminated. My friend from Memphis (Dr. Leroy) shows that miscegenation is one of the prime factors in the production of the disease; but we had miscegenation in the days of slavery. There were mulattos all over the country, plenty of them, nearly as many as we have now. Miscegenation, however, is gradually dying out — at least, I hope so, for the sake of the Caucasian race. The food given in the antebellum days was three and a half pounds of middling hog meat, a quart of molasses, and a peck of meal for a week's rations. One of my professors used to say that the meat was an antidote for tuberculosis. I think that it is one of the prime factors in the prevention of the disease in the olden times. Dr. Leroy has graphically described the causes which have produced tuberculosis in negroes to-day.

Dr. J. H. STANLEY, of Beardstown: I want to correct the erroneous impression conveyed by the remarks of Dr. Leroy, that negro women knew nothing about abortion previous to the war. I want to say that the negro race knew all about it previous to the war. I remember hearing an old negro man who belonged to my father say he could take Gossypii Radicis Cortex and cause an abortion in twenty-four hours.

I have heard old slave owners say that previous to the war that they had to watch their pregnant slaves to keep them from causing an abortion on themselves. Cotton root tea seemed to be the sheet anchor.

Dr. W. J. ENGLES, of Smyrna: I wish to say a word or two in regard to tuberculosis among negroes in the country. I live in Rutherford county, and attended two patients this year who came from the city and only remained a few months, who had tuberculosis. They have about as much meat and about as much good food as they had in the antebellum days. They got good wages. I do not think the food accounts largely for tuberculosis in negroes. In the country they have syphilis, and they are hybrid. There is hardly a pure-blooded African. I have noticed that you see more cases of the disease in mulattos than in the pure-blooded negroes. Let them go to the city, and they come back home with tuberculosis.

Dr. JONES (closing the discussion): I will not take up the valuable time of the Association by making any extended remarks in closing the discussion. I tried to bring out in my paper the difference between the prevalence of tuberculosis among negroes prior to the war and now. So far as the hybrid portion of the race is concerned, that has not been my experience. We have a large number of negroes in our county, and in conversation with a physician who practices in our county, I find that his experience coincides with my own, that the full-blooded negro is as subject to tuberculosis in our section as is the yellow man. I think the condition that largely obtains now with the negro race is due to their manner of living in crowded huts and contaminated environments. I believe, too, that food is an important factor.

TUBERCULOSIS AMONG NEGROES*

EX-GOVERNOR W. J. NORTHERN
Atlanta, Ga.

Mr. President: The vitality of the negro may well be considered the most important phase of the race problem. Among

*Read before the Southern Medical Association, Atlanta, Ga., 1908.

all races of people. the negro has the least power of resistance to disease. The greatest element of danger. therefore, threatening the health conditions of the communities at the South, is the diseased negro.

The subject assigned me for discussion. Tuberculosis among the Negroes. covers only one aspect of the danger from the diseased negro. If to this disease should be added the loathsome diseases. directly traceable to the negro's excessive immorality. the evidence of menace would be so strikingly cumulative as to alarm the most indifferent citizen. in the most obscure community.

In discussing Tuberculosis among Negroes. I. of course. cannot speak as a skilled physician. I shall speak only as a layman and a citizen.

If a case of small-pox were located within the borders of the South. the fact would be heralded throughout every other city in the nation. within twenty-four hours after the case had been clearly defined. The authorities would erect barriers for safety. and those who were able would hurriedly escape to places of security from this dreadful and deadly disease.

If a case of small-po were located within the borders of any municipality or rural district at the South. the authorities in charge would run up the danger flag and quarantine all persons who had been exposed to the deadly contagion from this disease.

If a child should be stricken by scarlet fever or diphtheria. all the other children would be hurried rapidly from the home. and the unfortunate little one would be securely confined and locked in seclusion until the disease had run its course. guided by the most skillful physician accessible to the home.

If a case of tuberculosis. more deadly than all infectious and contagious diseases combined. were discovered anywhere in the community. nobody would be concerned and nobody would take precaution to prevent the spread of the disease. No danger flag would be hoisted to give needed warning. although the records show that 184 people for every 100.000 die in the United States every year from tuberculosis. while all other infectious and contagious diseases combined destroy far less than that number.

During the same year that 184 people from every 100,000 in the United States died from tuberculosis, only two people out of every one million of the population died from small-pox, while 160,000 died from tuberculosis. For the same year only 104,000 died from all the following diseases combined: typhoid fever, malarial fever, whooping cough, scarlet fever, measles, small-pox, diphtheria, croup, cholera, dysentery, yellow fever, influenza, leprosy, erysipelas, and all other epidemic diseases combined. That is tuberculosis destroyed 160,000 people in one year, while all other epidemic diseases, combined, destroyed only 104,000.

To more definitely localize: In the State of New York, the deaths from all causes for 1907 were 147,242. Of these, 14,406 or about ten per cent of the whole, were caused by Tuberculosis. That year in New York State diphtheria destroyed 2,372 lives; typhoid 1,668; scarlet fever 995; and smallpox only ten. The actual cost to the people of New York that year occasioned by tuberculosis, including the value of the lives destroyed, is authoritatively reported to be 70,000,000 dollars. All this vast value would have been saved to the people of that state, if this dread disease had been prevented.

In New York City alone, within one year, there were 1,740 deaths from diphtheria; 796 from scarlet fever; 740 from typhoid and 10,262 from tuberculosis alone.

In Chicago, croup destroyed 16 lives; peritonitis 24; small-pox 61; scarlet fever 79; measles 231; typhoid fever 339; whooping cough 239; diptheria 426, making the total deaths from all these epidemic diseases 1,864, while there were more than two deaths from tuberculosis for each one that occurred from all the diseases named.

In the little State of Rhode Island, the roll of deaths from preventable and communicable diseases for 1905 was as follows: Smallpox nothing; scarlet fever 35; measles 44; whooping cough 50; diphtheria and croup 9; typhoid 84; influenza 107; while tuberculosis alone destroyed 1,031, as against 419 for all other diseases named.

It may be objected that I am giving the death rate from Northern states and Northern cities that do not concern our conditions at the South. I am reporting upon these States and cities so as to be able to show that there is far more destruction of life from tuberculosis at the South than at the North and then, subsequently, to say, that the communities at the North are making most strenuous, intelligent effort to eradicate the disease, while the people at the South seem, practically indifferent to the alarming dangers that are all about them.

I have the authority for saying that, of the eleven cities reporting the largest population in the United States, it is left to a Southern city to report the highest death rate from consumption.

Giving the figures in round numbers: Pittsburg reports that seven per cent. of all deaths in that city are caused by tuberculosis. Cleveland reports eight per cent.; Chicago reports eleven per cent.; St. Louis, eleven; Philadelphia, twelve; Boston, twelve; Cincinnati, twelve; Baltimore, twelve; New York, thirteen; San Francisco, thirteen; while New Orleans reports that fourteen per cent. of all deaths that occur in that city are caused by tuberculosis.

In New Orleans 900 people died from tuberculosis in 1881. Of these 512 were white and only 388 negroes. The next year, 1882, there were 857 deaths from this disease; 507 were white and only 350 negroes. The next year, 1883, there were 845 deaths from tuberculosis, 505 being white and only 340 negroes. Since that date the death rate among the negroes has steadily increased, so that in 1904 there were 1,121 deaths from tuberculosis, 567 white and 554 negroes; in 1905 there were 1,060 deaths, being 532 whites and 528 negroes; 1906, 498 whites and 463 negroes; 1907 563 whites and 512 negroes.

The negroes make 27 per cent. of the general population of New Orleans and furnish 48 per cent of the deaths from tuberculosos. This shows a most remarkable difference in the death rate between the races in that city, and yet other Southern cities show conditions quite equal and even more alarming.

In Atlanta, the negroes make 40 per cent. of the population and furnish 58 per cent. of the deaths from tuberculosis.

31

In Jacksonville the negroes make 51 per cent of the population and furnish 72 per cent. of the deaths from this disease. The negroes in Augusta make 47 per cent. of the general population and furnish 66 per cent of the deaths. In Indianopolis the negroes are only 9 per cent of the population and furnish 24 per cent of the deaths. Baltimore has a population 2.5 per cent. negro and they furnish 32 per cent of the deaths from tuberculosis. Nashville has 36 per cent of the general population negro. and during the past four years these people have furnished 60 per cent of the deaths from tuberculosis. The population of Raleigh. U. C., is 35 per cent. negro and they furnish 60 per cent. of the deaths. The population of Washington is 23.5 per cent negro and they furnish 56.6 per cent of the deaths from tuberculosis.

These localities. widely separated as they are. and yet holding about the same proportion of deaths as between the races. go to confirm the statement just made as to the menace that threatens the health conditions at the South because of the presence of the diseased negro.

A closed study of condition seems to indicates that the death rate among the negroes is determined by local environment. Where sanitary regulations are enforced. as is true of the whites. the death rate is greatly diminished. Under these conditions the rate for the negroes varies from two to seven times that of the white man. It has not yet been definitely and satisfactorily settled as to whether the negro is naturally more susceptible to tuberculosis than the white man. or that his excessive death rate is caused by his bad life-habits.

Statistics show that mortality from consumption. 15 to 44 years of age. according to birth place of the mother. rate per one hundred thousand. for all nationalities dwelling in America has been as follows:: Poland. 80: Hungary. 120: Russia. 150: Italy. 175: Wales. 175: United States. 180: Scotland. 225: Canada 225: Germany 235: France 245: Scandinavia 260: Bohemia 165: Ireland 455: Negro 615. That is 615 deaths for the American Negro against 180 deaths for the American white man.

When we compare these figures with conditions before

the Civil War, we are forced to know that the negro is paying most frightfully for his civilization, while he becomes a frightful menace to the health conditions of our communities. The same relative condition is true of the American Indian. While in the savage state, tuberculosis was practically unknown among the Indians. Since they have been put to live in tents and houses, they are dying in great numbers and unless relief is given all the American Indians will soon become extinct. The same would be true as to the negroes if they were not so unusually prolific. However, it remains to be seen whether or not these people can continue to increase in numbers under the destructive life-habits of this generation.

There is hope for the race, and for the whites as well, if we can induce them to avoid the breeding places of tuberculosis. If we fail, these people are just as sure to be wiped out as that death follows disease. If they continue to go out in bodies as they are now going, they will carry proportionate number of the white race to certain death along with them.

All the known breeding places for tuberculosis are easily open to the masses of the negroes, under their present practices as to individual and home living.

Possibly the most fruitful source for disease among these people is found in their excessive and corrupt immorality, giving lodgment for the germs of turbeculosis and breeding places for all other diseases. This is proverbial and patent everywhere. Whilst immorality is not necessarily allied to tuberculosis, it necessarily weakens the vital forces and prepares the soil for the seed of the disease.

A prominent physician in this state is the authority for saying that every negro minister in one Georgia county has been treated for loathsome diseases resultant from the grossest kinds of immorality. If this can be true of their religious teachers, what is possible with the untaught. Leaders among the negroes themselves publish, in their race conferences similar statements, with the very deepest expressed regret and the severest possible censure.

Prof. Eugene Harris of Fisk University, in a lecture delivered before the Atlanta University (Negro) Conference, said:

"Be it known to all men that we, in this conference, are not the enemies of our people, because we tell the truth. We shall know the truth and the truth shall make us free, not only from the bondage of sin, but from vicious social conditions and consequent physical death. I am convinced that **the sine qua non** for a change for the better in the negroe's physical condition is a higher social morality. I am convinced that, for the black man's low vitality and his enormous death rate, we must look to those social conditions which he creates for himself. The diseases which are responsible for our unusual mortality are often traceable to our enfeebled constitutions, broken down by gross immoralities. This is even the source of pulmonary consumption, which disease is today the black man's scourge. Rome was destroyed because she had no mothers, and Babylon was blotted out because she was the mother of harlots."

The testimony is practically universal and uniform, that the masses of the negro people are thoroughly debauched through moral decay, and that their physical degeneracy is making a very hot-bed for all infectious and contagious diseases, that become epidemic in the communities at the South, destroying the white people as well as the negroes through infection and contagion that make the beginning of a plague and a scourge that science and skill and effort cannot prevent unless taken in time.

Another breeding place open to the negro, is Alcoholism. From the latest report by the Board of Health of the City of New Orleans, I quote: "The improvement in the general death rate of New Orleans during the past fifty years was brought about by the control and the decline of yellow fever, but by no means wholly so. Other causes operating have been gradual eradication of malaria from our midst; the marked diminution in infectious and contagious diseases, notably smallpox, since 1883; the fewer fatalities from diphtheria and croup, the progressive reduction in the death rate of infants, that, "barometer of public health," and the general advancement and ever-increasing interest of the masses in matters of public health and personal hygiene."

"The change is much less marked for the colored population. the mortality rate for which is now 56.6 per cent in excess in the white death rate. Tuberculosis and alcohol are today the greatest scourges of that race." We are diligently striving to prevent the spread of all other diseases, while we leave the most deadly to unhindered ravage and destruction.

This latter statement as to alcohol is quite enough to answer all arguments against the prohibition of the sale of whiskey within the limits of the States of the South. If we do not care whether the negro drinks himself out of existence, the whole race at a time, it quite enough concerns the white man for his own security from the dangers and the diseases that come to us from the drunken negro. The excessive dissipation by the negro through the use of whiskey as well as sexual immorality makes him an easy prey to tuberculosis, and all the community suffers, in this way, from his degeneracy.

Another breeding place for tuberculosis among the negroes and open more from ignorance than dissipation or irregularities, is found in the manner of living in their homes. Large families eat. sleep. do their washing. cooking and all their home duties in houses with only two and many times only one room. Many times half a dozen or more occupy these quarters for all these purposes. Their homes are constructed without regard to ventilation or light. They most frequently close up all such places, if they find them, few as they may be. The negro has a strange and peculiar habit of sleeping with his head covered, and when several occupy the same bed. they not only get no fresh air, but they breathe the breath of each other, with most debilitating and deadly results.

Only few homes among the masses of the negroes are tidy and clean or well kept; they are constitutionally opposed to personal cleanliness; their indolence and improvidence and the general lack of the spirit to accummulate, leaves them without the means to provide for their necessities, and, in consequence, they are more often than otherwise, without good food and proper clothing; they have few changes of clothing, because they decline to work to buy enough of them; they are exposed to the rains and often sleep in damp clothes; they have no regard for regular hours and they are often prowling all during the night time, to supply their needs without taking the day time to do this by honest work. These are the conditions of the masses who are destroying the better classes of the race, as well as scores and thousands of the white people through infection.

The diseased ones know little and care less about the harm they are doing the community by infection. They spit where they please: sleep with those who are not diseased: eat promiscuously, using the same spoons, knives and dishes: breed flies by the millions: know nothing of disinfectants and would hardly use them if they did. There is only one remedy known to science that the masses among them use for cure, and that is abstaining from overwork and taking plenty of rest.

These are the main sources or breeding places for tuberculosis among negroes: none of them prevailing before the Civil War, or, if at all, in a most limited way.

A tuberculous negro was almost an unknown quantity at the South before the war between the states. And yet, they did not rest then as much as they do now: they were furnished good comfortable clothing: they were given plenty of wholesome food: they understood and practiced personal cleanliness and they were required to meet its demands: their work was almost constantly in the open air, their houses were comfortably built and required to be kept clean: their morals were looked after because the master's interests demanded they should be: no man ever saw a vagrant slave: no man ever heard of a drunken, debauched negro before the Civil War: when, from any cause, they were ill, the physician was promptly called just as he would have been to any other member of the family: they were put to bed regularly and prevented, by public officers, from strolling in the night time, and all necessary health laws were enforced and uniformly complied with. Conditions are altogether different now, and the negro is paying for his civilization and his freedom at most desperate cost in the enormous death rate that is destroying the race in hecatombs.

As my testimony on these points may not be convincing, it may be well to quote authority, although I lived for thirty years among the slaves at the South, and know whereof I speak.

Writing of tuberculosis, Mr. Fred L. Hoffman, everywhere an acknowledged authority on vital statistics, says, a volume could be written on this one disease and its influence on the destiny of the negro race. This most to be dreaded of all diseases, he says, is constantly on the increase among the negro population of the country. He says further: "The opinion of southern physicians who practiced among negroes before the war is practically unanimous, that consumption was less frequent among the negroes than among the whites. The death rate of the two races now, from consumption is nearly four times as great among the colored as among the white population."

Dr. E. H. Scholl, an ex-president of the Medical Association of Alabama says: from 1856 to 1862 a large proportion of my practice was plantation work among the negroes, who were well fed, well clothed, well housed and carefully nursed when sick, and well treated. I cannot recall, in my practice for those six years, one solitary death from consumption among the slaves of my district, when the population was not in the rate of one black to two whites, but at least eight or ten blacks to one white."

Dr. . C. McIntosh of South Carolina, had large practice among the negroes before the Civil war. He says: "Phthisis was a disease unknown among the negroes before 1860. Among all those around me as I grew up, I cannot recall a single case, and now, since 1865, in families in which there had not been a single case of pthisis, to my knowledge, for twenty years previous to that time, parents and children have yielded to this fell disease, and entire families have disappeared. In a family of sixteen children, ten have died from scrofula, and phthisis with the father and mother still alive."

Dr. James Evans also of South Carolina says: "The death rate among the slaves on the rice plantations was very low from pulmonary tuberculosis, even though they were much exposed to the weather, repairing dykes, cleaning out and digging ditches, etc., etc." He then says: "In Charleston, during the thirty-one years that immediately followed the war, there died from tuberculosis 1,525 white persons and 4,915 negroes.''

Dr. Oertel of Georgia says: ''When one takes into consideration the well known fact that during slavery, a case of tuberculosis in the negro was almost unheard of, and that now his death rate from this cause is about twice that of the white race, it seems that there must be some cause for thorough investigation.''

In presenting this phase of the question, it must not for one moment be supposed, that I am defending or supporting slavery. With all good men in the south, I am heartily glad slavery is dead. I can, however, never endorse nor accept the manner of its going, but I am glad myself to be free from the burden the institution brought to the people of the south. I am comparing conditions simply to show that, if we do not save the negro, the negro will destroy us, and that his salvation can come only through the methods practiced during slavery, when the negro was free from disease. At the close of the Civil war, the south presented to the nation a race made up of the finest specimen of physical manhood, the world has ever seen. These people had among them, less by far of disease, than any race the world has ever known. The negroes were physically more vigorous than the white people of the same generation. They had been made to respect and obey the laws of health, enforced by the white people, who themselves violated almost all the laws of health. White people at the south drank whiskey to excess and became debauched; slaves at the south never did; white people entered upon all kinds of dissipation that enervated the body and broke down their vitality; slaves were not allowed to; white people, many of them, were vagrants; slaves never were. The world had never seen and probably never will see, any body of people so thoroughly perfect in physical manhood, as were the negro slaves the day they were made free and then promptly made citizens of the Republic. Only a very short removed from savages and yet, in the judgment of the nation, worthy to be entrusted with all the rights and privileges of an American citizen.

It may be well to consider in what ways these people are now a menace to the communities in which they live.

Dr. Knopf tells us the germ of consumption may enter the human system, first, by being inhaled; that is, breathed into the lungs. Second, by being ingested; that is, eaten with tuberculous food. Third, inoculation; that is, the penetration of tuberculous substance through a wound in the skin. Negroes can communicate tuberculosis to white people in all these ways. The fact that the disease is so rapidly on the increase among them, makes the danger to the whites the more alarming. The sputum of the tuberculous negro mingles with the dust all about us and we enhale it in unobserved particles. Expectoration in pastures where cows feed, communicate tuberculosis to cattle and we drink the milk. We are at all times exposed through wounds in the skin, to become poisoned through tuberculous particles deposited by tuberculous negroes.

Let us see. To the homes of these people we send our laundry, the first day of the week and the clothes remain the entire six days to be burdened with the germs deposited there, in immeasurable number, to be brought again into our homes for the unguarded spread of disease. For the lack of better place to keep what we send to their homes, our laundry is kept in their one room, or at best their two room cabins and shoved under their beds to get out of the way of their inmates, and into the way of all things tuberculous.

Negroes are employed to nurse our children when we have no conception of the evils they bring with them. Not that they want to do harm, but purely from their affection for our little ones, they kiss them over and over again and sow the abundant seeds of disease and death.

They are our cooks. In passing over our premises they expectorate when and where they please and we inhale the sputum; they prepare all that we eat, tasting as often as they like, and we taste what they leave; they drink from all our kitchen utensils and we do not know whether the vessels have been properly cleansed when we use goblets, knives, forks cups, and dishes. They sneeze and cough into our cooking utensils and into our food and we swallow the germs they deposit.

Negroes are our office boys, draymen and coachmen and men of all work, and they come and go, carrying disease and death at every turn and in every way. We touch these people at all points of service and every turn of our going, and our vitality is open to be broken down by disease every itme we meet them, or take in by infection what they may have left behind when they are gone.

In the midst of these dreadful conditions that are all about us, and immediately confronted by an outlook that is absolutely apalling, the state is dead asleep, the municipalities are criminally indifferent and the people, the large masses of the people, are in stark and painful ignorance of the plague that is spreading over the land.

I have presented the negro at a great disadvantage, as a constant menace to the community. Now let me say, it is not altogether his fault. He came into his new relations totally unconscious of the condition upon which he had fallen. He did not know, and does not now know, and nobody is telling him. It is not his fault if he is not made to know. It is the fault of the white man.

Now, finally, hear this grave and serious charge, deliberarely entered. At the close of the Civil war, because of his indolence, his impudence and his new made criminal character, the white people at the South told the negro to go to the Devil, and the negro promptly obeyed and went. He has now come back, and he is loaded with infections and contagions and crimes that appal the nation. Because of all this, the white people of the south are chargeable, distinctly chargeable, with great sin against themselves, sin against the negro, sin against the church, sin against the state, sin against the nation and great sin against God, and they have left the negro to himself to desolate the land with his wickedness, scattering death by his diseases and blood by his crimes and laying waste all along the track of his miserable going. For much of all this the white man is to be blamed because of his neglect and his indifference.

TUBERCULIZATION OF THE NEGRO
A Letter

BY H. J. ACHARD.

(The contents of this letter furnish the justification of its appearance here. The Journal will be glad to publish a reasonable amount of comment on the thoughts here advanced.—EDITOR.)

Chicago, Ill., May 28, 1912.
Dr. C. V. Roman,
   1303 Church St.,
     Nashville, Tenn.

Dear Doctor Roman:

For a long time I have been intending to congratulate you on the splendid Journal which you are getting out in behalf of the colored medical and allied professions. I enjoy reading the numbers as they come out and appreciate the excellent work which you are doing for your race.

If, after this "pat on the back," you will permit me to make a small criticism, I should like to say something by way of supplementing the remarks of Dr. E. M. Boyle in his fine paper in No. 2 of your Journal, page 124.

The doctor discusses on page 127 the question whether the Negro race is particularly susceptible to tuberculosis. While he is essentially correct, his words, as they stand, are open to erroneous interpretation.

In the days "before the war" pulmonary consumption was so exceedingly rare in colored people that the Negro, as a race, was considered to be immune to the disease, the infectious nature of which was then, of course, not understood, and it is said, that somewhere in the fifties, if my memory does not decieve me, one case of consumption in a Negro was demonstrated to the physicians in Cincinnati as a curiosity.

All this was changed by the war or rather by the different conditions of life caused by the war and by its outcome. The Negro acquired tuberculosis in its acute miliary form and died of rapid consumption in great numbers; in fact, a slow chronic type of phthisis was hardly known to occur. In the last ten and fifteen years, however, rapid acute cases are less frequently in proportion, and it is often possible to observe cases of the disease that assume the chronic prolonged course with which we are familiar in the Caucasian race. Even today, however, the census reports show that the mortality from tuberculosis is greater among Negroes than it is among Caucasians. Out of 100 Negroes, a greater number become tuberculous and consumptive than out of 100 Caucasians in similar conditions of life, and of all those who had acquired the disease, the mortality is greater in the colored people.

Dr. Boyle is undoubtedly right

when he says that "the various influences operating, either directly or indirectly, potently or feebly, whether within or without the host, the housing conditions, habits, and so forth, must all be arranged to ascertain to what extent they have made predisposition possible in the victim," and this is exactly the explanation that is afforded. Before the war the Negro was, as a rule, well taken care of, because he represented an investment in money, and represented a definite monetary value. He was housed and clothed and fed, was attended to by physicians when ill, lived almost entirely in the open air and was obliged to maintain a certain degree of cleanliness. All these comparatively favorable conditions obtained, Mrs. Harriett Beecher Stowe's "Uncle Tom's Cabin" to the contrary, notwithstanding.

After the war all this was changed. The Negro, who was almost entirely uneducated, had been made a free man and could follow his own sweet will. It stands to reason that after the conditions of enforced work which had prevailed before the war, this sweet will would first of all lead him to indulge in dolce far niente and in taking an unaccustomed rest from the labors of the past years. Unfortunately, this prolonged rest did not keep the pot boiling, nor did it keep the cabin clean and the rent paid, and that proportion of the race that had no desire to improve its conditions soon descended to a mode of living that you know perfectly well to have been and to be horrible. Dirt, irregular living, alternating between stuffing and starving, excesses of various kinds, often indulgence in alcohol, crowded, unventilated quarters and insufficient clothing—everything contributed to lower the physical standard of the unfortunate Negro, and to make him a ready victim to tubercular infection which took terrible toll from the race.

This was the more easily possible because your race had not, like the white race, become accustomed to the disease through centuries of continued tuberculization. In the white race consumption is as old as its history and in the many generations a racial resistance to the disease has developed, which makes the tubercle bacillus far less harmful than it was formerly when tuberculosis was as vicious and fatal a disease as are now scarlet fever, diphtheria or smallpox.

Take the Jew as a race because Dr. Boyle mentioned him. The doctor would find contributions to literature from the pen of Dr. Maurice Fishberg of New York of great interest in this respect. Fishberg has explained in a number of articles which mostly appeared in the Medical Record (for instance of 1907) that the Jewish race has for centuries lived in crowded, unhygienic, filthy quarters; that is, has become urbanized long since, and the Jew has paid his toll to infectious diseases, acquiring in return resistance to them so that it is hardly ever possible to observe, for instance, a case of acute tuberculosis in the Jew, as the disease assumes almost always a slow and protracted course, more so than in the Gentile, and fibrous healing is frequent.

Here then we find, what is to my mind, a most important explanation of the relation of the Negro race to tuberculosis. The Negro readily became tuberculized owing to his mode of life which is unfavorable in many things and in many respects. He is frequently exposed to infection and has not the same resistance to the disease that the Caucasian enjoys. Therefore he is more susceptible to its ravages and it will take him generations before he will be able to resist the disease even as well as his white brother.

My dear doctor, I did not write this in any caviling spirit. I wish you would send my letter to Dr. Boyle if you will, and let him tell me if he differs from my position in the matter. I have given this problem a good deal of thought while in Asheville, N. C., where I spent three

years in the exclusive study of tuberculosis.

If my opinions may help Dr. Boyle to a clearer understanding of the problem of the Negro race, it will please me. Your race will not have to pay the terrible price for tuberculization that the Caucasians had to pay, because you have the benefit of modern research in immunity and in immunization; you profit from modern endeavor in sanitation, and you have the advantage of a comparatively large number of men who are far ahead of the rest of the race in their development, and in their striving and endeavor, and who are lifting their race, and aiding them to a better position in life. The evolution through which your race is passing will require decades where it took conturies for the white race. The results will mature far more rapidly and will be more prompt and more emphatic.

43

THE NEGRO AND TUBERCULOSIS

E. MAYFIELD BOYLE, M. D.

WASHINGTON, D. C.

July 22, 1912.

Dr. H. J. Achard,
Chicago, Illinois.

Dear Sir: Your letter to Dr. Roman, dated May 28, 1912, was sent to me several weeks ago in compliance with your request.

I read with much eagerness your comment, or "criticism," as you preferred to put it, which, to my mind, is mainly an amplification of the underlying causes I gave of the spread and mortality of tuberculosis in the "American" Negro. But, curious enough, after unavoidably quoting and accepting the premises of my views in the matter, and even contrasting the circumstances of slavery and of freedom in their relation to the Negro's physical well-being, and admitting that many customs and usages following emancipation have increased the vulnerability of the Negro to tuberculosis, you wound up by saying, "therefore he is more susceptible to (the) ravages" of tuberculosis "and it will take him generations before he will be able to resist even as well as his white brother."

The death rate of American Negroes from tuberculosis is undoubtedly large, and larger than that of American whites; but this is of itself no proof conclusive that the former is more susceptible than the latter. Every effect has its underlying cause or causes; and the sway of tuberculosis among Negroes of this country is by no means an exception to the rule.

The statistics from official sources, confirming the prevalence of tuberculosis among American Negroes, present figures and array of figures which have served their supreme ends, in myriads of instances, to bedeck the writing of many superficial and perfunctory investigators in pathology, with whom this country is infested, as well as increased the spectacularity which often accompanies agreement with every view or preachment purported to silhouette the Negro as the handiwork of an "apprentice creator." But these writers have proved nothing. They have simply observed that certain races behave variously in their contact with certain diseases; but they do not know, and have not looked well enough for, the whys and wherefores.

One does not resent the idea of being susceptible to any disease any more than one deplores the fact that all mankind must die. But the erroneous inference indulged in by men who are supposed to know better and the peculiar contagiousness and dissemination involved are, to say the least, revolting. . . One is forced in this connection to record the familiar words of Virgil with reference to "fama:" "*mobilitate viget viresque aquirit eundo.*"

If the mere prevalence of tuberculosis among American Negroes and its less prevalence among American whites need no further explanation than that the Negro's body is inferior to that of the white man and can only come to par with the latter through centuries of tuberculization, then one may also infer that the prevalence of, and almost exclusive tendency toward, suicidal tendency in the white race and its scarcity among American Negroes is indicative of inferior brain structure or mental endurance in the whites and the reverse in Negroes; that the Negro has emerged from centuries of suicidal mania through which your race is now wending its weary way. What an open sesame wouldn't this be if it were workable.

The death rate of the Irish in Ireland, as compared with that of the Britons, exceeds the ratio of the blacks and whites in the United States. And yet this people, like the Britons, have been white throughout their generations and, therefore, in your language, have acquired the immunity possible from centuries of tuberculization. But, on the contrary, we find that away from the squalor and hardships and privation and dejection and starvation of their native heath and on the Western Hemisphere with better housing conditions, larger wages and sufficient supply of wholesome food, first-class sanitary surroundings, this same people soon loose their physical weakness, become robust, hardy and fat, so much so that one often hears the by-word, "as big and fat as an Irish woman." What then is the matter with the acquired immunity of the Irish obtained through centuries of tuberculization? Is it possible that living in such close proximity of the Britons, the Irish could, like the Negro in Africa, have steered clear of the pathway of infectious diseases, particularly tuberculosis? Granting that the Irish possesses this immunity because of his identification with the white race and also because of his better health in the United States, why does it (this immunity) so persistently show such terrible differences of potency on the other side of the Atlantic?

That the manifest physical resistance of the white race to infectious diseases, particularly tuberculosis, is a legacy from generations dated centuries back, wakens the thought of a perpetually accelerating potency, rather than its reverse, of this immunizing agency in the white race. But ostensibly there is much contradiction here from what we know of the behavior of the white race with respect to infectious diseases. Perhaps your meaning is that the varied acquaintance of your race with infectious diseases has led to its immunity for tuberculosis. But if I am not mistaken, it seems to me that the necessity for vaccination once every seven years has not been urged from courtesy to the Negro, nor yet the various precautions in vogue to limit possible re-infection and re-reinfection, and so on *ad infinitum*, by the many infectious and contagious diseases of your acquaintance. If there were such a thing as a congenital immunity in the white race why isn't it demonstrable in mulattoes, quadroons, octoroons and the like who are practically white and yet perishing annually by thousands from tuberculosis and other infectious diseases? The answer may be that the victims do not live long enough—certainly hybridity can not materially affect it in view of the omnipresence of race admixture all over Europe, for example, long before the dawn of remote history.

Whatever may be contained in history relative to the physical white man does not necessarily eclipse corresponding facts about the Negro, because history is silent on him. History, secular and sacred, at best is imperfect. It is in reality an epitomized record of a small portion of the white race; and mention of the Negro is made only when it is unavoidable at certain junctures of a narrative. The white man wrote history of his ancestors and showed pretty good sense in doing so. At best, he could not say all he might and he had neither space nor time, not even the tolerance, to record the doing of other peoples, except as I have indicated. Jewish historians, for instance, wrote particularly about the Jews, and incidentally mentioned the Samaritans, Simon the Cyrenian, the Queen of Sheba, etc. The circumstances which have always inevitably brought races together are legion; and the most rabid display of race caste has always afforded loopholes for clandestine and other intercourses in the ages past and will continue so to do in the future. All along the way of the dead and forgotten past the white and black races have mingled and intermingled; and the opportunity for the transmission of infectious diseases by all races has always been ample. The white race has never had a monopoly of infectious diseases—certainly not of tuberculosis which has always claimed, and still claims, its booty indiscriminately whither the chances of sway are facilitated by factors whose principal object is to lower vital resistance and prepare the pabulum for the militant bacillus tuberculosis.

From bacteriological and other data gotten from the examination of Egyptian mummies and from the fact that most Egyptologists have died from tuberculosis, it has been inferred, and justly too, that many, perhaps most, ancient Egyptians died of tuberculosis. The primitive mode of living, the religion and custom of the people, and the unhealthy sanitary conditions ushered by the inundation of the Nile, tended to lessen the physical resistance of the people and render them easy of destruction by tuberculosis. In other parts of Africa you will see that natives contract tuberculosis either less rapidly than the American Negro or almost never at all. In South Africa where certain hardships are being forced upon the natives by unscrupulous and Negrophobic Englishmen, we notice tuberculosis as a disease to be reckoned with; but elsewhere, particularly on the West Coast, where, with more outdoor life, plenty of wholesome food and less oppression, tuberculosis is so rare that its detection is often construed by natives as a "hoodoo spell" put on by some secret enemy. In a period of ten years I know of less than half a dozen fatal cases of tuberculosis to develop in Freetown, Sierra Leone, West Africa. As a native of West Africa I can speak with authority in this connection.

On the other hand, the death rate of civilized Africans, from other causes than tuberculosis, is higher than that of the uncivilized, owing largely to the modernized mode of living and other civilized indulgences. The thatched houses, the characteristic native costumes, the native foodstuffs, etc., are variously substituted by corresponding devices of civilization.

That the health of the American Negro during slavery, as you have pointed out, was better than it is today leads to the same observation I have made between the civilized and uncivilized Africans and more too, perhaps. Those who once exercised the right of tutelage over "body and soul" have, with a younger generation, become, in a large measure, the freedmen's oppressors. Whereas during slavery Negroes were engaged in all manner of physical endeavors and counted efficient as workmen, as freedmen they are vigorously opposed in many a line of industry and labor, wherein their employment was once indispensable. When employed their wages are so small that, to many of us, it is no wonder that many so often fail to "keep soul and body together," seeing that they have to pay the same prices for food and higher rents than the whites who are paid higher wages for the same work. The necessity of corresponding with modern mode of dress, either for beauty's sake or for the sake of being in style, has also forced upon colored Americans such death traps as "ventilating" shirt waists, thin shoes, gauze and linen underwear in winter and summer, light hose, overcoats made only for their appearances instead of for comfort. Think of these transgressors! Think how imperfectly heated the dwelling of the average colored family is in winter— how it may be about blood heat in one room and at freezing point in another; how these persons are thus forced to dress and undress in cold rooms, walk about or ride in unheated cars. Is it not a wonder to you that the census still shows an increase of Negro population in the United States?

Among the numerous other causes of tuberculosis in the American Negro may be mentioned the following: Ignorance of personal hygiene, particularly in the winter; superstitious ideas and the dissemination of erroneous views on health and disease; unwholesome and improperly prepared food; unsanitary and unmodern houses; too much indulgence in spirituous liquors; poverty and its allied disadvantages; promiscuous kissing; crowded apartments; sleeping with consumptives and in unfumigated apartments of consumptives; moving from house to house, not knowing and not even caring to find out the health conditions of the previous occupants. I have further noticed that the death rate of (colored) Baptists, especially among the ignorant and fanatical worshippers, is comparatively greater than that of nearly all other Christian denominations (of colored) put together. As revival services are held chiefly in the winter, new converts who wish to become members of the Baptist church believe (as they have been taught by the "older heads") that cold immersion is just the thing for the "new birth," and that once truly born of the Spirit one cannot be affected by the coldness of the water. There are people who, I am told, would even break ice in the water before baptism. But this is not all. Undressing and redressing take place in apartments which, like the auditorium itself, may be very imperfectly heated. Then comes going home through the cold streets with dampened bodies and half wet hair, especially in the case of women. People who do these things, whether they be white, black brown or yellow or what not, will surely pay the debt either with their health or their lives.

In view of all that I have said I cannot but conclude that the record of the American Negro with reference to infectious diseases, tuberculosis in particular, as in the case of the Irish in Ireland, is due to other than the existence within the host of an inherent susceptibility; and the supposed immunity of the white race handed down through centuries by preinfected ancestors has no foundation in fact. On the contrary, the greater stability of health in your race in this country is the result of superior intelligence, better circumstances, and more wholesome environments. When the American Negro has attained these excellencies of living he will be just as healthy as the white man.

I have, however, said more in this letter than I intended to say at the outset. If I have expressed myself very frankly it is because the nature of the subject before us demands it. If I have enabled you to understand a bit more of the subject which you are giving much attention to I shall feel doubly rewarded.

THE NEGRO, A PUBLIC HEALTH PROBLEM.*

By C. E. TERRY, M.D.,
Jacksonville, Fla.

In presenting this paper I wish at the outset to state that I appreciate fully the magni-
tude of the subject as well as my inability
to more than touch upon certain points to
which the attention of the sanitarian is most
frequently directed. Throughout what follows it will be quite evident that my object
has been rather one of query and suggestion
than of solution.

It must daily occur to the Southern health

*Read in Section on Hygiene and Preventive
Medicine, Southern Medical Association. Seventh
Annual Meeting, Lexington, Ky., November 17-20,
1913.

officer that there are operating, as causes of mortality among the negroes of each community, potent factors which are so little understood as to almost preclude any intelligent efforts at control. Indeed I know of no portion of the great problem of health conservation in which our armamentarium is so completely lacking in effective weapons as that concerning the unduly high negro mortality and its relation to the white mortality in our section of this country.

In preventive measures amongst our own race, throughout those countries in which modern preventive medicine is practiced, there are recognized certain fundamental and fairly definite methods of procedure. These methods are of course changing from year to year, but their development is in the nature of a continuous and logical evolution. When, however, we try to apply these same methods in preventive work among the negroes, it is almost as if we had entered a foreign land expecting our own language to convey our ideas to its people. We find ourselves, in fact, confronted by an alien, and not only does this racial difference render our task most difficult, but this very alien has been but recently transplanted to conditions of life which are entirely foreign to his nature. To our own ignorance of him is added his of his surroundings. His value in the labor market is probably better understood than any other of his attributes, but, even while fully appreciating how far sanitation has lagged behind other sciences amongst our own race, it is almost inconceivable that in view of our close association with the negro in the South we should have made so little effort to keep in sanitary touch with him.

This may appear to be a sweeping statement, but it is based upon comparative figures that are startling and that I fear may be but partially explained by the claim of racial inferiority. In a review of the annual reports of the health departments of nine of the larger Southern cities I find that the negro, as a health problem, is discussed at some length in but one, that of Richmond. In the other eight, outside of a casual mention in two, the only evidence of his existence is shown in the bare figures of the mortality tables. I feel that we are justified in assuming that this absence of mention is a fair measure of health conservation efforts in his behalf.

A glance at the mortality statistics of the U. S. Bureau of the Census should serve to direct our attention most forcibly to the problem which confronts us. The mortality rates given for the registration area of this country are, for 1911, 1373.7 for the whites against 2396.0 for the negro per 100,000. This great disproportion affects the total mortality of the registration area but slightly, the total figures being 1415.9, but it must be remembered that but a small portion of the South is included in the registration area, only three States. Were the whole South, with its universally high negro mortality, within this area, the death rate of the country would be considerably higher.

Another fact strikingly illustrates the apparent inadaptability of the negro to life in our larger cities. This is the marked difference shown between his death rate in the registration cities and that in the rural portions of the registration States, 2604.3 for the former against 1890.2 for the latter. Or to present this in another manner, the death rate of the negro in the registration cities is 714.1 higher per 100,000 than his death rate in the rural portion of the registration States, while the white death rate in the cities only exceeds that of the rural districts by 119.5 per 100,000.

For further comparison I have chosen fifteen cities of the North, East and West and nineteen Southern cities in which the negro comprises 10 per cent or more of the total population. The North, East and Western cities chosen were Los Angeles, San Francisco, Wilmington (Del.), Chicago, Indianapolis, Kansas City (Kan.), Leavenworth, Boston, Kansas City (Mo.), St. Louis, Columbus, Carlisle, Philadelphia, Cincinnati and Covington. For the Southern cities Birmingham, Mobile, Montgomery, Washington, Jacksonville, Key West, Atlanta, Savannah, Lexington, Louisville, New Orleans, Baltimore, Wilmington (N. C.), Knoxville, Memphis, Nashville, Charleston, Norfolk and Richmond.

In these two lists I have compared the average white and colored rates per 100,000. Those cities of the North, East and West give us an average white mortality rate of 1478.2 against a white rate of 1690.4 for the Southern cities, while the colored rates are 2430.5 and 3087.5 respectively. A comparison of the white and colored rates of these two groups of cities show for the South an excess in the white rate of 212.2 and 657.0 for the negro. In other words, the death rate of the Southern negro as compared with the Northern negro is more than three times as high as that of the Southern white over the Northern white.

Granting that the poorer equipment of the South in sanitary matters will account for the increase in the white death rate, it still remains difficult to explain why the same conditions should apparently affect the negro to a so much greater extent. The South has come to be regarded as a more natural habitat for the negro than the North, but these figures would indicate that the negro thrives better in almost any other section of the country. To this it may be objected that for the greater part only the more intelligent negroes, and hence those better equipped to protect themselves against disease, seek homes in the North, while those mentally and physically more deficient remain where they find themselves and add their constitutional weaknesses to outside factors contributing to their mortality. Such an explanation would be comforting to a degree, but I feel that it will not wholly explain the discrepancy. It would appear instead that in the North the negro lives under better sanitary conditions and is affected by closer and better organized supervision than in the South. The truth of this

assumption is borne out, I believe, by a comparison of the mortality rates of the two races per 100,000 from certain causes.

Still using the figures from the cities named and for the year 1911, I have chosen nine important causes of death, typhoid fever, pulmonary tuberculosis, measles, scarlet fever, diphtheria, whooping cough, pneumonia (all forms), diarrhoea and enteritis (under 2 years) and congenital debility. These causes are commonly considered preventable with the exception of the last named. An average of the mortality rate from these causes for the two races shows that in the Southern cities the white rate is 4.4 higher than the white rate in the Northern cities, while for the negroes of the South the rate is 14.1 higher than for this race in the Northern cities. Presented differently, we find that from these causes the Southern negro loses 146.6 per 100,000 more over the Northern negro than the Southern white does over the Northern white. The details are shown in the following table:

Average Rate Per 100,000 Certain Causes.

	North, East and Western Cities.		Southren Cities.	
	White.	Col.	White	Col.
Typhoid	21.1	35.3	54.8	71.9
Tuberculosis lung	149.2	447.7	137.6	395.5
Measles	7.9	4.6	20.4	15.3
Scarlet fever	10.3	3.8	3.9	0.7
Diphtheria	15.6	15.4	12.6	7.4
Whooping cough	8.2	19.5	19.5	54.2
Pneumonia	142.2	276.4	109.6	310.1
Diarrhoea and enteritis	67.7	89.1	94.8	142.2
Congenital debility	79.4	87.2	88.0	158.1

A scrutiny of this table shows that tuberculosis of the lungs affects the Southern negro proportionately less than the Southern white whereas pneumonia (all forms) causes a far greater proportionate loss among the Southern negroes than among the whites. As an explanation of the apparent anomaly in these two diseases of the respiratory system, both of which cause an unduly high mortality among the negro race. I would suggest that the figures for tuberculosis are possibly influenced to no small degree by the fact that this disease is usually excluded from those for which companies, insuring negroes, will pay a death claim. At least I am aware that in Jacksonville it is not at all uncommon to find malaria or some other incorrect cause named on the death certificate of negroes so insured, where pulmonary tuberculosis was the actual cause of death. This factor would unquestionably apply to a greater degree in the South where the larger portion of the negro indemnity insurance is carried on. Not only might the death rate from tuberculosis be lessened but that from pneumonia be, for the same reason, increased. I mention this merely as a tentative explanation.

Whooping cough shows a marked predilection for the Southern over the Northern negro, while the other acute contagious diseases of childhood tabulated, measles, scarlet fever and diphtheria, do not figure largely in the mortality rates of either race. Diarrhoea and enteritis (under 2 years) serves to augment considerably the Southern mortality rate, especially in the case of the negro, 89.1 for the Northern negro against 142.2 for this race in the South.

Under congenital debility and malformation we find the greatest sectional variance of all. In the Northern cities named the negro rate from this cause is but 19.5 more per 100,000 than that of the whites, while the Southern negro rate exceeds the white by 70.1 per 100,-000. While this cause of death is not to be classed as preventable, in the ordinary acceptation of the term, yet we are forced to admit that physical surroundings, social and economic influences, occupations and customs, housing and institutional provisions, in other words modern sanitary supervision, unite to augment or lessen the number of deaths thus classified, nor is it possible for us to explain away this immensely disproportionate rate on the grounds of inherent racial weakness.

I shall not attempt to explain or answer the questions implied in the above general considerations. These are matters that may only be settled after years of united study and ob-

servation on our part. A statement, however, of a few specific, local facts and figures may prove of interest as offering in some small degree a partial explanation.

In Jacksonville for the five-year period, 1908-1912, inclusive, the negro death rate has been 23.0 per 1,000 as against 14.9 for the whites. For the same period the negroes have shown a birth rate of 17.31 per 1,000, 5.7 lower than their death rate, while the white birth rate has exceeded the death rate by 3.5 per 1,000. During the past four years, 1909-1912, still-births have constituted 13.80 per cent of all negro births and 6.29 per cent of white births. Aside from the influence of congenital weakness in this high still-birth rate, there enters another factor of importance and one obtaining, for the most part in the South, namely the practice of midwifery. For the four-year period named the still-birth rate in the practice of the midwives has been 15.62, that in the practice of physicians 8.21. Nearly all the negro babies are delivered by these women and their ignorance operates chiefly against this race, though it is felt to some degree amongst the whites.

It is needless for me to attempt to picture to this gathering the woeful shortcomings of the negro "granny." Her influence extends beyond the confinement bed and we find her a common and sole attendant upon the negro babies during the early months of life and no small number who escape her upon their entrance to life, succumb to her later ministrations. Tetanus, obscure "convulsions," "teething," "hives" and "colds" appear with disquieting frequency upon the death certificates of negro babies above the signature of this midwife or that, while ophthalmia of the newborn and fatal infection of parturient women follow in her wake at all times.

A further reference to the death certificates of Jacksonville for the past five years (1908-1912) shows that of all the negro deaths (exclusive of violent deaths and suicides) 16.88 per cent occurred without medical attention, while of the whites dying during this period only 4.48 per cent were unattended by a physician. To this total absence of treatment in 16.88 per cent of negro deaths must be added a very large percentage receiving scarcely better service at the hands of physicians of their own race. I can only speak for my own city, but there. at least, may be found as fine a collection of ignorance among the negro physicians as one might care to view. Not only does their paucity of intellect and training enter as an unquestioned factor in a high mortality, but their mercenary motives are daily evidenced by the fact that, however grave the condition they may be treating, their visits are, for the most part, numbered by the fees collected at the door of the sick room. Their patients seem to expect no more and, throughout the dangers of typhoid, pneumonia. infantile diarrhoeas and other grave infections, appear contented with

past two years with colored district nurses. I am convinced that, in proportion to the amount expended, no other single means is more valuable in lowering the death rate of this race, especially that of infants. Nor does it fill a less important role as a means of sanitary education. No white man or woman can do this work, in the far South, as well as can a colored nurse, providing her mentality and training are adequate to the requirements.

I can not close this already long paper without reference to the high mortality rate of the negro from communicable and preventable diseases as shown in the following table. These figures are for the five-year period, 1908-1912, of Jacksonville. Divided as our population is almost equally between the two races, we offer an especially favorable community in which to make these racial mortality comparisons.

DISEASE	1908 W	1908 B	1909 W	1909 B	1910 W	1910 B	1911 W	1911 B	1912 W	1912 B	Avg. Rate W	Avg. Rate B
Typhoid (residents)	20	25	20	23	31	16	18	8	1	9	6.45	5.42
Malaria	5	18	7	28	2	29	6	35	5	10	1.72	8.03
Measles	1	1	0	1	0	0	6	3	2	0	.59	.24
Scarlet Fever	0	0	0	0	2	0	4	0	0	0	.40	.00
Whooping Cough	3	6	0	9	0	5	2	0	0	2	.32	1.48
Diphtheria	2	0	3	0	1	1	4	2	1	3	.77	.33
Influenza	1	6	2	3	0	4	3	8	2	8	.51	.59
Tuberculosis (lungs)	53	142	40	111	19	95	48	100	34	102	13.35	36.64
Tuberculosis (other forms)	2	2	10	4	3	3	10	8	6	0	2.19	1.16
Venereal Diseases	5	12	2	24	0	9	7	32	1	31	1.06	6.91
Pneumonia	28	57	34	44	24	57	23	43	17	43	8.83	16.21
Diarrhoea (under two)	9	11	9	6	13	36	28	43	18	25	5.27	8.00
Diarrhoea (over two)	25	24	24	27	5	7	8	15	5	7	4.75	5.39
Totals	154	303	151	280	100	262	167	297	92	240		

a weekly or biweekly visit, and whatever the outcome, it is accepted as inevitable and with cheerful indifference by the family.

In this connection I may say that we are solving in some measure these two problems by the employment of a negro district nurse who follows the midwives and cases of reportable diseases and undoubtedly secures for such cases more careful medical attention, as her connection with the health department puts the attending negro physician on notice that we are in close touch with his case and his methods. From our experience during the

These causes are responsible for 40.1 per cent of all negro deaths as against 29.3 per cent of white deaths. Were as large a percentage of negroes as of whites attended by physicians and were the diagnoses of the negro physician more accurate I am confident that this negro toll to preventable disease would show still greater: I feel that not only is the negro mortality of the Southern city increased by these diseases from the lack of preventive measures amongst this people, but that the white mortality and morbidity is raised by these same causes. through their prevalence in the other race. To quote from another paper on this subject:

"These negro citizens, amongst whom we find such an undue prevalence of diarrhoeal diseases, tuberculosis and venereal infections, who live under the worst of sanitary conditions, through circumstances, racial inferiority and our neglect, mingle with us in a hundred intimate ways, in our stores and factories, our kitchens and nurseries. They knead our bread and rock our babies to sleep in their arms, dress them, fondle them and kiss them; can any one doubt that we may not escape this close exposure? The missed and carrier cases of typhoid and other intestinal diseases that wait upon our tables must exact their toll nor is this lessened by any habits of personal cleanliness discernible."

In conclusion I would state that the burden of this great health problem must devolve finally upon the Southern sanitarian and sociologist. It has, I believe, been sadly neglected by us all in the past and yet it is most intimately concerned with the welfare of the entire South; accurate observations, careful social surveys, experimental methods must all play a part. No field is probably so barren of sanitary achievement as this and none offers a more worthy occasion for painstaking effort with promise of far-reaching results of the utmost import to the Southern states.

DISCUSSION.

Dr. Fred J. Mayer, Opelousas, La.—In approaching any problem in hygiene and state medicine, whether the inhibition of mosquito or fly life, soil pollution, food and drug adulteration, vital statistics, drainage, or eugenics, we find that all roads lead logically to one point, viz., the education of the public in the true cause, nature and prevention of communicable diseases, and particularly in the relation of insects and animals to the public health.

As was said by the great Kentuckian, Lincoln: "With public sentiment everything will succeed; without public sentiment nothing will succeed. Consequently he who moulds public sentiment goes deeper than he who enacts statutes or pronounces decisions; he makes statutes possible to be enacted." Shall we go a step further and say, after enactment possible of execution?

In so far as the negro is concerned in his relation to public health, it is but one phase of that sinister problem that looms large and lowers low on the horizon. Speaking as an ex-white leaguer, who has served his apprenticeship in preventing the Africanization of the ballot-box in his native state, and therefore not to be misunderstood, I have no hesitancy in declaring that now that the negro is removed from the plane of political action, his social and political status as a child race thoroughly understood and settled forever in the South, we are confronted with a sacred duty, the duty of improving his material welfare and especially his health. Of course, as a carrier and transmitter of disease, he is a standing menace to the white race, and therefore self-interest points to this improvement, but I prefer to place it on a higher plane than self-interest and to view it as a humanitarian duty. Duty, in the words of the South's most venerated chieftain, is the sublimest word in the English language. The question then arises, is the negro susceptible of being educated in the fundamental principles of hygiene? We have had the affirmative proofs in Louisiana in 1905 and 1906, where along with the whites he was led out from the fallacious fomites theory of yellow fever transmission into the true mosquito doctrine and did yeoman service in exterminating stegomyiae, the epidemic being suppressed before frost, and a recrudescence the following year prevented for the first time in epidemic history.

We should, through our boards of health, and other educative agencies, start an educational movement among them on hygienic lines, through illustrated lectures and especially in their churches, secure the co-operation of their preachers in teaching them the A B C of hygiene and especially that "Cleanliness is indeed next to Godliness," and by pointing to the twenty-third chapter of Deuteronomy, warn them of the sinfulness of soil pollution. We should also improve their houses, making them healthful instead of the existent dens of filth and contagion, which they now are. In Louisiana Dr. Dowling, the eminent head of our health service, intends after the carnival season starting such a campaign, which doubtless will bring forth good fruit in an eventual lessening of morbidity and mortality rate among the negroes and reflexly affect beneficially the white vital statistics.

Dr. R. M. Cunningham, Birmingham, Ala.—I did not expect to be called upon to take part in this discussion. I regret very much that I did not hear the paper, but the negro problem embraces its hygienic and sanitary aspects, as I understand, and if that is the case, it is one of very great importance. I caught enough of the last gentleman's remarks to get the drift of the discussion. We have practically sterilized the negro, and therefore it is up to the white people to do his voting and make for him the best possible conditions.

I have had considerable experience in practice among negroes around public work, and I am free to confess I have left alone all those that did not have the rudiments of sanitation, and hence their education is of very vast importance. My personal observation has been, however, that with the exception of tuberculosis and lobar pneumonia, they have been a rather remarkably healthy people, notwithstanding I do not know how to account for it. We have a good many cases of typhoid fever among them, but it is rare, and malaria also is rare, notwithstanding the presence of flies in abundance and mosquitoes. Whether this is an acquired racial immunity that has been gradually developing for years or not, I do not know. But I do know that to be a fact, and I know that appendicitis is not rife in the negro race. I made that statement before a meeting of the Southern Surgical and Gynecological Association, and they all jumped on me. I have had as part of my clientele from 1,000 to 5,000 negroes embracing a period of thirty years, and I must say that appendicitis is one of the rarest diseases with them. I explain that in this way: The work in which I have been engaged for thirty years is contract practice; the negroes pay so much a month and get the value of their money, and it is their constant practice to take pills at least once a week, particularly compound cathartic pills. In my judgment that accounts in a very large measure for the few cases of appendicitis. Possibly of other diseases that is not so much the question.

Where I have been for thirty years the employers of this labor have taken up the question of sanitation and hygiene and have employed experts for the purpose of teaching these people. We have at Ensley and throughout the district the property of the Tennessee Coal & Iron Company. Dr. Nolen, who was at Panama for a number of years, has charge of the general proposition, and the company has screened the houses, drained the ponds, and has issued bulletins on sanitary methods. I remember there was one written on flies about a year ago in relation to the spread of disease, and another one on mosquitoes, and the people took considerable interest in these articles. In the cities and in the country the regulations have to be enforced, and the law is enforced by the legal officials. I have been struck with the remarkable manner in which these people are controlled by the law; how they take an interest in the law and its enforcement. When the superintendent or foreman of this great corporation says, "Johnny, this house must be cleaned up or you git," he immediately cleans the house. And that is what counts with the negro race. It takes authority to execute these things and that is being done.

In my work at Ensley we have what was once the old Birmingham, but now the Greater Birmingham, embracing Ensley and Wylam, an incorporated city, and just across the railroad, northwest of the works, are the convicts' quarters, absolutely under the control and the authority of the officials of the Tennessee Coal & Iron Railroad Company. We have had but two or three cases of typhoid fever in the quarters, as we call it, in a year, either in the white or black. We had a number of Italians that came from Mississippi and located on the white stream, and they were the hosts of malaria. There were a few mosquitoes, and from this intermediate host there was quite an epidemic among the white people, but not among the negroes; whereas in Ensley, and in parts of the Greater Birmingham now incorporated as one of the villages of the state, we have not had a great many cases of typhoid fever, notwithstanding we have good sewerage, whereas in the quarters we have the dry system, but it has a system of closets which are cleaned, disinfected and the filth is removed and destroyed.

Now, there is no comparison, as we all know, between the wet system of sewerage and the dry system when left to the people to execute them, but with a man behind them with authority to tell them to make a move or to get off the premises, it works well. I do not know just how much education has done towards this very great revolution, but I know authority has done a great deal for them, so that I believe in solving the problem of the negro race, and in considering every possible relation of life, we should consider him as a part of the white man's burden, and we should all do what we can for him in every particular. Where I am living the negroes work around public works, the schools are being conducted properly, the public playgrounds are being kept clean, and the houses are kept in good sanitary condition, and they are taught personal hygiene, and whatever the reason is, with the exception of lobar pneumonia, to which the negro race as such is particularly predisposed, whether in the aggregated or segregated relation, we have had wonderful success. I believe education should be carried on through the preachers and the negro doctors; that mass-meetings should be held and illustrated lectures be given. If you show them pictures and point out the practical application of sanitary and hygienic measures, you will accomplish something.

Some work has been done along the line of prevention of the social diseases, with no success, nor will there be success in that particular line for years to come. But along the line of infectious diseases being transmitted through the air or body hosts, or through carriers, something over which there can be co-operation and control, we have had wonderful success.

Pneumonia is as yet, as we all know, the crux of the medical profession. We do not know how to prevent it. We do not know how to treat it. We know more about it than Hippocrates did as to the means of its propagation, but we do not know much more about the treatment. It is particularly fatal in the negro race, and it is one of the things we have to deal with.

Tuberculosis is diminishing. I do not know why. For many years I was physician to two large prisons that employed 1,000 or 1,200 men. Thirty years ago tuberculosis prevailed to the extent of 80 per cent among these people. The history of these cases was that there was a chronic nidus somewhere either in the lungs or lymphatic glands. Under the environments then existing we found cases of acute tuberculosis. I saw then a good many cases of typhoid fever, but typhoid fever is diminishing. There are not so many cases of glandular tuberculosis among the younger generation as there were twenty or thirty years ago. You do not find as many scars on the necks representing healed scrofula, which we know now to be tuberculosis. With the white folks I do not know what has done this. Negroes spit on the street and in public places, and we know disease is communicated in that way, yet authority is being exercised in regard to that. But you cannot watch everybody. Upon the whole, the negro question in relation to sanitation and hygiene, where there are white men in control, who know themselves what ought to be done, and who have the authority to hire others to do it or to get off the premises, is working well.

Dr. Henry S. Hanson, Jacksonville, Fla.—There is one feature in connection with the negro as a source of infection not only to the white people with whom he comes in contact, but his own people, to which I desire to call attention, and while Dr. Cunningham was speaking of malaria among the negroes and the relatively few clinical cases of malaria among them, that does not however mean that the negro cannot be a source of infection to white people with whom he comes in contact.

In the State Board of Health in Florida we made a number of determinations among apparently healthy schoolchildren as to the presence of malarial carriers. We found that among from 500 or 600 schoolchildren, white and black, from whom we had taken blood smears, and who at the time showed no symptoms of malaria, an average of about 4 per cent of malaria carriers among the children: they harbored the sexual forms of the tertian and estivo-autumnal parasites. In one section we found that in one school we had 33 per cent of carriers among the negro children; 9 per cent of these harbored estivo-autumnal parasites. This, of course, indicates they can be prolific sources for infection of mosquitoes, who bite them, and transmit the disease to the white population. Every one who has gone through the negro hovels of the larger cities and seen the unsanitary conditions under which most of these people live can have no doubt as to their being a source of infection to the children whom they nurse and care for. As has been said, they have not very exalted ideas of hygiene or cleanliness, and wherever the infectious intestinal diseases prevail, such as dysentery or typhoid fever, it is easy to see how these people can carry these infections over into the kitchens of the white families where they are employed as cooks or as nursemaids.

Dr. D. M. Molloy, Manila, Philippine Islands—As a visitor I should like to add just a few words to the discussion of this paper. I am heartily in accord with the sentiments expressed by the first gentleman in discussing it, namely, that of the duty of the white man to the negro. We cannot fail to take cognizance of that great democratic principle under which the humblest individual in a community is taken into account in all efforts to prevent disease in that community and without it no community can be said to be protected.

The question raised by Dr. Krauss, that of the individual danger of negroes in their relation to the white people is one of the most important things brought out so far in the discussion of this negro problem as a health problem. We have had a great deal of experience in the Philippine Islands (and I may say here, I am from the Philippine service and our work in the Philippine Islands is principally among Filipinos and as regards sanitation and education in sanitary matters they do not compare favorobaly in some respects with the negro race in the South), and we have for some years recognized that the ignorance of the ordinary Filipino servant did not constitute a danger to himself alone, but it constituted a grave danger to the white people in the Philippine Islands who are laboring for his welfare and attempting to eradicate diseases from among the people. We have, of course, in the Philippine Islands taken into account the protection of the races against

certain tropical conditions which prevail there. For instance, amebic dysentery was the bete noir of all Americans in the early days of the Philippine Islands. Many of the civil employees, soldiers and many people in various walks of life in that country contracted chronic amebic dysentery and were invalided. Recent work has convinced us that much of our effort to prevent amebic dysentery among the white inhabitants there was directed toward the wrong source. The white people in the Philippine Islands would contract amebic dysentery after having observed all of the usual precautions, and the question would naturally arise, where did they get it? They boiled their water; they did not eat uncooked foods; they excluded raw vegetables from their diet, and possibly protected themselves against flies and other carriers of infection; yet numerous individuals contracted amebic dysentery. We have recently learned that intestinal amebiasis is very prevalent in the Philippine Islands, and it may be said the great majority of Filipinos are ameba carriers. The amebae may exist in the intestinal tract of an individual just as typhoid bacilli may exist in the intestinal tract of man without actually producing the disease, amebic dysentery, in that individual, and yet he is a great menace to the people with whom he comes in contact on account of the fact he is a carrier of amebae; and since through his ignorance he is careless in his habits he constitutes a grave danger to the white people whom he serves. This is particularly true of the negro in the South. We all know, the negro in the South comes in close contact with the white people in the capacity of servant, and in many instances he is thrown into closer personal contact with the white people than the white people are thrown in contact with one another. In that way he constitutes a grave danger to the white people as a carrier of disease.

Dr. Litterer in the discussion on milk referred to an epidemic of typhoid fever at Athens Female College, and a carrier was responsible for this epidemic of eighty-nine cases. This carrier, as he told me, was a negro who was employed as a domestic in this college or as a servant in the dairy from which they got the milk. This negro servant was responsible for this very acute epidemic of eighty-nine cases of typhoid fever in that institution, and I believe he told me there were eight deaths. This is likewise true of malaria. We know malaria is comparatively rare among the negroes in one respect, as Dr. Cunningham has said, but most of us with large experience with malaria know that certain people, certain individuals, may act as repositories for malarial infection, and they themselves not be suffering from acute attacks.

I believe that the negro, while not actually suffering from clinically pronounced malaria, constitutes one of the greatest difficulties to be encountered in any organized effort to eradicate malaria from the South, on account of harboring malarial parasites, thus constituting repositories for the malarial infection, sources from which the mosquito may become infected, and thus convey the infection to the more susceptible white people among whom the carrier lives.

Dr. R. H. von Ezdorf, Mobile, Ala.—I have been studying one special disease, malarial fever, among the negroes and white people, and I have been doing this work with a view to establishing a malarial index in some of our Southern states. I find that the negro is a very receptive individual in the educational side of preventive medicine. He wants to learn something about it, and I have been frequently invited to discuss before negroes the subjects of malaria and other diseases with special reference to the methods of prevention. In the talks I have given in colored schools I found the teachers as well as the children were very much interested in this subject. If we are to begin with the education of these people we ought not to lose sight of the schools and ought to do what we can to help and educate the youths, and particularly the negroes in the schools. In some of the cities and towns where I have been I found that they were not provided with the best facilities for schools, and in some places the amount of appropriations are limited and proportioned by taxation; that is to say, where a negro pays a small tax, they are given a proportionately smaller appropriation for educational purposes. When we make an inspection in our towns in the South we will find the negroes are living in the outskirts, where the houses are built on cheap lands and the houses built cheaply. You will find them where the land is not properly drained, nor provision made for proper lighting, water supply and sewerage. Who is to blame for that, I would like to ask? We are trying to educate them to bring about the best sanitary conditions, and yet these are the conditions the white people provide for the negroes. It is no wonder we find these unsanitary and unhygienic conditions, and until they are remedied it does not seem to me that we can accomplish much except through education, and endeavor to have them do what they can for themselves individually. For the sake of the general good we must certainly make better provisions for their living.

With reference to malaria, I have found in taking indices in the South that the negro is a larger factor in spreading infection than a great many imagine. I find a larger percentage of carriers among the negroes than I do among the whites. Some years ago I practiced in the North, and my belief and idea was that malaria did not exist among the negroes; that they were practically immune. However, when I came South I soon learned I was wrong and have since been able to confirm the fact that the disease is quite common among the negroes, and that the negro is a larger factor in spreading the disease than we have heretofore believed.

Dr. J. A. Stucky, Lexington, Ky.—I am very sorry all of the papers of this symposium were not read, for the reason I wanted to hear what each man had to say on each subject, to enlighten our brothers across Mason and Dixon's line, who are asking important questions about the negro. Living as I do on the border line here in Lexington, I cannot answer the question from a distinctive standpoint of the true Southerner. I am in hearty accord with all that has been said, and especially with what Dr. Cunningham has said. Somebody must get behind the negro with authority and tell him that he must do so and so or "git." We must do the same thing with the poor white trash. The poor white man must clean

up or get out, and self-preservation, if for no other reason on earth, demands that we scientists, we humanitarians, should give these negroes a fair deal, a square deal, and a fair chance, and teach them the sanitary laws that are so necessary not only for their own protection but for ourselves, because they are carriers of disease.

One question that I would like to ask and have answered is, although it may be out of place, with regard to enlarged tonsils and adenoids. I am often asked more particularly by physicians in the North whether we find diseased tonsils, adenoids and mastoid disease in the negroes of the South, the same as we find these diseases in the whites in the East and Middle West and the North. Up until six or seven years ago I answered no, we do not. But in the last five or six years I am meeting with a larger number of cases of young negro children, especially the mulattoes, with enormously enlarged and diseased tonsils and adenoids, and I have had more mastoid cases to operate upon among the negroes in the last five or six years than in all my previous medical experience. I would like to know if the present way of living of the negro in the South has anything to do with the lymphatic diseases that are on the increase. We do not hear so much about scrofulous diseases. We know what they are. I would like to know if the nose and throat men are meeting with a number of cases of diseased tonsils and adenoids, and if they are meting with a larger number of cases in the negro with mastoid complications that require operation.

Another thing I have noticed here in Lexington in the last five or six years is, that I am meeting with a larger number of negro children who need glasses, who have refractive errors, who cannot get along at school until the refractive error is corrected. Are you meeting with these cases in the far South? If these questions, Mr. Chairman, are out of order, I wish you would so rule, but I should be glad if some of you who live far South would tell me what your experience has been in regard to these diseases, so that I can tell the practitioners in the North who ask me questions in regard to these diseases.

Dr. H. H. Martin, Savannah, Ga.—In answer to what Dr. Stucky has said, in my own town, Savannah, the population is a litle over 50 per cent negro, and probably 90 per cent of these are blacks. I think I can safely say that enlarged tonsils and superfluous adenoid tissue in the throat is very rare. I have service in the negro hospital of about one hundred beds or something like that; I visit the institution almost every day in the year, and I do not recall in thirteen years fifty cases of tonsil operation or operation for adenoids. I can recall but three mastoid operations on negroes, and these were specific necroses. In my work on the ear, nose and throat I find 90 per cent of the cases among negroes are syphilitic; that the ravages of syphilis in the colored race do not seem to be so great as in the white, and they yield more promptly to treatment. But I repeat, that 90 per cent of these people who come under my service have this disease, either hereditary or acquired, mostly acquired.

In answer to the question raised by Dr. Krauss as to the danger of a negro communicating diseases to the family for which he works, I think it more imaginary than real. Why, I do not know. I have often wondered when I see so many young girls who have syphilis, who are nursing white children, and I see young men, middle-aged men, who are cooks and waiters in restaurants, and grown men and women who are about houses as negro servants, as they are in the South, why there are not more diseases transmitted or communicated to white people, but I can now recall but one single instance where disease was communicated, in my town, from a negro to a white family, and that was smallpox. I have had the members of my white families ask me when they send a negro to my office (and I must tell them that negro has syphilis), "Must I keep this negro in my employ?" My answer is, "Yes, why not?" They are afraid the negro will communicate syphilis to the family. Theoretically that is possible, but there has never occurred within my knowledge such a thing except in the one case I have mentioned.

The other question brought up by one of the speakers is one that has been on my mind during this entire discussion. Dr. Cunningham says we must get after these people with authority, and Dr. Stucky says we must do so with the white, while Dr. Mayer spoke of educating them. In my visit to the poor white people and poor negroes in my own city I find the negroes physically better than the whites; but they are huddled and crowded in tenements, in houses not fit for human habitation, and one of the most important methods that this or any other organization should advocate is creating a higher state of physical wellbeing among the negroes. The members of our profession should do this, and try to influence the people who build and rent houses to these people to construct better houses.

Dr. Stucky wants to know about refractive errors in negroes. My experience has been that negro children require glasses in the same proportion as white children. Unfortunately for them we do not give them quite as much time as we do the white children, but whenever I had occasion to examine a negro child's eyes for refractive errors, I have found them in the same proportion as among the white.

One other point in my experience, and that is trachoma. You know trachoma is not very communicable, but I have not in my fifteen years of experience in Savannah seen a case of trachoma in the negro. I have seen plenty of cases of ophthalmia neonatorum, but never one single case of trachoma.

A Member—I have had some experience in treating negroes. I believe we all recognize the importance of the negro as a carrier of disease.

Answering Dr. Stucky's question, I can say that I have been finding a lot of diseased tonsils among the negroes, but not so many cases of adenoids. I recognize the negro as a pretty good imitator, and they have about the same diseases as the white people. I believe we can accomplish a good deal for them by education. They want to do the best they can, and we should prepare places for them to live with greater comfort and with special reference to hygienic and sanitary measures. I am sure, by directing our attention in this direction, we can accomplish a good deal.

Dr. V. H. Bassett, Savannah, Ga.—I would like to say a few words with reference to the possibility of infection being conveyed from servants to members of the family, and on family hygiene. As Dr. Martin has said, I think the number of instances of infection from servants to families is small when one considers the instances of infection among these people, but they do occur, and some of the saddest cases we see are those of syphilis innocentium, or syphilis in the innocent, that occurs through such infection. I saw a little fellow, a three-year-old child, brought in from the country with a lesion on the tongue. On examination this proved to be a primary syphilitic lesion. The father and mother were healthy. Examination showed that the colored nurse was syphilitic, and there is no question the child contracted that infection from the nurse.

I also saw during the past year two cases of tuberculosis which developed in a child within a year after a nurse had been dismissed, who had afterwards died with tuberculosis. The general principles should be carried out that servants in the family should be under the medical care of the family practitioner, and as a matter of family hygiene it should be insisted that every colored or white servant be examined before being engaged in work and then being re-examined at frequent intervals. This would prevent infections passing from the servants to the members of the family, and they should be examined especially for two diseases—tuberculosis and syphilis.

Another point with reference to family hygiene is this: I believe it is bad practice to allow soiled linen to leave the household to be taken to the house of a colored woman for washing. It is bad practice to let soiled linen go out of the house to any other house. It may go to a well-conducted steam laundry. The washing should be done in the house or sent to an up-to-date or modern steam laundry. In my trips of inspection I have seen clothes soiled which had been laundried, spread over the bed, with a tuberculous patient on the bed spitting freely about him. As a matter of family hygiene, the soiled linen should not go from the house to the house of a negro woman to be washed, but it should be sent to a steam laundry.

THE NEGRO HEALTH PROBLEM.

L. C. ALLEN, M. D.,
Hoschton, Georgia.

Read before the General Sessions, American Public Health Association, Jacksonville, Fla., November 30–
December 4, 1914.

The negro health problem is one of the "white man's burdens," and it is by no means the least of those burdens. It is at once the most serious and the most difficult health problem with which the people of the South are confronted.

The statement that "None of us liveth to himself, and no man dieth to himself" is as true today as it was when the Apostle penned it to the Romans nineteen centuries ago. And it applies with as much force to our "brother in black" as to any other man. Because of the fact that no negro liveth to himself nor dieth to himself the negro health problem is not alone a question of concern to the black man, but is one of equal moment to the white population in communities where the negroes are found in any considerable numbers. Disease germs are the most democratic creatures in the world; they know no distinction of "race, color, or previous condition of servitude." The white race and the black race will continue to live side by side in the South, and whatever injuriously affects the health of one race is deleterious to the other also. Disease among the negroes is a danger to the entire population.

Communicable diseases find their favorite propagating grounds in the dirty negro sections of our cities, and in unsanitary negro homes in the country. From dirty homes, in these disease-infested sections, negro people come into intimate contact with white people every day that passes. We meet them in our homes, offices, stores, in street cars, and almost everywhere we go. The fact is not pleasant to contemplate, but is nevertheless true, that there are colored persons afflicted with gonorrhea, syphilis, and tuberculosis employed as servants in many of the best homes in the South today. In every instance the employer is, of course, unaware of the risk being taken. Various diseases are often spread in this way.

It is undoubtedly true that the negro race has deteriorated physically and morally since slavery times. In some ways he is perhaps more intelligent, but freedom has not benefited his health, nor improved his morals. There is more sickness and inefficiency and crime among them now than before the war. All old physicians tell us that in slavery time consumption was practically unknown among the negro race. This fact, I believe, is thoroughly established. But how is it with them now? The figures speak for themselves. In the year 1911, as set forth in Census Bulletin number 112, the death-rate per one hundred thousand from tuberculosis of the lungs, in the registration area, was 162.2 for the whites, and

194

405.3 for the negroes.   In other words, the death-rate of the colored people from this disease *is more than three times the death-rate of the white population.* In Jacksonville the rate for the whites 154.4; that for the negroes is 319.5. In Atlanta the white rate is 109.9, the black rate 297.4.   In Savannah the white rate is 118, the black rate 328.   Everywhere you look the proportion is about the same.

Because of the excessive death-rate among the negroes from tuberculosis the impression has gone forth, and has been widely accepted as true, that the negro race has a peculiar susceptibility to this disease.   When all the facts are considered it seems to me that such a conclusion is not justified. Why was the negro free from tuberculosis during slavery time?   The answer is obvious.   Then he was disciplined; then he was made to bathe, and to keep clean; he was furnished a comfortable cabin in which to live, which he was required to keep scrupulously clean; he was given plain, but wholesome food, in generous quantities; he was made to stay at home at night, and rest, that he might be able to work; he was not allowed to roam the country, but was kept at work regularly, and was taught how to do his work in a skillful manner; he was not allowed liquor, nor indulgence in vicious pleasures; if he became ill the best physician obtainable was called to treat him. The health of the children was carefully looked after.   It was to the slave owner's interest to do these things.   The more efficient the slave the more valuable he was.   A sickly negro was of very little value—a dead negro none.   There was no more healthy race of people to be found anywhere in the world than the slaves of the South before the Civil War.

When freedom came, and all restraints removed, the negro began to indulge in all kinds of dissipation, and to practice all the vicious habits known to civilization.   He now had to "shift for himself," and not having any experience in providing a living for himself and family (because the master had always done this) and thinking that freedom meant release from all work, he got along very badly.   Like a child turned out in the world, homeless and penniless, he became the prey of any rascal who was disposed to take advantage of his situation.   To make bad matters worse, his unwise friends rashly gave him the ballot before he was sufficiently intelligent to use it properly.   Then, designing politicians, with insane political propositions and policies, proceeded to stir up all manner of race hatreds and prejudices, which had not existed previously to that time, and which has not yet entirely disappeared, but which, I am glad to say, is gradually passing away.   All this was bad for Cuffy—dreadfully bad.   Hurtful ideas got into his head. He became unreliable.   Criminal tendencies grew upon him, and evil ways overcame him.   He was prosecuted and persecuted.   He often went hungry, picking up food when and where he could find it.   His clothes became ragged, his home filthy, his children neglected.   Disease began to prey upon him.   From this deplorable condition into which the negroes were precipitately plunged at the close of the Civil War, they have not yet emerged. The present generation of negroes have grown up amid very unfavorable surroundings, and without home training, or discipline. Many of them have not had a bath since infancy. They live very irregular lives. They often roam about at night, some of them indulging in licentious debaucheries of the most disgusting character. Their homes are filthy, and their home language unchaste. Their girls early learn evil ways. Ignorance and superstition take the place of science and skill in the care of infants. I have never seen a negro mother who was unable to nurse her infant at the breast, but notwithstanding this fortunate circumstance the death-rate from enteritis and diarrheal diseases is excessive among them, being, in children under two years of age, 75.9 for the whites, and 111 for the negroes. It is the lack of physical and moral cleanliness that causes the death-rate to be so much more among the negroes than it is among the whites. Go into their homes and investigate for yourselves. You will never realize the true situation until you do. In the homes of the best of them you will find the front part of the house in pretty good condition, but the kitchen and back yards are neglected. In most instances the house in which the colored man lives is too small for his family. Miss Frances M. Kinney, a colored lady of intelligence doing social work among the negroes of my county, under the direction of our board of education, in a letter to me says: "I have in mind now a family of twelve living in a three-room cottage. They sleep without any ventilation whatever, and are as filthy as pigs. They go half-clad, and from three to four sleep in one bed, some sleeping in the cook room." Again she says: "The men and boys are stronger and healthier than the women and girls." She says the women in the rural communities do more work than they are able to do, often doing as much work in the field as the men, besides doing the cooking and housekeeping. She continues: "The next generation of negroes will be weak, yes, consumptives, unless something is done to strengthen and protect our girls, who are to be the mothers of the next generation." Miss Kinney goes on to say that her people are very careless with contagious diseases, allowing children to eat and drink after patients afflicted with consumption, and to sleep with such persons.

Again, old physicians tell us that in antebellum days the negro race was practically free from venereal disease. Now syphilis and gonorrhea are very common among them. In fact very few negroes escape one or the other of these diseases. Many negro women have gonorrhea, and pay little attention to it. This is a very real menace to our white boys, and through them, after marriage, to our innocent daughters also. For, despite our best efforts, many boys are going to sow wild oats. Even Solomon the Wise, in his mature years earnestly exclaimed: "Remember not against me the sins of my youth." Evidently the old king had reference to his youthful wild oats. Sterility among the negro women is becoming quite common as a result of the activity of the germs of Neisser. The birth-rate among them is diminishing. The tremendous amount of evil that venereal disease is doing the negro race is incalculable. If the spread of syphilis, gonorrhea and tuberculosis among the American negro is not checked, this once physically superb race will become extinct with a few generations.

I contend, then, that it is not a peculiar racial susceptibility to tuberculosis that is causing this disease to destroy so many people among the negro race, but his environment—his bad habits and his insanitary conditions of living. The same causes operate to produce a high death-rate from other filth diseases. Take for instance puerperal fever. The death-rate from puerperal sepsis in the registration area is just about twice as great among the negroes as it is among the whites. But for the circumstance that all negro mothers nurse their infants at the breast the death-rate among their babies would be appalling. I suppose that when negro women adopt modern styles of dress, and modern social customs, they will also begin to give their babies the bottle. By an examination of the Census Bulletin referred to above, and other health reports, it may be seen that those diseases that are caused from filth, contagion, carelessness, insanitary living conditions, and exposure to cold have a high death-rate among the black population. The death-rate from pneumonia is 128.4 among the whites, while among the negroes it is 252.2. Other diseases that have a notably high death-rate among the negroes are: smallpox, typhoid fever, whooping-cough, rheumatism, influenza, and organic heart disease. It is worthy of remark that the negro race possesses, apparently, a notable degree of immunity to scarlet fever, the death-rate from this disease being eight times as high among the whites as it is among the negroes. According to my personal observation enlarged tonsils and adenoids are extremely rare among them. Mouth-breathers are infrequent.

Negro children, as a rule, are neglected, not receiving proper training at home. Their ailments are given too little attention. Food is often lacking. Parents are incapable of giving their children proper care and training. The schools teach only book-learning. Many are allowed to grow up in idleness, and often acquire habits of indolence and vice.

The negro's health condition will remain bad until his intelligence is greater, and until his financial condition is improved. On account of his poverty, his food is of the cheapest variety, and it is badly cooked. It is a real wonder how millions of negroes manage to live and do good work on the kind of food they are forced to eat, and the character of cookery they get. Frances Kinney, herself a negress, has lived and worked among negroes all her life and knows what she is talking about when speaking of the negroes. In a letter to me Miss Kinney says: "The average colored family live principally on meat (bacon) and bread, which is poorly prepared, especially for school children. The meat is generally fried, and lunches are put up hot in tin buckets, and on opening at lunch time the food has a very disagreeable odor, often driving away the appetite of a delicate child. The meat is soft and soggy, and the bread is in about the same condition."

In answer to a question Miss Kinney says: "The colored people do not have any regular hours to take their meals. They are very careless indeed about going to bed, but get up at a pretty regular hour. It is common for a family to sit up until 12 or 1 o'clock at night, and get up at four in the morning. Many of the women work until a late hour, but when not at work they naturally sit up from force of habit. This habit was handed down to us from a former generation."

I asked Rich Young, a preacher and schoolteacher, if it were true that his people, as a rule, sit up late at night. He answered that it was true, and that many of them *stayed up all night*, and that many of them roamed the neighborhood at such times.

There is no doubt that the habit of staying up late at night, and even all night, is common throughout the negro world. This habit is helping to undermine the negro constitution. It was not allowed in slavery times.

A noticeable defect in the negro character is the want of initiative. He waits to be told. Give him orders, tell him what to do, and set him at it, and he is all right. This lack of initiative in the negro character has far-reaching effect on the condition of the race, But I cannot go into this here.

Habitually careless about most things, the negro is especially careless about caring for the sick. Frances Kinney says: "The day has come throughout the country that you suffer when you get sick if you are not a member of some good society, or club. In the church it takes all the money for the preacher, and he hardly ever has anything. The negroes are only too ready to shield and protect a criminal, whom they regard as a sort of hero, but a sick negro they often regard as a nuisance. In the majority of negro families the sick are never bathed, and their clothing and bed clothing are not changed for weeks at a time. The room is not aired, nor kept clean. In rural communities the negroes often live inconvenient to physicians, and they have no money with which to employ medical attention. In my county it is a common practice for landlords to employ physicians to look after their tenants. Physicians also do a great deal of charity work among them, but they cannot do all that needs to be done."

The negro is not lazy. He is not afraid of work. He will undertake hard jobs which the white man shirks. But he loves carnal pleasure, and he lacks self-control. In other words, *he possesses powerful propensities for pleasure, but his inhibitory centers are rudimentary and weak.* This important fact should never be lost sight of in studying any negro problem. This peculiar mental make-up accounts for many of his follies, and most of his crimes. He is unable to withstand temptations and enticements. In slavery times his master's authority restrained him. For this effective control our preaching and teaching have proved a "broken reed."

The negro men love to frolic with the women; and the women love to frolic with the men; so they frolic. The negro loves to drink—and he drinks. He is especially fond of congregating with other negroes, and this is the reason he stays up so late at night. He attends church regularly—unless there is somewhere else to go. He goes to all the shows and picnics. He attends all the camp-meetings, and—all the dances. At such places he often gets into a scrap with some other negro, and shoots him or stabs him, or else "gets it in the neck" himself. It matters not how grassy his cotton, if the railroad runs an excursion anywhere he will go or die. He never misses a funeral. I once had working with me a negro man who made me a good hand, except that he would sometimes get drunk. But every time a negro died anywhere he had some excuse for going to the funeral. He would come and ask permission to go, stating that the dead negro was his uncle, or his aunt, or his cousin, or some other relation. Never a negro died anywhere that was not some kin to him.

In going to these places of amusement the negro loses a large part of his time, and causes his employer much annoying inconvenience and loss.

Every one conversant with the facts admits that the negro health problem is an important problem, which imperatively demands attention. The question is: What are you going to do about it?

After all, the problem does not differ greatly from the same problem regarding certain portions of our white population. Ignorance and poverty are everywhere associated with disease and vice. Filth and contagion, coupled with ignorance and indifference, always bring about disease and death. The remedy of greatest importance is—*education*. But by the term "education" I hope I shall not be understood to mean the kind of learning the negro has been getting for the last fifty years. Millions of dollars have been spent, and thousands of teachers and others have devoted many years of earnest labor to the education of the negro, and as a result of it all we find the negro race as a whole in a worse condition than they were in slavery times. True a few negroes have accumulated property; a small number have become markedly intelligent; a few have become skillful laborers; but the great mass of common negroes are today densely ignorant and poverty-stricken. Most of them are unskilled laborers, working for small pay; not a few are vagrants; some are in our almshouses; a very large per cent. of them are diseased; and quite a large number of them are in our jails and chain gangs. These facts cannot be denied. I contend, therefore, that the kind of education we have been trying to give the negro has been a disappointment.

Every negro child has had what we may term a preliminary education. This preliminary education was begun several hundred years before he was born. His education can be continued and finished successfully now only if it is conducted in accordance with his preliminary preparation. Human beings show a great many grades of intelligence, and a great diversity of talents. Some are so defective in intelligence that they have to be cared for like infants. Now I contend that in the education of any child, of any race or color, it should be taught according to its capacity and grade of intelligence, and its probable opportunities in life. What the negro needs is an education that will take the place of the discipline which he received in slavery times, and that will fit him for some useful employment that is open to him. The negro will remain poor until he becomes sufficiently skilled to earn better wages than he now gets. But no matter how much he *earns*, he will still remain poor until he acquires habits of economy, and quits spending his money for liquor, and on loose women, and quits squandering it in gambling, and in other ways that hurt him instead of help him.

The negro should be taught to work, and trained to keep regularly at it. He should be made to understand the value of time. He should be taught thrift. Proper ideas of cleanliness, sobriety, chastity, honor, and self-reliance should be instilled into his mind. These things are indispensable to his welfare. Some of the wisest negroes are beginning to see the wisdom of giving the negro an industrial education instead of teaching him Latin and Greek.

The physician should be consulted, and his expert knowledge made use of, in the education of the negro race. What is the object of an education? Evidently, it is to fit the child for the duties of life; to train and develop its physical, moral and mental potentialities so that it will be able, in the "struggle for existence," to fight its own battles, and to prosecute successfully whatever calling or business it may undertake for its life work. To succeed in life it is as necessary that a person be efficient physically as it is that his mind be developed. Good character, good habits, and skill in working with the hands are more valuable than a knowledge of the elementary branches of an English education. And an education that does not teach cleanliness and the proper care of the body is a defective education.

A large per cent. of the negro schoolhouses are dirty and insanitary. They are not ventilated, especially during the winter time. The privies are unspeakably filthy, and infested in summer with swarms of flies. At some schools there are no privies, and the children have to go to the woods, which means the spread of intestinal parasites transmitted through the soil. Children with physical defects, in both the white and the black races, are being neglected because their parents are not sufficiently intelligent to have them given proper medical attention. If a child with any of the more serious diseases or defects, such as hookworm or adenoids, is allowed to grow up and reach maturity with such troubles unremedied, such a child will be seriously handicapped for life. Having had his development retarded during his formative period of life, he finds himself at maturity weak in body and mind, and burdened with disease, and unable to cope with strong men in any calling or pursuit. Hence our educational methods should be changed. The development of a sound body should be the first object of an education. It is a regrettable fact—an exceedingly regrettable fact—that very much of the physical and mental inefficiency seen on every hand today among adult men and women could have been prevented by intelligent care during childhood. The remedy for these evils is the medical inspection of schools. This should not longer be put off. Sound principles of economy alone justify it. Every sentiment of humanity and patriotism demands it.

I am convinced that we cannot depend upon the negro churches for much help in bettering the condition of the negro race. The churches are in a rut, and cannot get out. In them there is too much sentiment, and not enough sense; too much praise, and not enough piety; too much glory-hallelujah, and too little sound morality.

A colored lady of intelligence says: "Our preachers are not what they ought to be; they go in too much for money, and not enough for the happiness and welfare of their people. They would do more good if they would stop preaching so much about heaven, and teach the people how to *live right*, in neat clean homes—homes that are clean physically, mentally and morally. More stress should be placed upon the word *live*."

A good friend of mine, a physician, says: "You might as well try to teach sanitation to mules as to try to teach it to the negroes." With this opinion I do not fully agree. I admit the task is a hard one. Progress will be necessarily slow. But the negro is not incapable of learning. It is our methods that are at fault. In some of the schools in our county, thanks to Frances Kinney, they have individual drinking cups, and nice lunch baskets made with their own hands. In this respect they are more advanced than some of our white schools. The trouble with the negro is not so much his inability to learn as it is his carelessness and indifference in doing that which he is taught to do.

Clubs of various kinds have been organized among the negroes of my state (and I suppose in other states), and from what I learn some of these clubs are doing valuable work, more valuable in character than that which their churches are doing. Parents meet with the children in these clubs, and all are anxious to learn. This work, however, is quite limited at present. I am told that mothers who have been instructed in these clubs are trying to keep their homes cleaner and more sanitary.

It occurs to me that these clubs give us a clue to a solution of the negro health problem. Improvement clubs, formed somewhat after the manner of the boys' corn clubs, and the girls' canning clubs, organized at every schoolhouse in the land, would offer a sane and practicable method of solving the problem, or at least greatly improving the present conditions. On account of the negro's gregarious proclivities it should not be difficult to secure a large attendance at these club meetings. Capable teachers, physicians, and social workers should be induced to help in this work. These clubs should be a kind of school for all ages. In addition to improved methods of farming, stock raising, poultry raising, etc., hygiene and sanitation should be taught at these meetings. Prizes might be offered for various things, as for the woman who has the cleanest house and yard. By teaching these people a few simple facts an inestimable amount of good might be accomplished. The women should be instructed in cooking, and the care of infants. The manner in which tuberculosis spreads from the sick to the well, and the approved methods of preventing the same, should be explained. They should be made to know that typhoid fever is an infectious disease, and instructed in methods of disinfection and cleanliness, and informed of the benefits of typhoid vaccination. They should be told how the mosquito spreads malaria, and instructed in methods of prevention. They should be told of sanitary privies, and that houseflies are as dangerous as mad dogs. They should be especially instructed concerning the two twin enemies of the negro race—gonorrhea and syphilis. Many other things will naturally suggest themselves to you. Let them understand that disease, for the most part, is under man's control. Divest their minds of the vague superstitions which most of them harbor concerning the causation of disease, and make them understand that disease is caused from uncleanness, alcohol, germs, bad habits and bad morals. The negro should be inspired to think more of himself, and to place a higher value upon his life. Call their attention to the remarkable old age which many of their ancestors reached, but to which few of the present generation can hope to attain. They should be taught the great value of sleep, which they do not seem to appreciate.

In conclusion, the health of any people is the foundation upon which their happiness and prosperity and usefulness rests. If the individuals of any race yearly diminish in stature and physical strength, that race is doomed.

The negro race in America is deteriorating, and at a rapid rate. The death-rate among them from filth diseases is alarming. The race is headed toward destruction. Unless something is done to arrest the spread of disease among them the race will go as the American Indian went within a few generations.

The educational and religious efforts that for fifty years have been employed to better the condition of the negro race have been disappointing. Our educational methods should be changed radically.

Every influence that helps to increase the negro's efficiency, everything that encourages him to become productive and self-sustaining, and that helps to make of him a better citizen lessens the "white man's burden."

The fundamental source of disease, as well as of vice and crime, among the negroes is shiftlessness, ignorance, and poverty. The remedy is a systematic, *disciplinary* training of his physical, mental and moral powers.

THE NEGRO AS A PROBLEM IN PUBLIC HEALTH CHARITY.

Lawrence Lee, M. D.,
Savannah, Ga.

Read before the General Sessions, American Public Health Association, Jacksonville, Fla., November 30–
December 4, 1914.

In considering the question of the negro as a factor in public health, first let us look into the type of diseases with which he is most commonly affected. Dr. C. E. Terry in his article read before the American Public Health Association in Washington in 1912 and before the Southern Medical Association in 1913 at Lexington, Ky., shows that tuberculosis and other respiratory diseases and still-births cause a death-rate of 917.9 per 100,000 against a rate of 354.7 for whites. The Savannah Board of Health reports show for 1913 the death-rate from the same causes to have been 1,185 per 100,000 for negroes against 375 per 100,000 for whites. The disease most prevalent among the negroes, however, does not show in these figures.

I have found from personal experience, and I am sure that those doctors present who have had the disagreeable duty of treating any large number of the negro race have found, that venereal diseases are present in over 50 per cent. of those presenting themselves for treatment. Syphilis has as much to do with the high death-rate in the negro as any other single factor. It does not show on the death certificate, but as a complication of bronchitis, pneumonia and tuberculosis, it reduces the chance of a successful fight against these diseases, and as a cause of arterio sclerosis, endocarditis, cerebral hemorrhage, nephritis and still-births it seems to be ever present.

As city physician during three years I treated 1,426 negroes, 486 of whom (about one third) had syphilis in some evident form, to say nothing of those who came to me with minor injuries, biliousness, etc., who only paid one or two visits and in whom the disease was latent, and in whom I did not make the diagnosis. I personally believe that more than 50 per cent. of the colored race suffer with this disease, either inherited or acquired. If this be the case, as I believe it is, syphilis is almost *the* important factor in the high death-rate of the negro race.

How much through the negro race the white race is affected with this disease I am unable to state. I have never seen a case in a white contracted innocently from a negro and have heard of but few. This goes to prove that syphilis must be very slightly contagious in ordinary daily contact. The negroes live in our homes, care for our children, wash our clothing, cook our food, and if syphilis were very contagious from ordinary contact

207

numerous cases of syphilis of the innocent among the whites would have been reported.

As long as conditions exist as they do at present in negro homes, schools and hospitals, the prevalence of infectious diseases, especially such diseases as syphilis, tuberculosis, respiratory diseases, typhoid and malaria will increase rather than diminish. Negroes do not seem to be particularly subject to other infectious diseases, except smallpox, and vaccination is the prevention for it.

Let us look briefly into these conditions. I can speak from personal knowledge only of conditions in Savannah, but I am sure that conditions here are no worse than in the average southern city.

Their homes are usually one-story cottages, built in long rows of tenements, close to the ground, with small windows. In these homes a large number of people crowd, so that the negro section is very densely populated. In the district where the negroes live the house drainage system has not been installed as yet in all the houses, although rapidly being installed, and there is still a good sprinkling of the old-fashioned privies.

Living under such conditions typhoid, while never to my knowledge epidemic among them in Savannah because they cannot afford milk, and the water supply is fine, is always endemic and a constant source of danger to the city with the added danger of an epidemic among the whites through negro carriers working in a dairy.

The negroes hate cold, and it is almost impossible to get them as yet to open the windows of their homes in winter or if they are sick. Crowded as they are and fearing ventilation no wonder tuberculosis and respiratory diseases are so prevalent.

Into these homes our washing goes, and I have seen it more than once on the sick bed of a tuberculous patient. From these homes negroes come into our homes and, as our servants, are in most intimate contact with us. I know of one man who in the course of two years had three servants who had tuberculosis. He was a doctor and when he heard a suspicious cough had his servants examined, and the tubercle bacilli were found. Most employers, not realizing the danger, would fail to have the examination made.

Most of the negro houses in Savannah are on the outskirts of the city, in or near the district where the drainage is not perfect (this condition here is also being improved at present). The stagnant water in the low ground breeds mosquitoes. I have found in my practice that the negro is not immune to malaria but is moderately susceptible. He therefore is a carrier of this disease as well, and a frequent carrier in my opinion.

Their Hospitals.—It is no surprise to me that the negro is afraid of a hospital. The negro hospitals I have seen are warranted to repel and even terrify people less superstitious than the negro. In Savannah I know of no negro poorhouse, so that the hospitals have to take care of the aged, infirm, paralyzed and blind.   As a result they are horribly overcrowded. In the largest colored hospital in Savannah frequently when night comes there are ten or fifteen more patients than beds, and no matter how hot the weather two patients have to sleep in a single bed, and some on the floor or in chairs.

During the six months, April to September, 1914, inclusive, on 667 occasions patients were without individual beds.   In April there were only five days on which there were sufficient beds on which to accommodate all the patients.   In May, three; in June, six; in July, ten; in August on no day were there sufficient beds.   Since August, by the establishing of a house surgeon, and having such surgical patients leave the hospital as could and return for dressings, the wards have been kept from overcrowding as in previous months.   In September there were only four days in which all the patients did not have beds, and in October one.

By establishing a negro free out-patient department, and a negro poorhouse the present hospital facilities might be sufficient for a few years more.

The South has a tremendous burden in the negro, and it is remarkable how much is being done with the funds available, but if healthy conditions are to be established here much more must be done.

Their Schools.—Savannah has just completed another modern school building for negroes, but in 1913 out of 10,699 colored children between the age of six and eighteen there was only provisions in the public school for 4,086.

The South, as I have said, is carrying a heavy burden.   In Chatham County the tax returns for 1914 show for the whites, $42,508,970.00; the negroes, $1,160,839.00.   The taxes paid in by the negroes amount to almost nothing, and he gets an infinitely greater proportion out of the state, county, and city, than he pays into it, and it is claimed by some that we are generous to a point of extravagance with him.   Suppose, however, that they were only given their dues.   Suppose that we even went further and that as an editorial in the *Columbia State* recommended, the negro not be educated at all until education was brought to the door of every white boy and girl in the state, so that no negro could have any advantage of education over any white no matter how poor the opportunity of the whites had been.   Suppose further that this idea was carried out in all the public charities, in the schools, hospitals, poorhouses, district nursing, etc.

Suppose that under such conditions every white had been given every advantage it was possible to give him, the negro none.   Can you imagine that a city under such conditions could be a healthy one?   Half the population in absolute ignorance; poverty, disease and immorality infinitely worse than they are at present.   This would drag the other half down.

3

No one can deny that such a state of affairs would be bad for a community. It is impossible to keep one half of the community clean, with the other half dirty, one half moral with the other half rotten, one half healthy with the other riddled with disease.

The difference between this imaginary state of affairs and the present is only one of degree, and what is so evidently bad for the community under these exaggerated conditions is bad for it to a less and less extent only as the conditions approach the ideal.

Every dollar spent in improving the conditions of the negro race benefits the whites as well.   If the whites and negroes live in the same community

STATISTICS FOR YEAR 1913.

	White, 37,000.		Colored, 42,000.	
	Rate per 100,000.		Rate per 100,000.	
Still-births.........................	48	129.73	230	547.62
RESPIRATORY DISEASES:				
Pneumonia.........................	32	86.48	84	200.00
Broncho pneumonia..................	6	16.27	16	38.09
Tuberculosis.......................	48	129.73	135	321.42
Whooping-cough....................	1	2.70	1	2.38
Bronchitis.........................	1	2.70	10	23.80
Influenza..........................	3	8.10	20	47.62
Pleurisy...........................	....	....	2	4.76
Total Respiratory Diseases..........	139	375.65	498	1185.61

TEN–YEAR INTERVALS.

	Tuberculosis.				Pneumonia.			
	White. Number of deaths.	Colored. Number of deaths.	White. Rate per 100,000.	Colored. Rate per 100,000.	White. Number of deaths.	Colored. Number of deaths.	White. Rate per 100,000.	Colored. Rate per 100,000.
1874–1883....	549	975	346.07	610.35	....	....	....	....
1884–1893....	543	1,092	277.55	506.99	157	480	80.25	222.85
1894–1903....	541	1,333	214.46	499.20	289	653	114.57	238.97
1904–1913....	472	1,369	52.41	421.58	379	968	122.33	298.20

the health of the whites cannot improve unless the health of the colored also improves. The health of the negro cannot deteriorate without dragging down the whites.

Selfishness, therefore, even if there were not other motives, demands that the negro be provided with better public charities, better schools, especially industrial schools, better hospitals, and the out-patient departments and visiting nurses that should go with them, better poorhouses or homes for the aged and infirm, and last but not least better laws governing their dwellings and the crowded conditions existing in them.

It will take time to accomplish these advances on account of the large sums of money required to build, equip and run such institutions, but if the absolute necessity of such institutions be constantly impressed on the public their accomplishments will be brought about at a much earlier date.

By themselves the negroes will not better themselves. Where they came from they were savages, left to themselves they remain little better than savages. Their nature is such that benefits such as public charities provide, have to be given to them, almost forced on them. It takes much persuasion to get one into a hospital.

The Japanese are a people of a different type. Already having a high grade of civilization, when brought in contact with our customs, they did not have to be forced on them. Being enterprising they adopted much of ours and in a few decades have equaled and even outstripped us in many ways. The negro in closer contact and with better opportunities remains down.

By the education of the negro he may be made a better citizen, and a more useful member of the community, and come to live in better homes and more healthy surroundings. Instead of being a burden he may come in time to look after himself. This time will be a long time, generations of time. Until this comes to pass it is necessary that the whites, out of their own pockets, in order to protect themselves, furnish the negro with public charities and better public charities than exist at present.

Finally, this paper would fail to accomplish its purpose, if it did not contain a recommendation that increased facilities should be afforded to furnish the negro with better schools and with better hospitals. It must also be recognized that the presence of this inferior race puts a burden on the white race, a burden that must be met with increased appropriations for public health purposes. This must rest on the moral obligation of a higher race to an inferior race dependent upon it; and further on the practical and selfish ground that it is impossible to protect the white people and neglect the black.

REMARKS ON THE HEALTH OF THE COLORED PEOPLE

*BY J. MADISON TAYLOR, A. B., M. D., Assistant Professor of Non-pharma-
ceutic Therapeutics, Medical Department, Temple University
Philadelphia, Pa.

Health is the most important asset any human being can possess, and much more so in proportion as he is poor in finances. With health a poor man or woman can be happy and can earn a living; without it he or she cannot. A rich man may get along with poor health and not suffer for essentials of life.

I personally feel the deepest interest in the colored people because my childhood was spent on the plantation of my grandfather and among his slaves, one of whom, a boy of my age, was given to me and became my most beloved companion until we separated in later life, he to remain on the "big place" with many others long after freedom, I to come north to school.

The colored people of the United States are in great danger of loss of health, even extinction from two

*Address to the Colored Convention, Varrick Memorial Temple, February, 1915.

sources; one the unsuitable climate and the other narcotic drugs.

The colored people in America were brought here by force of conquest hence without capital, or land grants, or special privileges. Since freedom they have done as well as could be expected under their disadvantageous circumstances. Hence it is far more necessary for each and every colored person to save all they can and invest it securely. The best investment is to gain and keep all the physial and mental vigor in one's power.

Let us look into the conditions which make for this essential possession.

The first condition is, to live in such a place as is most likely to furnish the best elements for health. Races of people who have lived for thousands of years in certain climates become adapted in their make-up to survive and flourish under similar conditions. They inevitably suffer if suddenly removed to other climates or environments whol-

74

ly different, and for which their structure, skin, color, nostrils and the like have become entirely unadapted.

Now all that I have here stated is of scientific knowledge, verified by overwhelming testimony of masses of facts. Certain of the many races represented here in America fail to survive or maintain vigor if they persist in living in cities. For instanse, the blonde Scandinavian people usually fall ill and their children become feeble and readily die, unless they live in the country. Furthermore, they tend to perish unless they keep as far north as possible. The dark-haired, yellow-skinned Latin peoples, Italians, Portuguese, Spaniards, some French and other races from South of Europe, do very well in the United States; they also increase and multiply.

It is well known that the original Anglo-Saxon stock, the English and Germans, also Swedes, who settled this country, now have very few children, and these are likely to become attacked by certain kinds of sickness, whereas, the newer, darker peoples are not. In the same way the children of the English and German stock grow sickly in hot countries, in India, in Ceylon, in Java, in Egypt and in our newer province of the Philippines and the Sandwich Islands. All this is the inexorable law of nature which there is no use in disputing or denying or resenting. It is simply a fact to be accepted and reckoned with.

It is true some exceptionally vigorous individuals seem to adapt themselves when suddenly called upon to live under these climatic disadvantages. Not so their children and less so their grand children. It is also true that races from the North can move to the south, from the cold and cloudy

regions to the hot, glaring tropical regions, but only by gradual approach. There always have been and always will be what is called Racial Trends, tendencies for people to move from one region to another for a number of compelling reasons. When this trend or movement is gradual, when the people live some hundreds of years a few miles further and again further south, they become adapted to each place and can then safely move yet further south.

Then, as all history proves, people have moved gradually in different directions, coming slowly into diversifications of locality and climate, adapting themselves and developing into stable, efficient, powerful nations far removed from their original habitat.

Whenever any attempt is made, however, to exceed a certain speed or rate of movement, the people so doing, no matter how vigorous, inevitably deteriorate and die out. They do not merely mix in, breed in with the local and established people, who have attained a racial equipoise, they die out, perish, root and branch, disappear, evaporate and leave no descendants whatever.

No amount of wishing it might be otherwise, no fervency of prayer, no degree of hoping ever did or ever can change these inexorable laws of the expansion or contraction of races.

Bear in mind, this statement is of radically unlike peoples suddenly transplanted.

The Goths, the Huns, the Vandals, the Norsemen, the Vikings who went down and conquered the peoples in the Mediteranean Basin faded from the map and left no trace.

There is no known instance of a purely tropical people like the natives of Equatorial Africa having invaded the North except the large body of Afri-

2

cans who were conquered and brought to America.

Now the United States is somewhat different climatically from the corresponding countries of Europe by reason of Isothermal lines. This means we have here colder winters in proportion to our summers. Few realize that London is on the same line of latitude as some place 200 miles north of Quebec, Canada. New York City is on the same line as Naples, in Italy; Philadelphia as Madrid, Spain. Nowhere short of the most southern of our States is there a climate warm enough to suit the Equatorial African.

The African is a peculiarly adaptable race, originally of extraordinary vigor; some of them at least, notably the Kroo Races of the west coast and the people from the highlands of Central Africa.

Most of the Negroes or black people in the United States came from the lowlands of Equatorial Africa; hence they cannot possibly be expected to do well in a country where it freezes hard during the winter. The fact remains they have survived remarkably well so far, but the progress of the race is not continuing in the north, and only hold their own in the far south. While they multiply rapidly, they are unusually susceptible to certain diseases.

It is a matter of stern fact that four Negroes die to one white of tuberculosis, even in the south, and about five to one in the north. It is also true that mixed people, part white and part black, are much less vigorous than pure bloods. Many other facts could be cited and proven by statistics to show that the tenure of life of the rising generation of mixed bloods is growing feebler. This loss of vigor is especially marked in the city dweller, and less so in those who live in the open country.

This contribution is merely an outline sketch of a very large subject. It is only possible here and now to point out some inevitable conclusions.

In order that the Afro-American shall survive or even to maintain a fair measure of health, it is imperative that he shall keep out of the big cities and live in the open country. Also that he go and live in the warmer regions, and avoid the cold seasons for which he is not structurally adapted, or he will surely die out in a few more generations, just as the other races have done who violated the inexorable laws of race expansion.

Moreover, it is a fact that mixed bloods inherit the weaknesses of pure bloods. The mulatto, the quadroon, the octoroon, has the same leaky skin, the same wide nostril, etc., made for life in a tropical climate. The white and black races will not fuse; they are too totally unlike in racial characteristic and in conformation. Unless the colored people as a body realize these facts and adapt their forms of life in accord with them they will disappear. No denial, no protest, no prayer will change the laws of nature.

Now as to the second great menace to health, the use of narcotic drugs. All primitive peoples, that is those whose stage of racial evolution is nearer to the original forms and who have existed till recently under the so-called savage circumstances of life, are only strong so long as they continue to do so and fall into evil states on their earlier contact with civilization. Civilization is only of value to those who survive the hurtful effects of sophistication and artifical condition.

For example the Esquimaux and Northern Indians are dying like sheep wherever they are compelled to live in houses yet do very well so long as they live in tents or igloos. Also these people, as well as our brothers of African descent, go all to pieces when they use alcohol, or any other of the "dopes," opium, cocaine, and the like. The chief reason for this is that simpler organizations act more on impulse than on deliberate judgement and it requires many generations to acquire dependable, self-restraining safe-guards and the race often dies out before these safe-guards are achieved.

One dose of alcohol weakens anyone's capacity for decision, hence the temptation to take another is made over strong, thereupon excesses follow. The same is true of other "dopes." It is a fact that many white men are similarly affected but not those who are of the higher grades mentally, that is, more highly specialized or equipped with the most essential quality for efficiency and survival, namely, self-restraint, inhibition.

It is a well known phrase, "Whom the gods would destroy they first make mad." Artificial madness is "dope." Narcotics in any form create a madness. Repeated use of this universal mind perverter, inevitably tends to destroy a race, not always the individual but his children and grandchildren.

The scientific facts on which these statements are made, are all on record; any one can verify them in spite of any strong current of opposition, any of which is based on resentment against facts, or contradiction grounded upon false wishes, hopes, on vitiated feeling tones.

It is well known that in a family in which there is a tendency to drunkenness it is only safe for each individual member to remain an abstainer. All the evidence points one way, viz.: it is only safe for those who wish to survive and remain efficient breadwinners to avoid alcohol and opium and cocaine which seems devised to kill off the weaklings. They will continue to be used till the weaklings are weeded out and the race purified.

For example, note the effects of the Russian Czar in forbidding the use of vodka. In less than six months the efficiency of the laboring classes has so increased as to more than offset the loss of revenue from the tax on vodka. The French have forbidden the use of absinthe. The Kaiser has done the same thing in Germany, and now the British Government is preparing to do the same thing in England. To be sure, those whose taste for grog has grown strong, should protest violently. The governments should know their duty as it has been shown them.

JOURNAL OF THE NATIONAL MEDICAL ASSOCIATION

PUBLISHED AT TUSKEGEE INSTITUTE, ALABAMA, ON THE 15TH DAY
OF FEBRUARY, MAY, AUGUST, AND NOVEMBER.
Editorial Office: 1303 Church Street, Nashville, Tennessee

Entered as Second-Class Matter, March 29, 1909, at the Post Office at Tuskegee
Institute, Alabama, under the Act of March 3, 1879.

Subscription Price: $1.50 per year in advance. Foreign subscription, $1.75 per year.
Advertising rates on request.

Communications concerning the Publication may be addressed to Dr. John A. Kenney,
Tuskegee Institute, Alabama.

Articles intended for publication in the Journal should be sent to Editor-in-Chief,

Editorial Staff

C. V. ROMAN, M. D., 1303 Church St., Nashville, Tenn.   -   -   -   Editor
J. A. KENNEY, M. D., Tuskegee Institute, Ala.   -   -   -   Managing Editor
W. G. ALEXANDER, M. D., Orange, N. J.   -   -   -   -   Associate Editor
U. G. DAILEY, M. D., 5 East 36th Place, Chicago, Ill.   -   Associate Editor
ROSCOE C. BROWN, D. D. S., Richmond, Va.   -   -   -   Associate Editor
JOSEPH J. FRANCE, M. D., 803 Glasgow St., Portsmouth, Va.   Associate Editor

Elsewhere in this issue of the Journal appears an article by J. Madison Taylor, M. D., of Philadelphia, Pennsylvania, entitled, "Remarks on the Health of the Colored People." Whether we agree with all the writer has to say or not, the article is certainly food for thought, and most serious thought, on the part of the serious minded among our profession. It should be studied in an impassive and unprejudiced manner. We must confess that we are not sufficiently conversant with all the statements and deductions made to thoroughly agree with the writer or to render an adverse opinion, but as mentioned above we do say that the article is at least interesting and is deserving of most careful consideration.

His remarks concerning the Negroes in the United States should be read several times before we try to reach conclusions concerning them. This statement for instance:

"Most of the Negroes or black people in the United States came from the lowlands of equatorial Africa, hence they cannot possibly be expected to do well in a country where it freezes hard during the winter."

The conclusion here seems to be logical, but he continues:

"The fact remains they have survived remarkably well so far but the progress of the race is not continuing in the North and only holding their own in the far South."

If this latter statment is true (and

who of our readers is prepared with figures and statistics to assert that it is or is not?) it shows a very serious condition of affairs for our people. We cannot boast of very large observations in the North but from what we have seen we have had the distinct impression that, taken as a race, our people in the North were not only holding their own but are making progress. With reference to the South where most of our time has been spent, having come in contact with our people in most of the Southern States, and seeing them in their homes, daily lives and activities, we certainly are not prepared to accept the statement unreservedly that we are only holding our own in the far South. A people only four million strong when emancipated 50 years ago, in ignorance and poverty, who can boast of having more than doubled its population in a half-century, who has reduced its illiteracy from about 90 per cent to 30 per cent, who now own 225,000 farms, pay taxes on $700,000,000 worth of property, who own 695 drug stores, 51 banks, 20,000 grocery stores, who own 20,000,000 acres of land, and has produced about 4,000 physicians, with large numbers of other professional men and women in nearly all walks of life, and these being added to yearly, in my opinion should hardly be spoken of as "only holding their own."

"In order that the Afro-American shall survive or even maintain a fair measure of health, it is imperative that he shall keep out of the big cities and live in the open country."

This it seems to me is good advice for any people; for is it not a fact that were it not for the young fresh country blood being constantly poured into the cities that decay would be inevitable? Back to the farm is the universal slogan not alone to the Negroes but to all those hordes who are merely eking out a more or less miserable existence in our large cities.

"The white and black races will not fuse. They are too totally unlike in racial characteristics and conformation. Unless the colored people in a body realize these facts and adapt their forms of life in accordance with them they will disappear."

This seems to be the last word on the subject of miscegenation. The races even though they have been intermingling for the past 250 years will not fuse and the advice to the colored people to realize these facts seems to us a little far-fetched; for it is a fact well known in the South, at least, that it is not the colored people who are responsible for the racial fusion, and that whatever mixing of bloods there may have been, in almost every instance, has come from the side of the whites; for it is very seldom indeed that we meet with a mulatto whose mother is a white woman. Hence, it would seem that such advice would be more properly rendered to the members of the white race as a whole.

His allusion to what he terms the second great menace to the health of

the race, narcotic drugs, seems time-
ly.   It is hard to controvert the statement which he makes that the older
races by reason of generations of acquired dependable, self-restraining
safeguards are more able to resist the
temptations and inroads of alcohol
and other "dopes" than a young or
primitive people.   Alcohol and cocaine as we well know have certainly
made great inroads on our people.

Again we call upon our readers to
study the article carefully, thought-
fully and without prejudice, and may
we not in future numbers of the
Journal have some very interesting
discussions and facts brought out as
a result of it.

————————

Public Health and the Negro

By Algernon Brashear Jackson, M.D.,

Director School of Public Health, Professor of Bacteriology and Public Health—School of Medicine
Howard University, Washington, D. C.

Two years are not a very long time, but with me they have been laden with many experiences and most careful observations touching the matter of Public Health and its application to the Negro. Two years ago I came to Howard University with certain preconceived ideas born of certain experiences, to initiate a Public Health program which we hope to make far reaching among our people. Today I come before the medical men and women of my race with a confession of perfect faith and partial failure. Perfect faith, because I am convinced of the absolute integrity of our medical men and women and their willingness to co-operate with any program which means the betterment of health, social and economic conditions among Negroes. Partial failure, because I am convinced that the problems of ill health and high mortality among our people cannot receive, for the present at least, the same treatment from our medical men and women, as that administered by the white profession for their group. Many reasons assemble themselves.

Theoretically, the Public Health movement in America stands for the health preservation of all the people and really seems so to function. But actually—with very few exceptions—the various state, county and city boards of health erect a political and social barrier, which prevents the cooperation of the Negro profession toward the solution of a problem which is always a specific one, to be met only in a specific way, and in thus missing the mark, only a part of the program functions.

On the other hand we must very frankly admit that we have very, very few trained health workers, and without the proper training we can be nothing but a mis-fit in such a program, bringing down upon our heads only chagrin and failure. With the idea of answering this need, which we believe to be a very definite one even though not freighted with countless opportunities, the School of Public Health was initiated at Howard University. It may be some years before a Negro will be called to an administrative position in the Public Health field, but proper training and personal adaptability will do much to break down the barriers so that he may become at least a part time health officer. But first of all the big thing, the biggest thing we can accomplish within our entire profession, is the development of the *Public Health Consciousness* and the *Will* to intelligently apply the same, which eventually are bound to serve as the "open sesame" to the largest phases in this great humanitarian movement. Where there is the will there is usually the way.

While there are so few opportunities which welcome our services in a public way, there are countless opportunities in which we can and must serve our people in an individual way. Every physician, dentist and pharmacist should regard himself a private health officer, whose duty it is to apply his whole scientific knowledge to the health preservation of his race, his state and his nation. I remember when writing the announcement of our School of Public Health this thought came to me and I set it down as follows: "A training in Public Health tends to make good doctors—better doctors." Such is the burden of this article in its attempt to show the place Public Health knowledge and training should occupy in the daily practice of our profession. Unquestionably the tendency of modern medicine is toward the prevention of disease, in which the social and economic phases of life are duly emphasized. In the future the trend shall grow more definite and decided as the medical profession awakes to a larger consciousness of its whole duty to mankind. The Public Health movement is paving the way toward this finer altruistic idea and accomplishment.

It must not be understood by this that the practice of medicine and its allied branches is drifting toward a maudlin sentimentality *sans* its treasured heroics, *sans* its highest scientific aspects, of which we are all a bit jealous. In fact it is rather the rapid progress made in medical science that is lifting our profession from the old rut and placing it high, indeed highest of all human endeavors. Each day gives us a finer and more perfect knowledge of disease, its causes, its cure and its prevention, whose application the modern physician must make in his daily practice in order to render his full duty to those who put their trust in him. Public Health therefore, means the translation of all that is best in our science, into terms of humanity and its application to human needs and public welfare. Public Health places the physician upon a pinnacle which he has never occupied before and gives him a leadership over the affairs of all mankind absolutely essential and undisputed. Public Health is lifting the physician from the position from being merely a watchman over sickness to a place in which he stands as director and guide over life, with the idea of adding to its length, comfort and happiness. What can possibly be more heroic, more scientific and a greater contribution to civilization?

When I was first ushered into the field of Public Health education, I came with the idea that the Negro profession should receive the same training as that given the whites. Today I am taking a different stand in the matter, which has all come about by careful observation and study of racial needs and short-comings. I still believe there is a need and a field for a few specially trained Negro health officers. There is a great need and a large field for many specially trained Negro Public Health Nurses. But the big need of today in attempting to work out the most beneficial Public Health program for Negroes, is *more well-trained physicians, dentists, pharmacists and nurses.* With only two Medical Schools turning out a limited number of graduates each year, and our population on the increase, we as a race are losing ground all along the line toward better health. Even a better distribution of the Negro profession would do much to help clear the situation, but that being always a personal matter is difficult to regulate. Almost all the large cities North and South could and would gladly spare a goodly number of their professionals to the rural districts where they are needed and would fare better financially. The Public Health problem of the Negro is almost entirely a clinical one. In far too many instances the sick Negro is not getting the skilled, careful, conscientious medical attention he should have, for which he is ofttimes paying at a high rate. Contrary to the thought and assertion so often projected, the white physician *is not* as great an offender in this direction as is the Negro physician who should feel a double urge—racial and pro-

fessional—to give his best service to his own people. There are many who give their best, honestly and conscientiously, but their best falls short of the mark. They are blissfully ignorant, but could nevertheless be made a power for good, with a little post-graduate training. In other words, their hearts are right and they have a large opportunity for helpfulness. We must find some way to get these men back to school and give them a new knowledge and inspiration. But sadder still there are many who know but are too lazy and careless to give the fullest value of their knowledge. They belong to the trade union wing of our profession, and through exploitation of the ignorant and trusting gullibles are reducing the greatest profession on earth to an unprincipled trade. These are the types who should have awakened within their hearts and souls the Public Health consciousness—the altruistic consciousness, which must always be emphasized within our profession.

For some time to come the Public Health burden of our people must be borne by the general practitioner, who must strive for early diagnosis, better and more careful diagnosis, treatment, care and prevention backed up by good judgment, an open mind and progressive ideas. Such is the ideal physician and he is the type upon whom we depend to bring about an improvement in health, social and economic conditions among our people. For this sort of physician the training which would make him the race's biggest asset in projecting the Public Health program, should be along clinical lines and an attempt to familiarize him with the latest methods in physical examination, laboratory deductions and interpretation. And just here we run upon a stumbling block for we do not have enough physicians taking post-graduate work, and those who do seek it do not find themselves welcomed to those institutions which offer such courses.

Now we come to the crux of the whole situation. In this country we have but two institutions specializing in the medical education of the Negro, and they, Howard University and Meharry, are limited in their resources for giving post-graduate instruction. However the main reason for their limitation is due to the fact that the Negro profession is not making sufficient demand for advanced training. Let us once begin to make the demand, and in some way the resources will be forth-coming. This indifference displayed by the Negro profession toward post-graduate study is our weakest link in the Public Health program, and until our attitude is changed we shall not progress as we ought in this movement for humanity. In almost every state there is a law expressed or implied which directs all school teachers to take post-graduate study in order to modernize educational methods. Almost all members of the Medical profession agree that this is as it should be as touching the teachers of their children. Why not apply the same rule to themselves? Can it be that they believe Public Education more vital to the race than Public Health? I rather dislike to think of the day when the public shall awake to the indifference of our profession, and write upon the statute books a law forcing the guardians of their health to take advanced study or lose their license to practice the health-giving professions.

The future for Medical Education and Public Health for the Negro looks quite gloomy unless we as a race can find and make possible for ourselves a way to increase the number of our Medical Schools and Hospitals in which to train physicians, dentists, pharmacists and nurses. The number of all is all too few for the increasing numbers of our people, the vast majority of whom are now turning to Negro professionals as the guardians of their health. Think of it, only two class "A" Medical Schools offering unhampered and unembarrassing opportunity for the education of the sons and daughters of twelve million American citizens! We must find a way or our race shall lose much that it has gained, for the economic and social progress of any people shall always be measured in terms of its health and physical well-being. The passing of the Leonard Medical School of Shaw University was one of the grimmest tragedies in our modern race history, the significance of which was unrecognized until this moment, when we see the doors of most American Medical Schools slammed in our faces. Is there not some one, some group from among that wonderful aggregation of scholars and race patriots, alumni of Shaw University who will lead the way toward reviving and perpetuating their beloved Alma Mater? If there is, let him, let them come forth, make an appeal to racial patriotism, racial salvation, American preservation, and once again the lily of Shaw shall be seen to bloom where now the rank weeds of oblivion have all but stifled the very life and soul of a glorious past. The Negro race needs Leonard Medical School, America needs it; so let us together make a national appeal, and our hopes shall come to pass.

Another weak link in our Public Health program is the sad lack of sufficient hospital facilities. This is a two-edged sword which is cutting into the progress of our race at two most vital points. In every physician's experience there comes the time, again and again, when his patient's best welfare is served by his admission into a hospital. Many a life is saved which would otherwise be lost were it not for the care and attention a hospital only can give. In a hospital many a

spell of sickness is cut short which without institutional care would drag on to chronicity, helplessness, loss of earning power and dependence. The social and economic aspects of the hospital service bulks large in the final analysis of its worth as a public benefit. Without hospitals of our own in every community where our people are in large numbers, there is no possible way for our profession to render its full duty and its best service to those upon whom we depend and to whom we owe so much. The successful operation of hospitals among our people is doing much to bring about a higher degree of racial consciousness, racial respect and good will, all of which breed a confidence and faith in the profession which is destined to lead our race to a higher level, socially and economically. I have no misgivings as to my race, for I know that as soon as we have become convinced that self-preservation is the only safe and sane preservation we shall build for ourselves. At present however our race is not hospitalized as it should be for self-preservation, but the spirit is growing and it is the duty of the medical profession to carry the importance of this message to the people. We have no right to expect others to do for us what we can and ought to do for ourselves.

Let us turn to the other side of the picture. Our lack of hospital facilities decidedly and distinctly hampers our professional growth and development along the line of advanced ideas and methods which we should apply in serving our people. Strictly speaking the modern hospital should always serve as a post-graduate school from which much can be gained if we approach our work and study with an open mind. The properly organized hospital affords wonderful opportunities for physicians to develop a special knowledge of the several special branches of medicine, which they can carry into their daily practice. They need not be *specialists* but they can soon earn the reputation of possessing a *special knowledge* in some particular field, and thus be of greater service to each other and the public. The educational value of the hospital is almost unlimited. It is needed for the training of internes and nurses, all of whom are tending to make stronger our fortification against the invasion of disease and death. At present there are but a few hospitals in the country—all too few—equipped for the proper training of internes. More and more of the states are demanding the hospital year as a requisite to practice medicine within their borders. Here we as a race face an impasse, unless we create and properly equip more hospitals in which to train the young medical graduate. We must awaken to this situation now or we are destined to awake too late and find that our profession has received a tremendous setback. Also the training of nurses cannot progress without proper hospital facilities; and we must have nurses: for they are a most vital factor in our Public Health program. The present-moment demand for more and better equipped hospitals is a most urgent one, and we must find some way to answer it or lose much ground we have gained.

Summed up in a few words, we might as well face the issue frankly and agree that we must practice a higher and better grade of medicine than many of us are now doing. In order to do this we must learn how, and that means study, the development of hospitals, faithful attendance of our local, state and national societies, post-graduate work and finally the urge of the Public Health consciousness. We must do our *full* duty for those upon whom we depend, and nothing less will do. Every community should have its pre-natal clinic, child welfare society, health talks, and any and all methods calculated to stimulate the health idea. Many physicians seem to believe that such a practice is suicidal, but that is never the case. The present Public Health movement gives the profession the highest opportunity it ever had to get into the hearts of the people and take distinct leadership by pointing out to them the way to a healthier and happier life. When sickness comes—and come it always will—the people will turn to him who has best served them, imbued with the thought that he who has so faithfully served will surely save.

Public Health should not be regarded as a movement calculated to rob the physician of his practice, but rather a force directing him toward the practice of a higher grade of medicine and surgery in which care and conscience are duly emphasized. The public wants not free treatment but better treatment, more careful examinations, better diag-

nosis, the whole truth, and in the majority of cases they are willing to pay for it. The day of merely feeling the pulse, looking at the tongue, asking a few vague questions and writing the prescription is gone. The public is being educated to know that this is not enough and are therefore demanding more, for which they are willing to pay. State medicine will never come in America, so the practice of medicine shall continue to remain an individual contract between physician and patient; but patients are demanding that their physicians take a deeper interest in their welfare, and make a reasonable forecast as to their physical condition. Out of this thought has grown the idea of periodic examinations, which should be encouraged by every physician, and when made should be of the most thorough and searching character followed by an intelligent interpretation of his findings. Public Health is thus bringing the practitioner back to the realization that it is the personal touch, and human interest which are the big factors in keeping faith between people and profession. We cannot over accentuate this, and with the hope of broadcasting such ideas, I trust we shall in the near future be able to find a way in our School of Public Health to project short post-graduate courses which will duly emphasize the clinical and sociological phases in the practice of modern medicine.

The Negro profession cannot afford to be satisfied with the adoption of half measures, when we realize the tremendous responsibility placed upon us. We must develop more thoroughly the missionary spirit and carry the lessons of health, social and economic integrity to the very lowest stratum of our race. Each and everyone of us must become a teacher who regards it his most sacred duty to teach a race how to save itself—if we would save *ourselves*.

THE PART THE NEGRO IS PLAYING IN THE REDUCTION OF MORTALITY*

HENRY M. MINTON, M. D.,

Superintendent, Mercy Hospital; Clinical Supervisor, Negro Bureau, Henry Phipps Institute, Philadelphia, Pennsylvania

At the beginning of the discussion of such a subject as this I feel that I should at once call attention to the point I desire to make and that is that in this country wide effort to cut down mortality rates and to increase the span of life expectancy the Negro has not been in a passively receptive mood entirely. He has been anxious to assume his part of the burden and has wherever permitted taken his part in the greater fight. To a large degree he has conducted a battle against high mortality rates among his own group in ways that have seldom come to the public notice. He has realized that such things as lack of proper hygiene, poor housing, too great reliance upon patent medicines, as well as the low wage, have combined to create a mortality rate far in excess of that of the white group.

In regard to hygienic intelligence, this of course accompanies general intelligence, and must usually be supplied either in public schools or by means of health propaganda. Even in Philadelphia, where we have always had a large proportion of the Negro population hailing from the rural South where their education has been of the most meagre sort, any health propaganda about them but not especially directed toward them has not reached them. And then, too, there is required a certain amount of intelligence to appreciate any such campaign of preventive medicine.

The matter of poor housing and its relationship to disease has been assigned a place on the program of this conference, and hence I shall bring it to your notice in only a casual manner. Where this condition is accompanied by lack of hygienic intelligence its baneful influence on health is doubled.

I feel that the patent medicine evil has had a great influence upon the mortality rate of the Negro race in this country. Very frequently we find in colored persons suffering with some organic disease that they have exhausted the efficacy of two or three different patent medi-

---

*Read before The All-Philadelphia Conference on Social Work, April, 1924.

10

cines before consulting a physician. This may be the outgrowth of habits formed in rural communities where it was difficult to obtain medical attention and patent medicines were more available. I do know that with the oncoming of the Negro migrant from the South new patent medicines began to appear upon the drug store shelves, having come there by popular demand. Valuable time for early treatment especially in such diseases as tuberculosis, Bright's disease, diabetes and heart diseases is often lost and the opportunity of an arrest or a cure of the disease has passed.

The matter of low wage has many ramifications in its baneful effects. It has its influence upon housing conditions to a considerable degree. It often forces the Negro mother out to work, thereby causing neglect of her children. This is reflected in the high motality of colored children. It often prevents proper recreation, this being one of the prime factors in the lessening of resistance against infectious diseases.

The Negro is both a fatalist and an optimist. He accepts certain conditions as inevitable and tries to make the best of them. At the same time he has faith in the future, and believes that a way out will be found for his many difficulties. The fact that his mortality rate is abnormally high does not stampede him, yet he will readily accept any proposition to improve this condition. He has never shared the fear of many who contended that eventually his race in this country would become extinct on account of high death rates and lower birth rates.

Many years ago Booker Washington created a determination among the Negroes of the South to get out of the one room cabins with all of their unhygienic surroundings. As these people improved in their living conditions, and illiteracy began to lessen, their mortality rate began to drop. Ten years ago the National Negro Business League organized an annual Health and Clean-up Week. Members of this organization, whose president was Booker Washington, co-operating with the Negro medical profession, in all parts of the country, held public health meetings. In the rural districts and small towns members of their race were urged to clean up their premises, paint their houses and whitewash their fences. Later the National Medical Society, an organization numbering in its membership colored physicians, dentists and pharmacists in every portion of the United States, officially co-operated with the Business League. In every large city in the United States through its local branches it has yearly conducted a health week.

The Metropolitan Life Insurance Company in its Statistical Bulletin has shown by statistics from the mortality records of Negroes insured in its industrial department that in ten years, from 1912 to 1922, the expected life span of colored male policy holders at age of ten had increased five and a half years, or 13.1 percent. This appears most favorably especially when compared with an increase among the whites of 6.3 years or 13.8 percent. The exact figures were for Negro males 41.32 years in 1911-1912 and 46.74 in 1922. For white males the figures were 45.61 in 1911-1912 and 51.91 in 1922. A rather peculiar fact was noted that among Negro females at the age of ten the expectation increased from 41.30 years in 1911-1912 to 46.07 years in 1922, a gain of about five years or 11.5 per cent., while as to white females the increase was from 50.66 to 54.54 years, an increase of but 3.8 years or 7.5 per cent.

Such figures must make us feel that the Negro's optimism is not without ground and that his faith in the future is not by any means unreasonable. We must also recognize that some forces for good have been at work. Doubtless such general sanitary improvements as improved sewerage and elimination of mosquito breeding spots have had their good effects toward lessening both morbidity and mortality.

Together with these, larger efforts have been put forth by the Negroes themselves. Booker Washington's "out-of-the-one-room-log-cabin movement," instituted more than 20 years ago, has resulted in a better home for the Negro throughout the country. This and the Negro Health Week have certainly helped to bring about this lowered mortality.

Negro forces have been directed toward this effort in Philadelphia for the past fifteen years. In 1907 Mercy Hospital, before any other institution or organization, we believe, gave in a half dozen different churches lectures by members of its staff on tuberculosis. In later years this work has been taken over by the Philadelphia Academy of Medicine, the local branch of the National Medical Association. During Negro Health Week in 1923 this organization enjoying the co-operation of the State and City Departments of Health, reached 75,000 people through motion pictures, stressing baby saving, tuberculosis and housing. Seventy physicians and nurses spoke in many churches on Health Sunday. Thirty large industrial plants massed their employees at lunch hour and they were given health talks by Negro physicians and dentists. Many large mass meetings were held and thousands of pieces of health literature were distributed.

The Secretary of the Academy of Medicine, Dr. J. P. Turner, writes this expression of the Society's work and ambition, "The Academy of Medicine through lectures and talks is disabusing the minds of the ignorant Negro of the belief that tuberculosis is a racial disease and that because he is a Negro he has consumption. Rather, the Academy is making him realize through these means that consumption is to a large extent, especially in his case, a result of poor housing facilities and poor economic conditions. We feel that to give the Negro a new vision, a new hope, is to aid him to reduce his mortality through the consciousness that he must not have consumption just because he is a Negro."

The Academy has taken official notice of the problem of the unvaccinated in our city and is devising methods of reaching these individuals.

In the movement toward the reduction of mortality the hospitals must always play a large and important part. In Philadelphia we have two Negro hospitals, one having about 60 beds and one 106 beds. One is located in a densely populated Negro section of the city, the other in West Philadelphia, on a five acre plot of ground, yet within easy reach of the center of the city. The Negro hospital, as every other public hospital, does three distinct things. It ministers to patients, it gives young medical graduates their fifth year in medicine while they serve as internes and it instructs young women in nursing. So far as these two latter activities of a hospital are concerned, in the Negro hospital they are of relatively greater importance than in the white institution. The reason for this is that the demand is greater than the supply. With but seven approved hospitals in the country accepting Negro internes, there are many more applicants for interneships than can be accommodated. While nearly all of the white hospitals are complaining of a scarcity of nurse applications, we have at Mercy at all times a waiting list twice as large as our entering class. The same thing is true of all of the other hospitals.

There are in the United States about 150 small hospitals, some more properly termed sanitariums. The majority of these are in the South, for of the seven approved institutions all are located in the North or West with the exception of one, that connected with the Tuskegee Institute, Alabama. All of these hospitals are centers of disease fighting activities and preventive medicine campaigns. Not only have they developed Negro surgeons of ability, and specialists in all branches, but have sent out graduate nurses who have become pioneer emissaries for the propogating of public health movements in the rural districts and in the large and congested cities.

I have just returned from attendance at the annual conference of the John A. Andrews Clinical Society held in the John A. Andrews Memorial Hospital at Tuskegee Institute. Seventy-five physicians and many nurses from 16 southern and southwestern states were in attendance. The medical men represented the leaders of their profession. The most impressive thing about the conference was their intense interest in every paper read, every clinic held and every operation performed. The conference to them was in no sense a junket. These men are in a large respect responsible for the lowering of the mortality rate among the Negro in the South. Their sense of the importance of public health propaganda was most keen, and their experiences along this line were intensely interesting.

In many towns and cities, entirely apart from the hospitals, have been conducted clinics especially for Negroes by Negro physicians and nurses. Many of these have been either directly connected with churches or furnished accommodations by churches. Such a clinic is conducted here in Philadelphia at the Zoar Methodist Episcopal Church for babies with an average attendance of thirty patients at a weekly clinic.

The most spectacular reduction in mortality rates at the present moment is that in regard to tuberculosis. Dr. Dublin, statistician of the Metropolitan Life Insurance Company, at the meeting of the National Tuberculosis Association last Spring called attention to a 50 percent. reduction in the mortality rate of tuberculosis from 195.2 per 100,000 of population 1900 to 94.2 per 100,000 in 1922. These were the figures released by the United States Public Health Service and based upon statistical returns from the original registration area. Based upon statistics from the industrial insurance department of the Metropolitan Insurance Company, Dr. Dublin demonstrated by tables that among its policy holders the greatest reduction in the mortality rates occurred during the decade of 1911-1912 to 1921-1922. The actual reduction during that period for all ages over one year was for white males 55 percent., and for white females 41.5 percent., while for colored males the reduction was 43.1 per cent and for colored females 33.1 percent.

The Bureau of Vital Statistics, Philadelphia, gives the death rate from tuberculosis in this city in 1912 as 150.52 per 100,000 for white, and 327.93 for colored. In 1922 the rate for the white population was 86.30 and the colored 260.28. The reduction of the Negro mortality rate does not compare as favorably with that of the white mortality rate as was noted in the statistics of the Metropolitan Life Insurance Company.

I have mentioned these figures merely to remind you that mortality rates among Negroes from tuberculosis are on the decline though not as rapidly as among the whites.

Dr. Dublin goes into the discussion of the theories as to the causes of this great reduction of mortality from tuberculosis among the general population. He recognizes two groups of persons; the environmentalists, those who contend that the reduction is due to improved environments of the entire population, as to housing, working conditions and recreation facilities; and the geneticists, or those who contend that this reduction has been due to a natural immunity in those individuals who have withstood tuberculosis infection and have not succumbed to the disease. Dr. Dublin leans toward the first class who give credit to our increased knowledge and practice of personal hygiene and to the crusade of such organizations as the National Tuberculosis Association.

Granting that this theory is a more reasonable one, then it would seem that the lesser decrease in mortality rates from tuberculosis of Negroes as compared with that of whites represents fairly the difference in opportunities which the Negro has had to enjoy our new knowledge of preventive medicine as pertaining to tuberculosis.

Of all of the anti-tuberculosis movements which have had as their object the reaching of the Negro group the clinics at the Henry Phipps Institute have received the greatest attention. Ten years ago, feeling that the inability of the institute to attract but a very few Negro patients to its clinics was most unsatisfactory, Dr. Landis, director of the clinical and sociological department, conceived the idea that the establishment of a clinic for Negroes administered by a colored physician and nurse might improve the situation. This experiment, as it might be called, soon demonstrated its wisdom. From one doctor and nurse in 1915, the personel of this particular work at Phipps Institute has grown to three physicians and four nurses. The ready response of the Negroes themselves to this appeal has increased the number of individuals attending the clinics annually from about 25 to over 800. A short time after this was done at Phipps Institute the same thing was done at the Jefferson Hospital Chest Department. About a year ago a third clinic was established by the Phipps Institute, the Whittier Centre and the Philadelphia Health Council on Ridge Avenue in the northern section of the city. These three clinics have been nominally united, composing what is known as the Negro Bureau and under the supervision of a Negro physician. This Bureau has as its personel 10 colored physicians and 8 colored nurses. An average number of 450 individuals pay about 800 visits to these clinics each month. Following this plan there has been established during the past year at one of the colored hospitals a tuberculosis clinic under the auspices of the City Department of Health, but conducted by colored physicians and nurses.

This so-called Philadelphia plan has received much attention outside of Philadelphia and has been the basis of new arrangements for health work among Negroes in other cities. In addition to the clinical work, the Phipps Institute is training student nurses from Mercy Hospital in tuberculosis nursing and social service work in order that they may go forth into virgin fields with this specialized knowledge.

The Department of Public Health of Philadelphia is employing two colored medical inspectors in our public schools and five municipal nurses. This has materially contributed toward the betterment of the well being of our colored community. I feel that their numbers should be increased in order that the good results may be increased.

I have merely tried to tell you of some of the things the Negro has been doing toward reducing the mortality rate among his own people. It would be impossible in one short paper to tell you all that have come to my notice.

The Negro physician, nurse and social worker are enthusiastic in modern public health. They meet a spirit of co-operation in their own people. As their opportunities for carrying on their work broaden I feel certain their efforts will be reflected in a further reduction of mortality rates among members of their race. These, however, must always be influenced by those factors of living and working conditions to which I have called your attention.

Racial Health

(PRESIDENTIAL ADDRESS*)

By G. N. Woodward, B.S., M.D., Ft. Valley, Ga.

Members of the John A. Andrew Clinical Society:

I do but mildly express the fact when I say to you that I deeply appreciate the honor which you conferred upon me at our last meeting by electing me president of this splendid body of scientific workers. I thank you for your esteem and confidence and trust that it may always be thus.

We assemble at this time to plant the seventh milestone which shall mark the extent of our journey along the way of science and research.

The records of our activities during the past years are indeed commendable, and of such we can justly feel proud; and yet, with a continuation of persistent, careful, painstaking efforts, who will dare prophecy what still greater achievements shall crown our future labors?

I have chosen as the subject of my address, "Racial Health," first, because as a group our professional activities, as I believe they should be, are confined largely to our own race; and secondly,

because for obvious reasons, the question of public health is to receive generous consideration in our present program along with the observance of Negro National Health Week.

The law of "The survival of the fittest" holds as true today as ever before, and is indeed applicable to the Negro race; for, with the rapid changes in conditions due to the progressive march of civilization, the race will more and more be brought to the test as to its physical, mental, and moral status.

Therefore, we cannot afford to stand still, for that would mean ultimate extinction. The gigantosaurus, which was over a hundred feet long and as big as a house, the tyrannosaurus, which had the strength of a locomotive and was the last word in frightfulness; the pterodactyl or flying dragon, indeed, all the great monsters of prehistoric ages are gone. Why? Because they did not know how to meet the changing conditions.. They stood still.

Egypt and Persia, Greece and Rome, all perished when they ceased to grow. China, after years of toil in building a wall about herself, stopped, stood still and went to sleep for a thousand years and

*Read at the annual meeting of the John A. Andrew Clinical Society at Tuskegee Institute, Ala., April, 1924.

upon awakening, found herself to be a mere medium of exchange between the other nations which while she slept "Kept toiling upward in the Night."

But we are not sleepers; we are not stagnant; we are making progress along many lines and can boast of a goodly number of men, any one of whom would be a worthy asset to any group of medical scientists.

Still there is ample room and pressing need for improvement along all lines, especially along those lines pertaining to the development and maintenance of health.

Our esteemed friend and leader, the late Dr. Booker T. Washington, with his far-seeing vision recognized this need and sought to provide for it, in a measure, through organization of the forces of the race by the annual observance of Negro National Health Week; thus, vividly reminding the medical profession of our duty to the race and pointing us to a truly fertile field for real service.

We are intensely interested in general racial progress. But general racial progress is primarily dependent upon racial health, for it is as impossible for a race as for an individual to yield normal production while handicapped by disease and by impaired health. It is therefore advisable, in order that we may achieve our greatest possibilities, that we wage ceaseless and unrelenting warfare against disease in every form.

The responsibility for the initiative in such warfare rests largely upon the medical profession; for, although the laity in their various spheres of activity are capable of, and are giving, tremendous aid wherever and whenever there is an organized attempt at public health work; yet, because of his special training and peculiar fitness. the doctor is the logical leader.

It is indeed a great privilege, as well as a real duty, for the doctor to take the lead in his community in all worth while movements directed toward improving health and preserving and prolonging life. The question may arise as to the effect of public health work and improved health conditions upon the income of the doctor. The answer is that such work brings him in contact with all classes of people in his community in such a manner as to create in them greatly increased respect for, and confidence in, his professional ability, while their increased appreciation of the value of health and of the dangers of disease will at the same time increase their desire for the advice and services of the doctor; thus producing a counter balance.

There are difficulties to be met in the battle for racial health, and these difficulties will vary more or less with the location. For instance, those in a Northern or Eastern section, where laws and regulations governing public health and sanitation are more adequate and more im-

partially enforced will not be so grave as those of the South where yet reside the great masses of our race and where, in most cases, comparatively little consideration is given to them by those in charge of municipal affairs when arranging for the health and sanitation of a given community or state. For example, the state of Georgia has for a number of years maintained a tuberculosis sanatorium for whites, while no provision whatever has yet been made for the care of such patients among the Negro race.

There is also the segregation aspect, with its many disadvantages so conducive to ill health, as are, likewise, the rural conditions characteristic of the Southland and of the small cities and towns where large numbers of our race occupy sections which as a rule are undrained and unlighted or very poorly lighted. It is because of these difficulties and disadvantages that the need for organized effort and team work is the more urgent along all lines pertaining to racial health.

There should be a general united effort on the part of the physician, the dentist, the pharmacist and the nurse to, in some systematic way, give to our people the simple fundamentals of hygiene. and sanitation. It cannot be done at one sitting; but by carefully organized plans, made to suit the conditions of the particular community, great and lasting good can be accomplished.

As a profession, we owe the race more than mere diagnosis and treatment of already existing ailments. We should also endeavor to lessen the frequency of occurrence of such ailments by using every possible method to instruct the masses in the simple laws of hygiene and preventive medicine.

A very important factor in racial health, one which has given me great concern, is that mysterious apostle of ignorance and superstition—a living relic of witchcraft—the midwife. What shall we do with her? How can we improve the grade of service she is rendering and which it seems she will continue indefinitely to render to such a great per cent of the mothers of posterity?

There is no doubt that both infant and maternal mortality are greatly increased through the very poor handling of thousands of maternity cases by careless, ignorant, and superstitious midwives. Still it seems that they are to continue actively in the field for years to come.

Then had we not better gravely consider them in any program for racial health? They are usually shy of the doctor, and may be a bit hard to get hold of. But I believe great good can be accomplished by an earnest effort on the part of the physician to gain their confidence and co-operation in order to be in a position to instruct them in some degree in the simple methods of

93

caring for those who either from choice or necessity engage their services.

An effort might be made to call them together at intervals and give them plain, simple talks and demonstrations. Such endeavor would accomplish the double purpose of increasing their ability, and at the same time, of establishing better relations between them and the doctor; and would ultimately give the doctor a line of contact by which he could in a measure supervise their activities and in that way improve the grade of service they are rendering. We have plans arranged and will hold our first of such meetings with the midwives of my community in conjunction with our Negro National Health Week program about the middle of April. We may be able to report some good results in the future.

While records show improvement in the mortality statistics of the race, there is still too great a percentage of mortality per thousand. I will not burden you by attempting to quote statistics, since such is provided for in our program for a future session during this meeting, to be given to us by one who makes a specialty of collecting such data.

It is encouraging, however, to note the various movements and organizations already in operation in various places directed toward racial health improvement, and it is gratifying to note the vast amount of good which they are accomplishing. Still there is a crying need for yet greater and more extensive effort to instruct and encourage the masses along every line that will tend to improve health and prolong life.

Many of us are so busy with active professional duties, or are so situated that any worth while amount of study and research is practically impossible. We should, therefore, take advantage of such meetings as this to increase our knowledge and skill and broaden our vision of the field in which we have chosen to operate.

We are extremely fortunate, gentlemen, to have as our own, in this section, this splendid scientific organization with its annual feast of knowledge served to us by those who, by research, observation and careful gleaning, gather and bring to us new and newer ideas and methods in such wholesome and digestible form.

The results should be inspiration to better service and improved health conditions in our respective fields of operation—occurring as direct products of the John A. Andrew Clinical Society.

THE MODERN HOSPITAL

A Monthly Journal Devoted to the Building, Equipment and Administration of Hospitals, Sanatoriums and Allied Institutions, and to Their Medical, Surgical and Nursing Services

Vol. XXX   *April, 1928*   No. 4

Negro Illness and Its Effect Upon the Nation's Health

By EDWIN R. EMBREE

President, Julius Rosenwald Fund, Chicago

ANYTHING that affects the Negro today concerns the American nation as a whole. One-tenth of our total population is colored. And no longer is the Negro only a resident in the rural South. He has moved north in great numbers and he has gone from the farm to the cities both north and south. About one-fifth of the Negro population now lives in the northern and western states and a full third of this race is living in cities and towns.

The tendencies toward urban life are seen more clearly when one realizes that the great migration both north and south has been to the largest cities, and that while before 1920 no American

city had more than 100,000 Negroes, six cities had well above that number according to the 1920 census: New York, Philadelphia, Baltimore, Washington, Chicago and New Orleans. An equal number of cities is likely to be added to the group having a negro population of more than 100,000 in 1930, including such rapidly growing centers as St. Louis, Cleveland, Detroit, Birmingham, Ala., and Atlanta, Ga.

The economic and social conditions of a group so large and so widely dispersed cannot but affect intimately the other members of the population with whom they live. This is peculiarly true in the matter of disease. Bacteria have a disconcerting fashion of ignoring segregation edicts. Jim Crow laws have never successfully been set up for the germs of tuberculosis, pneumonia, typhoid or malaria. Many families in the old South most sternly refuse social contact with the Negro, yet live in closest personal association with members of that group who serve as domestic servants and nurses and guardians of children—the very relationships in which disease most easily spreads.

If the white folks take even the most selfish attitude toward the Negro they must from pure self-protection take an interest in his health conditions. That they have been slow to do so is witnessed by the shockingly inadequate facilities for hospital care and community health and even for certain aspects of elementary sanitation that exist for Negroes in this country. And this in a nation and in an age in which care for the public health is becoming almost a religion.

For purposes of analysis it may be useful to consider this matter from the standpoint, first, of what is often technically included under the term public health and, second, of individual hygiene and medical service. The first of these, that is,

public provisions for health, include purification of the water supply, sewerage, prevention of soil pollution and the control of the great contagions, such as malaria, yellow fever and plague, which involve mosquitoes, rats or other animal carriers. These are cared for by governmental and state authorities and, technically at least, protect alike all members of the population. Even then it must be remembered that in certain cities water supply for the Negro section is inadequate and proper sewerage nonexistent and that rural areas inhabited largely by Negroes are often not well protected against disease-bearing mosquitoes and the various types of intestinal parasites.

Negro Hospitals Are Few

It is, however, in the second category, that of individual health and medical service, that provisions for the Negro are largely lacking. Negro hospitals are few in number and inadequate in construction, equipment and financial support. Conditions of housing, nursing service, care of children, pure and proper food and the general community provisions against disease are, among the Negro, inferior to similar facilities for almost all white groups.

These diseases that involve simply human contact, and the control of which is closely tied in to general improvement in community health, are the main problem. These include such ills as tuberculosis, pneumonia, influenza and other respiratory diseases, the venereal group, the ills both to the mother and the child attending childbirth, infant and child welfare, especially care and nutrition of young children, and ailments traceable to teeth. These are the diseases from which the Negro suffers most in comparison with his white neighbor and steps need to be taken to aid him

Freedmen's Hospital, Washington, D. C., which is supported by Congress

A bulletin issued in February, 1928, by the State Department of Public Health of Illinois gives a striking picture of the difference between Negro and white mortality. This bulletin reports that during the four-year period 1922 to 1925 for the entire state of Illinois the annual death rate among Negroes was 23.0 per thousand as contrasted with 11.2 for whites. According to this bulletin tuberculosis in Illinois causes a mortality of 323 per hundred thousand among the colored, as contrasted with 71 per hundred thousand for whites; the Negro death rate from pneumonia is 330 per hundred thousand, as compared with 73 for whites, and diarrheal disorders take three times as many Negro lives as whites, in proportion to the population.

In fact in Illinois for the period from 1922 to 1925 the number of deaths exceeded that of registered births among the colored people, although the average Negro birth rate for 1925 was 22.5 per thousand, substantially higher than that for the whites. These conditions are not peculiar to Illinois. Wisconsin, Kansas, Minnesota, Iowa, Indiana and Michigan show death rates exceeding or approaching the traditionally large number of births in this group. Conditions in the South where, over a long number of years, the Negro has adjusted himself, show on the whole much better records both for sickness and death.

One should not be too much alarmed by the conditions reported for a few northern states during a period known to be one of transition and of adjustment of large masses of Negroes to new and trying conditions in industrial centers. The current records of the Metropolitan Life Insurance Company, which has on its books more than two million Negroes, a fifth of the total colored population, are on the whole much more reassur-

ing. These policy holders include men, women and children of all ages, working in every conceivable occupation, and living in all sections of the country. Dr. Louis I. Dublin in a recent article* reports, from the extensive experience of that company, that the average death rate of these two million policyholders has declined from 17.5 per thousand in 1911 to 14.6 in 1926. While in a sense the insured are a picked group, still the large number included makes the findings significant. Dr. Dublin's study indicates that Negro health has greatly improved during the past few decades, that it is in about the position of white health in this country thirty or forty years ago, and that further concerted and intelligent attack may be expected to show corresponding gains in years ahead.

Are Negroes Increasing?

Two things may be said about trends in the colored population in America. However bad conditions are in given localities there is no evidence that the group will die out or even diminish in number. On the other hand there is no likelihood that the Negro will increase at any rapid rate or begin to press the white man by sheer force of numbers. As a matter of fact, while the colored population of America has steadily increased in numbers since the first arrivals from Africa, it has for over a century quite as steadily decreased in proportion to the total population. The following table, from the official census figures, gives a

*Recent authoritative publications on Negro health include chapters in two books just off the press: Negro Problems in Cities, T. J. Woofter, Jr., Doubleday, Doran and Company; The American Race Problem, E. R. Reuter, T. Y. Crowell; and the following papers: Life, Death and the Negro, Louis I. Dublin, American Mercury, September, 1927; The Death Rate Among the American Negroes, James A. Tobey, Current History, November, 1926; The Negro Health Problem, Frederick L. Hoffman, Opportunity, April, 1926; The Tuberculosis Problem and the Negro, H. R. M. Landis, Virginia Medical Monthly, January, 1923. The annual volumes of the Negro Year Book also give much general and statistical information.

This hospital is the teaching hospital of the Medical College of Howard University

clear picture of the relation of the Negro to the total American population during the history of the nation:

Year	Colored Population	Decennial Increase Per Cent	Per Cent of Total Population
1790	757,208	....	19.3
1800	1,002,037	32.33	18.9
1810	1,337,808	37.50	19.0
1820	1,771,656	28.59	18.4
1830	2,328,642	31.44	18.1
1840	2,873,648	23.40	16.8
1850	3,638,808	26.63	15.7
1860	4,441,830	22.07	14.1
1870	5,392,172	21.35	13.5
1880	6,580,793	22.05	13.1
1890	7,488,676	13.80	11.9
1900	8,833,994	18.00	11.6
1910	9,827,763	11.20	10.7
1920	10,463,131	6.50	9.9

The Negro, as any other group in the population, begins to have smaller families as he rises in the economic and social scale. Better public health has not brought a great onrush of population among the whites in America and it will not do so among the colored. Fewer and better babies seems the established rule as prosperity, intelligence and health increase. As we begin to set greater value on human life we become more thoughtful to preserve existing lives and we also become more careful about assuming the serious responsibilities of bringing new lives into being.

Death is not the only index of health. While figures that will show the amount of sickness are much more difficult to obtain than those for deaths, it is evident that the higher death rates by no means tell the entire story of Negro health handicaps. Sickness in both mild and acute forms is known to be much greater among the colored people. Incapacities due to accidents and painful illness and malformations due to improper medical attention are conspicuous in this group.

Let us look for a moment at the actual facilities reported in the single field of hospitals. Although facts concerning them are by no means an infallible index of Negro health, they are the visible and material evidences of medical service to maintain that health. A list recently compiled by the National (Negro) Hospital Association reports approximately two hundred institutions throughout the entire country including regular hospitals, infirmaries, and sanitoriums, taking into account institutions supported by public authorities, by fraternal organizations, and private endowment or subscription or as the personal projects of individual physicians or groups of physicians.

While the total figure is sufficiently small, the picture is not seen at all until the conditions of most of these hospitals are kept in mind. Only nine of this total number are on the accredited list of the American Medical Association as proper institutions for the training of interns, and only fifteen are on the list of the American College of Surgeons as having adequate minimum hospital standards. This means that less than twenty hospitals for Negroes exist in the entire country that are of acceptable minimum American standards.

It should be said in order to avoid any possible misunderstanding that the Negroes themselves are not responsible for the existing conditions. In fact leaders among them have been struggling against great odds to improve things. But while they have been furnishing probably more than their quota of the labor of the country, they are still lacking in individual or corporate control of capital. The small number of Negroes who are now becoming prosperous are subscribing, probably beyond the average in America, to various aspects of social welfare, including hospitals, but relatively speaking there is little money in Negro hands. Furthermore the tax funds are still almost exclusively controlled by white groups. With few exceptions, small sums indeed have gone from Government sources to hospitals. The situation will be corrected as colored people get increasing wealth and as white groups that benefit both by Negro labor and by Negro taxes meet their fair share of the load.

Fortunately several of the acceptable hospitals that are available for Negroes are of excellent quality. They stand out as beacons toward which Negro hospitalization as a whole is struggling.

A Center for Research

An important institution is Freedmen's Hospital, Washington, D. C., supported directly by Congress and serving as the teaching hospital of the Medical College of Howard University. This excellent hospital is kept in a good state of improvement and equipment. It has a total of 278 beds, provides internship for twenty-eight colored medical graduates, maintains an excellent school for nurses, and is a center for medical teaching and research.

George W. Hubbard Hospital, Nashville, Tenn., with 140 beds, similarly serves as the teaching institution for Meharry Medical College. Plans are now under way for moving this hospital and the Medical College to land immediately adjoining the campus of Fisk University. On its new site with increased resources, which are confidently expected, this will become a great hospital and medical center. At present these institutions in

Washington and Nashville are the only ones that combine good hospital facilities with excellent medical school standards. Their influence on medical education and on hospital and nursing development is of the greatest significance.

Several other hospitals are of high standard both in care of patients and in facilities for interns and nurses, although they lack the medical school connections that make Freedmen's and Hubbard preëminent.

New York City has two hospitals in the front rank. Harlem Hospital, with 348 beds, a part of the municipal system, is one of the leading hospitals from the standpoint of the care of patients and of nurses' training. Unfortunately it is lacking on the side of facilities for colored interns. The classic school for the training of Negro nurses is that affiliated with Lincoln Hospital. The hospital itself, now under city auspices, serves, with its 350 beds, chiefly a white community and is staffed by white physicians. The nursing school has for years been of first rank, and under a new arrangement the endowment, built up over a number of years, continues under a special board of trustees, to be available for the support in perpetuity of a school for nurses for colored girls.

Hospitals for Negroes under the regular municipal system exist also in St. Louis and Kansas City Mo.; the St. Louis City Hospital No. 2, of 275 beds and Kansas City General Hospital No. 2, of 200 beds. This movement to have Negro hospitals supported directly by the city treasury is significant. It may be one of the natural approaches to more adequate support for colored hospitals. When tax funds can be adequately counted upon for building and maintenance of these institutions then their financial future is assured.

A striking hospital development in Baltimore points the way to cooperation between Negroes and whites, both in finance and in medical service. A group of physicians associated with Johns Hopkins led by Dr. J. M. T. Finney recently joined with the Provident Hospital, Baltimore, to raise both funds and standards. The building is being completely remade and repaired and adjoining property has been purchased for a nurses' home and for future building. The campaign was started for $175,000 and more than twice that amount was raised, in total somewhat over $375,-000. Of this $25,000 each was given by Julius Rosenwald and John D. Rockefeller, Jr. Over $170,000 was raised by Negroes in Baltimore, almost entirely from among their own people, and $160,000 was raised by a white committee. The group of white physicians will serve as consultants and will take direct personal responsibility for helping to keep the standards of medical

care and of training for nurses and interns at a high level. This is a notable demonstration of what can be done when a concerted effort is made under able leadership. The contributions of the colored group are little less than epoch-making.

Mercy Hospital, Philadelphia, with 100 beds, not only is doing a good work, insofar as its limited facilities will allow, but has an excellent informal arrangement whereby members of its clinical staff and of its school of nurses serve with the Phipps Clinic in out-patient work and in home visiting in the thickly populated Negro section of this city. Another hospital in Philadelphia, the Frederick Douglas, with 100 beds is also on the accredited lists of the American Medical Association and the American College of Surgeons.

In Chicago the Provident Hospital, in a sub-

Flint-Goodrich Hospital, New Orleans, La.

stantial brick building, erected nearly forty years ago, continues to do good work. Sixty-five beds provide facilities for a number of private patients, as well as for groups in wards. Dr. G. C. Hall and a group of Negro physicians are giving good service to patients although the necessarily high charges keep the daily census rather low. Facilities are offered here for the training of interns and nurses.

In the far South the Flint-Goodridge Hospital, New Orleans, has been making heroic struggles against great odds. Sixty-five beds in an old building have served a part of the colored community in New Orleans, and this service has extended far beyond the hospital walls by progressive developments in the form of out-patient clinics, prenatal care, and home visiting. Here plans are taking shape for rebuilding on a new site.

The Charity Hospital, Savannah, Ga., is another of those that has been maintaining standards against every handicap and that is also planning an entirely new plant.

The Dixie Hospital of sixty-five beds in Hampton, Va., while not a part of Hampton Institute stands on property immediately adjoining and may be expected to have even more intimate association with the institute as years go on. Plans have been discussed for a combined course looking toward academic work and nurse training, to be carried on jointly by the institute and the Dixie Hospital. The John C. Andrews Memorial Hospital, Tuskegee, Ala., a hospital of seventy-five beds, is directly associated with the Tuskegee Institute. These hospitals, in conjunction with these two historic schools, may play an increasingly important rôle, particularly in the field of nurse training. The St. Agnes Hospital of 100 beds, Raleigh, N. C., affiliated with the St. Augustine School, and the McLeod Hospital, Daytona Beach, Fla., connected with the Daytona Industrial School in Florida, are also making heroic attempts, although with much less adequate facilities than those at Hampton and Tuskegee.

The Burrell Memorial Hospital, Roanoke, Va., has made notable improvement in recent years. It is said now to have better medical records than any other hospital in the city. St. Philip's Hospital, Richmond, Va., with 176 beds, is one of a group controlled by the hospital division of the Medical College of Virginia. It is not practicable, nor would it be fair except on the basis of an extensive survey, to attempt to print here a list of Negro hospitals that were thought to have adequate minimum standards. In addition to those listed above I happen to know something of the work and standards of the following hospitals: People's Hospital, St. Louis, Wheatley Provident Hospital, Kansas City, Mo., Lincoln Hospital, Durham, N. C., and the Millie E. Hale Hospital, Nashville, Tenn.

Facilities Available for Colored Patients

In addition to hospitals exclusively for Negroes or under Negro management there are in many places other facilities for the care of colored patients. Many of the municipal and county hospitals of the northern cities have a large number of Negroes in their wards. The large Cook County Hospital, Chicago, and the Philadelphia General Hospital, Philadelphia, are said to be often more than half filled with colored patients who are accepted without discrimination. In the South many of the general hospitals, as notably the Charity Hospital, New Orleans, have wards that serve many Negro patients. While these services are of benefit to the sick they do not, save in exceptional cases, offer any facilities for the teaching of Negro medical students, for service by Negro physicians or for the training of interns and nurses of the race. Most hospitals for white patients, however, have no facilities whatsoever for Negroes.

Hospitals have been discussed at some length because, as I have said, they are the visible and material evidences of medical service. They by no means represent all the facilities needed in a well rounded program of health. In fact, except as bases and training grounds, hospitals are less important in the present day aggressive combat against disease than certain other arms; out-patient clinics for mothers and babies and for general work, visiting and public health nurses, and public health protection against pollution of water, food and soil, and against animal and human carriers of disease. The lacks in hospital facilities unfortunately are simply typical of equal lacks in these other aggressive branches.

Training for Colored Nurses Needed

In this paper I have attempted simply to state a few of the salient features of the problem regarding hospitals and health for Negroes. The facilities for institutional care and health protection are shamefully inadequate and this fact is reflected in unfortunate death rates and in a great amount of sickness and distress, not only among Negroes but, as a result, among their white neighbors. Any constructive program must include not only more and better hospitals but also a good organization for visiting and public health nursing, for practical instruction in the schools, and for aggressive out-patient services and clinics, which will emphasize preventing serious illness by checking it in early stages, thereby protecting the home and community. One of the prime needs is for extension both in numbers and in quality of the training of colored girls for nursing, particularly in its public health aspects, and the use of these nurses in clinics, schools and rural counties and city homes.

Happily there is evidence of renewed interest in the whole matter. The national medical, surgical and hospital associations have been conferring with the Negro Hospital Association concerning possible studies and standardization. Nursing associations have been discussing their aspect of the problem. One of the great Foundations has given substantial help to Howard and Meharry Medical Schools, and other Foundations and individuals are displaying active interest. Another decade should see great progress in America in hospitals and health for Negroes.

SOME SIGNIFICANT NEGRO MOVEMENTS TO LOWER THEIR MORTALITY

By Dennis A. Bethea, M.D., Hammond, Ind.

During the first thirty years succeeding the emancipation, the Negroes passed away so fast that many publicists were led to believe that this vexed race problem would eventually be solved by the Death Angel. The expected span of life for that period was between thirty and thirty-five as against forty-five for the white people. At the end of this period or about the close of the last century, there was a great health renaissance all over this land. While it was aimed at ameliorating the deplorable health conditions among the whites, the colored people were also greatly benefited. This increased attention to public health has lessened the Negro's sickness and death rate, but they are still 50 per cent higher than the whites. In the registration area in 1920 the colored rate was 18.4 per thousand and the white race was 12.8 per thousand. The Negro Year Book estimates that 450,00 Negroes are sick all the time, that 225,000 die annually, and that 100,000 deaths and a large proportion of the sicknesses are from preventable causes.

Physicians, ministers, teachers, social workers and all those, whose work brings them into intimate contact with the masses of the race, are agreed that the primary causes of this great mortality of the colored people are (1) ignorance, and (2) poor living conditions. Conclusions drawn from examinations made of recruits in the World's War appear to be that they have as good a physical machine as any other group. The prevalence of venereal diseases during those early days of freedom caused many to conclude that the race was grossly immoral. But studies by sincere seekers after truth have revealed that these people are not more nor less licentious than other races of like social conditions. As they realize more and more that "He who would be free must strike the first blow," they have begun to strike out boldly to free themselves from the scourges that have been leading them down to disease and death. Naturally the principal forces which they have set in motion are of an (1) educational, and (2) civic and economic aspect.

Educational

(a.) Health Week. Fourteen years ago Booker T. Washington, together with a few other far-seeing individuals, instituted what was called "Health Week," for the first week in April, and every since that time it has been religiously observed. On Sunday the ministers are asked to preach sermons on health and sanitation, or secure the services of some physician or social worker to give talks along that line. Meetings are held each evening during the week, when doctors, dentists, nurses, and welfare workers are asked to give talks or demonstrations on such subjects as tuberculosis, "swat the fly," care of the teeth, personal cleanliness, home sanitation and the like. One day is designated as "clean-up day." Prizes are offered the communities which show the most successful clean-up and health work accomplished. There is always a spirited contest between the various cities. The prize is given by the National Clean-up and Paint-up Bureau of New York, and awarded at the annual meeting of the National Negro Business League in August each year.

Health week is now being observed in twenty-one states and in almost every community where the colored people live in large numbers. Prominent organizations which have helped to make this observance a success are the National Tuberculosis Association, National Health Council, National Paint-up and Clean-up Bureau, the life insurance companies, the Y. M. C. A.'s and the Y. W. C. A.'s, the U. S. Public Health Service, and the Boards of Health of the various cities and states. Not only during health week but all through the year, welfare workers of both races work hand in hand in this great "Better Health Movement." As the sage of Tuskegee used to say, "the disease germ knows no color line." Dr. Algernon B. Jackson, director Public Health,

Howard University, Washington, D. C., in speaking before a public meeting at the National Medical Association, at Detroit two years ago, made this observation: "Health is the platform upon which white and black Americans can stand hand in hand as brethren working toward a common good, a common service, which shall build a greater white race, a greater Negro race, and a greater America."

The Commission on Interracial Co-operation has done more to promote National Health Week than any other force. This committee was appointed by the Federal Council of Churches, to study race relations and to promote general good will. Eight hundred county committees have been organized by this commission throughout the South. They feel that good will is best promoted by working together for the good of the community. For the most part, these committees can be depended upon to back any sensible health project. The headquarters of the commission is 409 Palmer Building, Atlanta, Ga. Dr. Will W. Alexander is the director and Dr. Thomas Jackson Woofter, Jr., is the director of education and research.

(b.) The National Medical Association, made up as it is of physicians, dentists, and pharmacists, of our race, represents the best instance of well trained men working for the good of their less fortunate brothers. Public Health meetings are held at the time of the annual state and national sessions are held, and there the general public has a chance to see and hear of what is being done in preventive medicine. These physicians take the lead in their various communities, in the promotion of day nurseries, baby clinics, boys' clubs, health centers and general recreation programs. Realizing that a great number of their people die from lack of the proper hospitalization, members of the association have set about to meet this pressing need. The work is carried on principally through the auxilliary, the National Hospial Association, of which Dr. H. M. Green, of Knoxville, Tennessee, is chairman, and Dr. J. A. Kenney, secretary. This committee has been assisted materially by Dr. Carl Roberts (a former president) of Chicago, who spent a great deal of time touring the country looking into this lamentable condition.

They found that in the larger cities there are a number of well-equipped hospitals and private sanitaria, but in the smaller cities and rural communties, these advantages are meager indeed. There are about 162 hospitals and nurse training schools conducted by Negroes, many of which are very small and poorly equipped. However, a heroic effort is now being made by the medical fraternity to bring these up to the standard of the American Hospital Association. A committee from the colored association met with a committee of the white association two years ago in Chicago, at which time plans were laid to raise a fund of $10,000 to put field men out to raise the standard of these hospitals.

Dr. A. B. Jackson, spent several months last year making first hand investigations for the committee. The hospitals of our group approved by the American Hospital Association are: John A. Andrew, at Tuskegee; Freedmen's, in Washington; Provident, in Chicago; Mercy and Fred Douglass, in Philadelphia; Hubbard, in Nashville; Flint-Goodrich, New Orleans; Harlem, in New York; St. Louis City and Kansas City General. The last three are city controlled and have mixed staffs.

During the past few years a number of surgeons who have had training in some of the great hospitals of this country and Europe, have started excellent private hospitals, where they not only have an opportunity to gain experience from the wealth of clinical material, but it gives the colored people a chance to get expert treatment from surgeons and clinicians of their own race.

Some brilliant examples of this are: Dr. J. Edward Perry, of Kansas City; Dr. R. M. Hedrick, Gary; Dr. A. M. Curtis, Washington; Dr. C. C. Barnett, Huntington; Dr. U. Grant Dailey, of Chicago; and Dr. John A. Kenney, of Newark, who was formerly surgeon-in-chief of John A. Andrew Hospital, Tuskegee.

Dr. Kenney had his formal opening in October two years ago. He has 35 beds, complete laboratory, X-ray, and complete surgical equipment that would do honor to a much larger institution. He has twelve persons in his employ, which includes secretary, stenographer, nurses, matron and other helpers.

The National Convention of Baptists, at its session in Detroit last September, voted to join hands with the National Medical Association in this hospital movement. The joint committee from both bodies recommended that there be three mammoth hospitals, in three widely different sections of the South.

It would seem that a large portion of the blame for the dearth of hospitals can be laid to the Negro himself. Men who have gone to the front and organized hospital groups, have had to wade through all manner of criticism. They were called enemies of the race, it was said that they were "fostering segregation." But this is not new. Every time a Negro attempts to stand upon his feet and do something for himself, these over zealous persons will raise a hullabaloo about segregation.

(c.) The National Health Circle. Probably one of the most significant pieces of health work being done by the colored people themselves is that of the National Health Circle. Miss Bell Davis is the executive secretary, 370 Seventh Ave., New York City. It has on its board of directors some of the most outstanding men and women of both races. The organization has given five scholarships to graduate nurses in Public Health Nursing at the Teachers College, Columbia University, and the Pennsylvania School of Social Work. Public Health Nursing has been inaugurated in a number of southern communities, and in some cases salaries have been paid. Besides they maintain field workers who distribute literature and give whatever instruction they can in the ordinary laws of health.

(d.) Fraternal Societies. One of the most discouraging situations that confronts the colored leaders is the appalling death rate among infants. The infant death rate per 1000 births in the registration area shows for whites 67 and for colored 113. Every hour 19 black babies are born, while 13 colored people are taken away by death. There are 201 white babies born every hour, yet only 102 white people pass out within an hour. This shows that the whites lose one half of their birth rate, while the colored lose two-thirds of theirs. Most of the fraternities carry an insurance department, and their losses are so great that they have begun to study in earnest the causes of this great mortality. The Elks are making an intensive study of infant mortality. At their annual session in New York City in September two years ago, they made an appropriation of $5,000.00 for the purpose of making a further study of the causes that lead up to this excessive rate.

(e.) The Press. In speaking of the influences that are at work to dispel ignorance and superstition, the press is one of the most effective. Of the 150 newspapers and magazines, a large portion of them give a liberal amount of space for health stories. Dr. Algernon B. Jackson, of Howard University, releases weekly articles to a large number of these periodicals. The Chicago Defender, which is possibly the most widely circulated weekly, has carried a health department for twenty years under Dr. A. Wilberforce Williams. For years I have conducted the health column in the Christian Recorder, of Philadelphia, which paper also has a tremendous circulation, especially in the South. This is the oldest Negro newspaper in existence. The Opportunity magazine, which is the official organ of the National Urban League, has always carried health articles by experts. If you go into almost any Negro home you will find one or more of the publications of his race, therefore the Press vies with the Church in its sway over the masses. It is here that such great services are rendered by such prolific writers as Dr. C. V. Roman, of Meharry Medical College, Dr. H. M. Minton, of Philadelphia, and Col. J. H. Ward, chief officer of the Veterans' Hospital, Tuskegee.

Civic and Economic Agencies

(a.) The **National Urban League.** The Urban League, which was organized for social service in 1911, came **into prominence during the** World's War, when thousands of colored people came North to take places in the various industries. These people were hurdled together in crowded quarters to a shocking extent, and not being accustomed to the rigorous northern climate, there was a great deal of sickness and many deaths. The league, through its many branches, rendered a great service in helping them to adjust themselves. Not only is employment secured for these people, but meetings are held in which they are instructed how to hold these jobs and how to save their money. They are urged to buy homes and keep them in good repair. The housing question has always been a serious one in the cities. The Negro is often forced to pay a higher rent for some dilapidated dwelling than others do for good apartments. In order to meet the high rent he has to take in more roomers than is sanitary. Congestion breeds uncleanliness and sickness. Negro workers are paid less than others. It has been said that "they are the last to be hired, and the first to be fired." In spite of all this, the colored folk are buying homes at a rapid rate, and the property is less likely to contain certain "ear marks" than it formerly did. The Urban League has been a great force in bringing about better living conditions among these people. Their headquarters is 1133 Broadway, New York City. Eugene Kinckle Jones has been the executive secretary from the very beginning.

(c.) Negro Health Clubs. Other groups which are doing signal service are the Health Clubs. They **are working under the** direction of the Philadelphia Health Council and Tuberculosis Committee. They maintain a number of clinics. **Their specific work is tuberculosis.** Negro physicians and nurses with reasonable knowledge of **the conditions of life among** their people, are employed in these clinics. Most of them are paid by the Health Council from money received from the sale of Christmas seals. An effort is made to have this "Health Club" idea

spread to other cities. A number of cities have community houses where much of this kind of work has been carried on. Dr. Henry L. Hummons, of Indianapolis, who has done considerable amount of work in the field of tuberculosis, has charge of a large clinic at the Flanner Guild of that city. As it is impossible to send but a small proportion of lung patients to the sanitaria, they are taught to care for themselves in their own homes. But above all the people are taught how to keep from becoming infected.

(d.) The Church. Undoubtedly the Church is the most powerful institution in Negro life. A larger proportion of people are reached through this source than any other. We have so few institutions that the Church has become the logical center of community life. Observers have frequently noted that these buildings are as much cummunity centers as places of worship, and that the successful pastor is the one who devotes as much time to community life as to preaching the gospel and financing his church. He teaches his members how to live as well as how to die. In the cities it is not infrequent that you will find these churches conducting day nurseries, baby clinics, health and recreation centers. And furthermore, nearly all of them serve as employment agencies to a greater or lesser extent. In almost any town, persons in need of reliable domestic help, will call up the colored minister, while the minister, on the other hand, is delighted to secure lucrative employment for his good members.

Conclusion

While the death rate among Negroes is on the decline, it is still very high. It has been considerably lessened by an increased general attention to health matters. The principal causes of this high mortality are (1) ignorance, and (2) poor living conditions.

The forces which the Negroes themselves are using to combat this high mortality are:

(1) Educational.
   a. Health Week.
   b. The National Medical Association.
   c. The National Health Circle.
   d. Fraternal Societies.
   e. The Press.
(2) Civic and Economic Agencies.
   a. The National Urban League.
   b. Negro Health Clubs.
   c. The Church.

530 Kenwood Avenue.

JOURNAL OF THE
National Medical Association

THE EDITORS ENDEAVOR TO PUBLISH ONLY THAT WHICH IS AUTHENTIC, BUT
DISCLAIM ANY RESPONSIBILITY FOR VIEWS EXPRESSED BY CONTRIBUTORS

| VOL. XXII. | JULY - SEPTEMBER, 1930 | No. 3 |

HOSPITAL SYMPOSIUM

THE NEGRO HOSPITAL RENAISSANCE

By John A. Kenney, M.D., Newark, N.J.

Editor-in-Chief, Journal of the National Medical Association; Member American
Medical Editors and Authors Association

During the meeting of the National Medical Association in the city of St. Louis, 1923, a small group of delegates got together and organized the National Hospital Association, as a constituent member of the National Medical Association. The purpose of the organization was to bring to bear all the forces possible in combating the unfavorable conditions existing relating to our hospitals, practicing physicians, internes, and nurses. Hospitalization for members of our race was seriously inadequate. Our physicians as a race were denied the privilege of the advantages to be derived from group practice in connection with hospitals. Year by year more states were added to the list of those requiring internship in a recognized hospital as necessary for a license to practice medicine. In spite of this legal requirement no provision was being made to prepare our medical graduates to meet the demands. The outlook for the coming Negro doctor was rather dark.

There were very few hospitals, whose diplomas were recognized, to which our girls were admitted to learn nursing. In our own nurse training schools there were no uniform regulations as to admission. There was no standard curriculum. Many of our hospitals were disjointed affairs, some entirely unworthy of the name of hospital or sanatorium. Many of the so-called training schools were really boarding houses into which our girls were inveigled with no assets in their favor except brawn. They could work, and that was the open sesame to the nurse training world. Too many of them awoke after their two or three years in "training." (working) to find that they had been hoodwinked. Worse still, this condition obtained in some of the white hospitals and training schools, where in order to get labor more cheaply, our girls were admitted ostensibly as nurses, but in reality as maids to do the drudgery which was beneath the dignity of the white pupil nurses. We are told authentically that these latter conditions were in evidence all too frequently.

These were some of the outstanding irregularities which our association was organized to combat. The officers elected at that first meeting were, Dr. H. M. Green, president; Dr. J. H. Ward, vice-president; Dr. John A. Kenney, executive secretary, and Miss Petra Pinn, R. N., treasurer. The Executive Board was composed of Dr. John A. Kenney, chairman; Miss Petra Pinn, R.N., Dr. John B. Eve, and Dr. L. A. West. The president, secretary and treasurer have been reelected from year to year and are yet serving—how well, is for the public to say. The work is only half begun, but many changes by way of improvement have taken place during these seven years.

The Hospital Awakening

While this association has no desire and makes no effort to take unto itself all or even any of the credit for the hospital awakening during this period, it at least has had the privilege of carrying on contemporaneously with other agencies which have been actively interested.

We can say with modest truth that we have

been, and are, on the firing line. Our president is an agitator. In season and out he has kept the hospital subject ablaze. His annual addresses on the hospital situation have always been full of vital interest. Early in our efforts we made important contacts with the big bodies: the American Hospital Association, with which we have a constituent membership, The American Medical Association, and the American College of Surgeons. These contacts have proven very helpful. While the survey of Negro hospitals in the South was made by Dr. A. B. Jackson of Washington, D. C., under the auspices of the American Medical Association, in 1928, this survey grew out of the activities of the National Hospital Association, and after much correspondence and several conferences between officials of the four bodies, Dr. Jackson was our selection. He did a good job and did it well, without fear or favor. He presented the facts. Some of them both good and bad were startling to the uninitiated, but the facts were necessary and will do good. In fact they are already bearing fruit.

The outlook for the Negro hospitals today compared with what they were in 1923 is as though we were emerging into a new world. Many fine and important things are happening. The whole country is aroused. Barring prohibition, perhaps the hospital question is the foremost in the country today, and Negro hospitals are sharing generously in the distribution of funds.

It is truly an awakening. From all sections of the country we gather reports of the wonderful strides taken. Of particular importance is the stress being placed on preparation and teaching and research. The modern hospital cannot completely function unless it has some teaching facilities. Not only should nurses and internes be prepared for their work, but it's the one unit in the community where the practicing physician is enabled to keep abreast of the times. In its laboratory and other departments research work and experiments are carried on. Not only are the hospitals which are connected with our medical schools expected to do this kind of work, but every large hospital should be a teaching unit in its community.

Howard University at Washington, has been strengthened. A new Meharry in Nashville is in course of erection. The New Provident Hospital and Training School in Chicago is taking the lead in this line. Mr. Julius Rosenwald terms it "one of the most epoch making steps in the development of the Negro race since Lincoln's Emancipation Proclamation." This unit as a de-

partment of Chicago University will fulfill the demands down to the last detail. Patients will be hospitalized, internes and nurses will be trained, post-graduate course will be given to physicians, research work will be provided for and encouraged, and last but of no less importance, public health will be taught by every conceivable means.

Just recently a big campaign has closed in New Orleans providing two and one half or three millions of dollars for the New Dillard University under whose auspices will come the Flint-Goodrich Hospital planned to be a great teaching unit in the South.

It is truly glorious. Not much did we expect in our day to see such a tremendous gain. Like the first locomotive seen by the backwoodsman, he assured his comrades that it would never start; but once it was under way he reversed himself and declared that it could never be stopped. While this hospital movement was slow beginning we believe now that the impetus is so great that it will go on and on till there are hospitals, and nurse training schools and internships adequate to our needs. In fact, with reference to nurses; the need now is not so much for more, but for better qualified nurses. The fact is that despite the announced entrance requirements in our training schools, in all too few of the applicants is the foundation sufficiently laid on which to build the nursing super-structure. The particular need today is better preparation for the course of nursing; better schools and better training. Quality now and not quantity is the keynote. In speaking of better training schools, we are doing so collectively; quite aware of the fact that there are some schools which do measure up.

We cannot leave this topic without asserting what we have said a number of times—modern nursing is a luxury. Only the well-to-do can afford it. Some years ago Dr. Mayo called attention to nursing in the hospitals on the Canal Zone.

A patient in a hospital wanting or requiring a private nurse paid three nurses in three shifts during the 24 hours $8.00 each, making his nurse cost him $24.00 per day. When the late Dr. Booker T. Washington was ill in a hospital in New York his day nurse cost him $12.00 per day for 12 hours and he did without the night special whose fee was the same. In our immediate recent experiences we have had a few patients who paid their day nurses $8.00 per day and their night nurses $7.00 or $8.00 per night plus hospital board and lodging for one or both. Thus we say nursing is a luxury and only the rich can afford it. This is all wrong. The poor and that great self-respecting middle class need the comforts and care of the nurse just as much as the rich. The estimate of the Metropolitan Life Insurance Company of $140.00 per year for the medical bill of the average American family will not go very far if the nurse's pay is included.

We wonder what one of our average doctors collects from the ordinary case of pneumonia that he treats. We'd say roughly $25.00 and feel certain that this figure is exaggerated. We are sure that our own average is far below this. Many a time have we attended a patient with attendant alarming pneumonia symptoms of high temperature, embarrassed circulatory and respiratory conditions and advised the nature of our findings and their seriousness, to be told by the householder, "We'll call you again if she 'pears to get any worse." On a few occasions we have felt forced to reply facetiously "No, if she gets any worse than now, you won't need us, you'll need the undertaker." The point we started out to make is the disproportion between the fees of the doctor and the nurse, in those few cases who can afford to have the nurse.

This is worth considering. In our section $8.00 per 12-hour day is the nurse's charge. A serious pneumonia case will need a night nurse, too. Thus $16.00 a day will be the fee. The average case will need the nurse at least 10 days. Thus the nurse collects $160.00 against the doctor's average of $25.00. Be it far from us to begrudge the nurse her pay. When the family can afford it, it is O.K. She should have it.

Those Who Need

Our plea is for that 999 out of the 1,000 who can't have the nurse at these figures, but who need her just as much as the one who can. The rich may go to a hospital or stay at home as they please, and have as many doctors and nurses as they fancy. The poor are frequently provided for in the hospital charity wards, or in the municipal institutions, but what about the self-respecting middle class who do not want to accept charity and can't pay the luxurious prices? This is a real problem and one to which we have been calling the nurses' attention for the past 15 years. It is up to the nurses to find some means to meet this situation. The doctors do. Again and again a doctor gives his service, for what the patient can pay and frequently for nothing.

Some months ago we had three operative patients in one group. In keeping with prevailing prices their fees for operations and hospital services would have amounted to $275.00. We gave them the service and collected in cash only $45.00 from the three, taking their I.O.U.'s for the balance. Needless to say not one of those notes has been honored or ever will be. The point we make here is that we try to meet the situation and serve suffering humanity.

If the trained nursing profession does not meet the situation it will eventually find a serious competitor in the experienced and practical nurse.

As to the training of our internes this problem is rapidly vanishing. With the hospitals that are already recognized as suitable for the training of internes and with those that will be on the elegible list in the next year or two, there will be enough interneships to take care of all of our immediate needs.

Hospitals in Large Centers

As above stated much has been done and great plans are under way for furnishing hospital facilities for our people. Quite naturally these are generally located in the big centers. With the clinching of these the work must spread to the small towns and rural districts; for after all it is among these that the most suffering and the greatest need exist.

The Small Hospitals

We must pay our respects to the small hospitals of proprietary ownership. These have been the mainstay of Negro hospitalization, particularly in the South.

The more rigid enforcement of segregation of practically everything between the races in the South caused the Negro doctor of that section to be more aggressive than his brother in the North in opening small private hospitals. Too much cannot be said in praise of the men and women who have been the pioneers in this work. Dotted all over the South and a few in the North, to the number of around 150, these institutions have relieved much suffering, saved many lives, and brought much happiness to members of the race. In addition to this they have been the only source of hospital practice for hundreds of our doctors. Many of these institutions are modernly equipped and up-to-date in every particular except in size. Others need the apology of Touchstone as pointed out by Dr. E. A. Balloch: "A very sorry thing, sir, but mine own." Of course, under such conditions it would be expected to meet many irregularities, and they do exist. But on the whole the founders and conductors of these institutions have been actuated by the proper spirit and the greatest number of offences have been due to poverty and ignorance. They have been errors of the head rather than of the heart.

In spite of all the good that these institutions have done, and all that may be said in their favor, their days are numbered. The handwriting on the wall says they must go. They do not and cannot meet the modern requirements, nor should they be expected to do so. There is one thing in which they do excel. They are man-killers as truly as is the man-eating lion. The clientele to whom they cater are not able to pay the prices necessary to carry the institutions with ease. Most of them, perhaps, 75 per cent, are conducted by physicians, but for which fact nine out of ten of them would close up quickly. They are eating cancers on the doctor's income. Most of the time he must use his surgical, office and visiting income to carry the hospital. If he succeeds in saving anything from his income more than a moderate life insurance, he is indeed a phenomenal man. The care of the sick is a community burden, and should be so assumed. No one individual or small group of individuals should be expected to carry this responsibility.

Modern medicine requires group practice. Both diagnosis and treatment demand the combined efforts and knowledge of the surgeon, the internist, and the laboratory technician. With great advantage to such a staff will be the addition of the dentist and the pharmacist. To these, depending upon the size of the institution should be added the various specialists with their individual departments. To the capacity limit of the hospital, patients should be admitted, and each one who enters is due the best that the institution and the staff offer. Hence the inability of the individual to properly function.

A Word of Thanks

In conclusion we want to thank the institutions and individuals who have so readily and generously assisted us with this piece of constructive work. We believe that this presentation will be accorded a warm reception by the interested public—regardless of profession. We also believe that this ensemble will prove to be a hospital classic to which reference will be made for a long time to come. Those who have contributed to it will have occasion to take pride in having done so. No, the list is not complete. For various reasons it cannot be. The most important of which is the expense and the lack of space. Not one penny has been collected or is charged for this presentation. It is the contribution of the N.M.A., to the cause. All could not be asked to contribute, and a large number of those who were asked failed to comply. While it has entailed a great deal of extra work on our limited time and resources, they have been cheerfully given. In fact, it has been a pleasure, for we believe it is a good cause.

With this preamble we bid you to the feast before you, believing that you will be wiser, if not better after partaking to the full.

134 West Kinney St.

HOSPITAL PROVISION FOR THE NEGRO RACE[1]

By Peter Marshall Murray, M.D.

Trustee, Howard University, Washington, D. C.
New York City

IT IS OF MORE than passing importance that the topics in this symposium on "Hospital Provision for the Negro Race" should center about the question of adequacy. It is recognized that the health needs of more than one-tenth of the population of this great country are being met "after a fashion" by public and private institutions, but this very meeting shows that intelligent

> *The grateful patient will contribute to hospital support as far as he is able, the public-spirited citizen will contribute as his interest dictates, but the substantial contributors will be drawn from the ranks of persons who can be taught, in addition to its humanitarian appeal, the valuable contribution an adequate hospital can make to the economic, moral, and social progress of a community both by its dircet service to the sick and by its educational value, which will ultimately touch the life of every citizen.*

opinion is aware of the fact that these facilities are far from being adequate in quantity or quality.

As to quantity, while the latest figures show that mortality and morbidity rates are several times higher among Negroes than among whites, the number of hospital beds available to this group is distressingly small as compared with their actual needs. Statistics tell us that the proportion of hospital beds to the entire population of the United States is one for each 139 persons. After making a most generous allowance for the poor economic condition of the Negro, a proportion of one for each 1,941 persons, which is the ratio for the Negro, gives in striking terms the true picture of the inadequacy in quantity of hospital facilities available to this group of our population.

Because the Negro occupies such a disadvantageous economic position—and this is an admitted fact—with practically no reserve on which to call in case of illness and because the livelihood of practically the whole race requires that they keep on the job, which is usually a physically exacting one, the health needs of the so-called white collar class, or persons whose incomes range from $2,000 to $2,500 a year and about whom so much concern is now being manifest, pale into utter insignificance when compared to the health needs of the Negro.

An heroic attempt on the part of the Negroes themselves to meet this dire need is seen in the nearly two hundred hospitals promoted and maintained by Negroes themselves. This sad state of affairs is not limited to any one section of this country. It constitutes a real problem in every section, North

---

[1]Read before the Annual Congress on Medical Education, Medical Licensure, and Hospitals, Chicago, February 18, 1930.

109

as well as South. A cross section view of hospital facilities in the entire country would give a picture ranging between two extremes. On the one hand, I would cite the Harlem Hospital, a municipal institution in the city of New York. Situated in the heart of the largest Negro community in the world, between 90 and 95 per cent of its patients are colored. In a house staff of twenty-seven, ten, or 37 per cent, are colored. Of 109 physicians on the staff of the out-patient department, fifty, or 45.9 per cent, are colored. On the indoor visiting staff nineteen out of forty-six, or 41 per cent of the physicians, surgeons, and specialists, are colored. The estimate of the success of this experiment after four years' trial, as expressed by Dr. John F. Connors, surgical director, is as follows:

"During the past four years since the question of color has been entirely eliminated I cannot see any marked change in the affairs of the hospital. If there be any it is toward an improvement in the interest of the patient, which, after all, is the most important duty of a hospital. This could not have been established if the colored doctor had not taken his place with the men on our staff, working as diligently and as effectively as any other member. Insofar as we are able to see, the colored doctor has progressed as far and as rapidly as any other racial group. We have tried in the past and hope to continue in the future to have competency the predominating factor in the promotion of the younger men who are associated with us. It is our definite policy to give all the men an opportunity to become proficient in their selected lines of medicine and surgery so as not only to fit them for our hospital but also to enable us when the time arrives to recommend them to take their places in other institutions."

The great city of New York thus records itself as permitting no discrimination against any of its citizens on account of race, creed, or color, and offers this successful experiment of what a community can do if it will face squarely its full duty to all of its citizens.

The city of Cleveland, after several years' serious study of this question, including the personal visit of a special committee to various cities with large numbers of Negroes, follows the lead of New York and on January 13, 1930 unanimously passed a resolution instructing "the city manager to make such appropriate arrangements as shall afford to all citizens of Cleveland seeking the same an equal and reasonable opportunity to receive training as nurses or interns at the Cleveland City Hospital and . . . . . further . . . . . that in accordance with the policy expressed in the Constitution and Laws of the United States of America and of the state of Ohio such opportunity shall in no event be denied or abridged on account of race or color of anyone seeking such training."

New York and Cleveland have taken advance positions along the highway of race relations and common justice. May their success point the way to others.

The other extreme might be pictured in the incident where a student of Fisk University, a member of the football team, was seriously injured. The facts in this case were furnished me by Dr. George S. Moore, clinical director of the U. S. Veterans' Hospital, Tuskegee, Alabama, the father of the boy, and are as follows:

The round table and section programs have never been better than they will be at this year's convention.

HOSPITAL PROVISION FOR THE NEGRO RACE

"About 8:00 A. M., November 4, 1927, my boy met with an automobile accident on the highway between Athens and Decatur, Alabama. A Mr. Gordon, who was at the time treasurer of Fisk University and in charge of the motor cavalcade, rushed my son, in his car, to Athens and Decatur in vain search for hospital accommodation. He was not only refused medical aid for his disability—fracture-dislocation of the third cervical vertebra with compression of the spinal cord—but was absolutely refused admittance to any hospital available in that territory on the ground that there were no hospital facilities for colored patients, regardless of the severity of the disability. An ambulance of the hearse ambulance type was finally secured after a wait of several hours and he was rushed to Huntsville, Alabama, a distance of some thirty odd miles from Decatur, and admitted to McCormick Memorial Hospital, where he received every attention and was rendered service far beyond the ordinary. He died the following evening at 9:00 P. M., November 5, 1927, from pneumonia, induced and aggravated by unnecessary exposure, lack of adequate medical care and treatment, and particularly on account of the inability of Mr. Gordon to secure hospitalization for him at a time favorable for recovery."

Neither of these two pictures is applicable to all sections of the North or South. It is not possible to predict geographically the adequacy of hospital facilities for Negroes—indeed, it seems that the Mason and Dixon line of hospital facilities would resemble more a tangled skein of yarn at the mercy of a playful kitten than a parallel of latitude.

A further complication is the question of hospital facilities for Negroes in the small town as against the large city. With a Negro population largely of the servant class, too small to warrant consideration of a separate institution, and with physicians of their own race denied opportunities in existing hospitals in the small town, the problem is most acute. The handling of the health needs of Negroes and of other underprivileged groups is truly an index of civic, social, and community progress. I venture the assertion that some of the communities in the South are exercising an honest concern and showing a degree of co-operation in meeting the health needs of the Negro population that are far more commendable than in some communities in the North. In this connection, it is only fair to quote further from the letter of Dr. Moore, already mentioned:

"I arrived at Huntsville in the early morning of November 5, 1927 from Tuskegee and found my son in the care of a physician who had just recently returned from extensive postgraduate study at Mayo Clinic on fractures of the vertebra column and compression of the spine, etc. This physician was untiring in his effort to save my boy and devoted his entire time to his care. In fact the personel of this hospital, and the x-ray diagnostician likewise, made every effort humanly possible to save him. However, his life was brought to an untimely end by pneumonia following the exposure mentioned above."

It would be a trite commonplace to repeat here that disease germs know no color line or that any racial group with a disproportionately high mortality and morbidity rate is a distinctly retarding factor in the progress of any community. Truly the concern of the health of the Negro is the concern of the whole community.

While the Negro still uses to a very large extent such free hospital facilities as are open to him, his experience leads him to feel that he will get better treatment if he pays something for his medical care. Consequently, his willingness to pay often exceeds his ability, and yet in the two hundred Negro hospitals practically all of the beds are pay beds. In the annual report of the United Hospital Fund of New York, Mr. Homer Wickenden, general director, said:

"The surprising thing is that practically all the poor people who need free treatment want to pay for it. They hate the idea of being charity patients and they will strain every effort to pay something toward the cost of their care ... it makes them feel more independent and happier." The general tendency is definitely that the patient shall bear an increasingly larger proportionate share of the cost of his treatment.

The practice well nigh general in this country of excluding Negro physicians from the staff of hospitals where Negroes are patients imposes a distinct psychologic handicap on the Negro patient and makes the result of treatment given him less effective. He is less inclined to apply for hospital service for preventive and early treatment and too often submits only after he has become a grave risk. *The Journal of the American Medical Association* editorially stated:

"In outlining plans for Negro health betterment, no factor is of greater importance than the part the Negro himself will play and particularly the part that will be played by the Negro physician. When the Negro physician enters the home of the colored patient or meets him in the dispensary or the hospital ward he greets him as one of his own people, adapts himself to the needs of the situation, and carries to his patient and to the home lessons of sanitation and health that he can enforce to a degree hardly practicable otherwise."

The experience of the Phipps Clinic in Philadelphia and the Harlem Hospital in New York abundantly attests to the tremendous increase in clinic attendance on the appointment of Negro physicians in the out-patient clinics.

Let us consider the question of the Negro pay patient. In the usual, or white, hospital when a Negro emerges from the charity class and pays something for his medical care, he as a rule has no choice in the selection of his own physician. It is only in the Negro hospital that his ability to pay permits him freely to select his own physician, for with some comparatively few exceptions Negro physicians and surgeons do not have staff privileges in other hospitals. With the growing tendency to require patients to pay something for their hospital care and with the rapidly improving economic conditions among Negroes, the necessity for providing adequate facilities for this class of patients is becoming more and more acute. If this situation is not met adequately we shall not only retard the development of the confidence of the Negro patient in the Negro physician and further retard the professional development of the Negro physician, but we shall fail to use a rich opportunity to convert the Negro public to its responsibility to pay its own way for medical service when able and to become contributors to hospital movements for the public good.

Dr. A. B. Jackson, in his report of his investigation of 125 Negro hospitals, states: "When the Negro pay patient compares the inadequate facilities of the Negro physician and hospital with the services offered him by a white hospital, though that service be of a poorer standard than that received by white patients, it is possible to understand his choice of the latter. In every instance where a first class Negro surgeon offers his people the facilities of a first class hospital he gets the Negro patient." This should settle the question of the natural preference of the Negro patient for the white physician. In years gone by this was probably true to some extent, but to-day, when the intelligent Negro is more acutely sensitive to incidents of discrimination and unsympathetic service, he is looking for the very best sympathetic care he can find. The plight of the Negro who is able, and wishes, to maintain his self-respect by not accepting charity demands serious consideration.

The two main aspects of any adequate hospital program which readily come up for consideration are:

1. The care of the sick.
2. Educational value to the physician and the public.

We have already seen that provision "after a fashion" is made for the Negro in the general hospital program of almost every enlightened community. In addition to institutions maintained by and for Negroes, many other hospitals offer facilities to some extent for Negro patients. Edwin R. Embree says: "The large Cook County Hospital in Chicago and the Philadelphia General Hospital, Philadelphia are said to be often more than half filled with colored patients who are accepted without discrimination. In the South, many of the general hospitals, as, notably, the Charity Hospital, New Orleans, are said to have wards that serve many Negro patients. While these services are of benefit to the sick, they do not, save in exceptional cases, offer any facilities for service by Negro physicians. Most hospitals for white patients, however, have no facilities whatsoever for Negroes."

The educational value of an adequate hospital to the physician and the community has a place of importance almost equal to that of the care of the sick. In defining the relation of the hospital to medical practice, Dr. Michael M. Davis in his study, *Hospital Administration: A Career*, aptly states: "Hospitals are intimately related to the whole medical practice of their locality. The physician who is deprived of opportunity to use a hospital for his patients is seriously handicapped professionally. The hospital is essential to the practice of surgery. Physicians who confine their practice to a specialty likewise must have affiliation with a hospital or a clinic. Statistics show that substantially all such specialists are in communities with hospitals and have some staff connection with them, whereas it is often true that from 40 to 60 per cent of general practitioners have no hospital opportunities. To develop and maintain a satisfactory relationship with the practicing profession of the locality is one of the important responsibilities of hospital management. To fulfill this responsibility means to benefit not merely a certain number of physicians, but also the whole community in which these physicians practice."

A Negro patient suffering from a ruptured ectopic pregnancy, an acute suppurative appendicitis, or an acute intestinal obstruction is apt to receive standard treatment anywhere in the United States when once admitted to any hospital. An adequate hospital program for Negroes in such a community would mean that prior to admission there had been early diagnosis, prompt reference to the hospital, and community confidence. These latter factors, the direct result of the proper community and professional relation to an adequate hospital, might surely mean the difference between life and death. "The hospital and the clinic are now agencies for the institutional practice of medicine."

New Orleans in October is like the month of May in the North.

113

It is my firm belief that in any hospital program for Negroes emphasis should be placed on the weakest spots in our armor of health. These are tuberculosis, venereal disease, and maternal and infant welfare.

The facts of the high death rate among Negroes from tuberculosis are too well known to demand more than passing mention. In order, however, to fix in your minds how urgent the need is for relief from this distressing condition, may I remind you that in 1926 in Chicago the Negro death rate from pulmonary tuberculosis was from two and a half to three times as high as the rate for the white population. Dr. Bundesen states concerning the death rate in Chicago among Negro children: "The very high death rate in Chicago among Negro children occurs under the age of eleven years, for tuberculosis is more marked in this group than for the population as a whole. Rates for Negroes in this group are from ten to twenty times as high as for the white children of the same age for the same period. In 1926, 41.04 per cent of the total deaths of children under eleven years of age were among Negroes who composed 3 per cent of the total population in this age group."

In 1928 there were 5,326 deaths in New York City from tuberculosis. Of these 823, or 15 per cent, were Negroes who composed only 5 per cent of the total population.

In addition to the study of the whole interplay of social and economic factors, this situation demands education on the part of the Negro profession and the Negro public. The Negro physician must be more public health-minded. The beginning of his public health-mindedness should be in his undergraduate days. The medical curriculum, at least in the two Negro medical schools, should place special emphasis on the problems which the Negro physician must face in his active professional life. Ideal tuberculosis hospital projects should be the atmosphere where the Negro student should learn what constructive work can be done in this fight against tuberculosis. I doubt whether any student, and very few physicians, can get the proper picture of what can be done for the arrest and cure of tuberculosis from observation of the "random" case. The very term brings to mind the hopeless, cough-racked, emaciated specimen rapidly succumbing to the disease. It is no wonder a great many Negro physicians have been charged with indifference to this problem. The good results of early diagnosis and proper treatment must be dramatized under ideal institutional conditions.

In connection with the two Negro medical schools there should be ideal tuberculosis hospital units for the proper instruction of students and for the continued postgraduate education of Negro physicians. Are you aware of the fact that there is no institution in the United States, to my knowledge, where a Negro who is able to pay for private attention may go for treatment of tuberculosis?

I have been able to locate among my professional friends about twenty-five Negro tuberculosis patients fully able to pay who have travelled long distances at great expense seeking some institution where they might pay for private hospital care. I am confident that the number of Negro tuberculous patients so fortunately situated economically who refuse to accept charity is not inconsiderable.

As I see it, as applied to the general population the question of venereal disease in all of its aspects is in no danger of an immediate satisfactory solution. Much of the alarming increase in deaths from heart disease in the middle and later decades of life can effectively be checked by a more thorough control of venereal disease in the earlier decades. Among Negroes this is especially significant. The solution lies again in the more effective education of both physician and public. Here, as in tuberculosis, the education of the physician should begin in his undergraduate days. The far reaching effect of venereal disease should receive proper emphasis. The late effects of syphilis, as evidenced in the syphilitic heart, and the high incidence of conditions resulting directly from gonorrhea which require surgery in the female give the question of venereal disease an importance almost equal to that of tuberculosis.

The third annual report of the Shoemaker Health and Welfare Center, Cincinnati, Ohio, states:

"The outstanding feature in the review of attendance figures and analysis of the entire service is the size of the venereal clinic. . . . The number of patient visits this year, 8,055, is nearly four times the number of last year, 2,773. . . . More patients are rendered unable to earn a fair living because of this disease than from any other encountered in the clinic. Yet continued treatment, although requiring a discouragingly long period of time, gives definite promise in most cases that the individual may return to a gainful occupation."

Under the direction of men or agencies who understand the full public health implication of venereal disease and by employing colored as well as white physicians for the work, venereal disease clinics could easily be the most satisfactory if not the most beneficial of all the clinics in any community of Negroes. It has been my experience that less than 5 per cent of Negro syphilitics can be persuaded to continue treatment beyond the first course of arsphenamine injections. With the idea prevalent and expressed among many laymen of this unfortunate stratum that gonorrhea is not much worse than a "bad cold" the educational possibilities as to the seriousness of these conditions are tremendous. Indeed, any hospital which would consider that it is doing its full duty to any large Negro community should have highly specialized, well developed services in urology and gynecology.

The Negro is also contributing more than his share to the high maternal and infant mortality and morbidity rates which place the United States disgracefully low in the list of civilized countries. No branch of health service responds so favorably to intelligent effort as the division of maternal and infant care. In the metropolitan area of New York last year 40 per cent of all births occurred in hospitals. Maternity services in centers of Negro population should be the focal points of attack on this problem. The work of the splendid agencies already operating in this field require adequate hospitalization to make their program most effective.

The progress that has been made in the last five years toward the solution of these problems is simply amazing. Philanthropy has been most generous

---

Enjoy a week of profit and pleasure at the New Orleans convention, October 20-24.

and whenever a broad, well considered program has been presented, co-operation has been easily secured.

Favorable results are already seen in the interest in this question due to the efforts of the National Hospital Association and the American Hospital Association and certain individuals and foundations. The Negro doctor has every reason to feel proud of the part he has played. "Of all the hospitals established and supported entirely by Negroes, 75 per cent were established by and are the direct financial burden of Negro physicians." With such tools as he has he has done a good job. The remedy then, as I see it, lies in (1) the removal of restrictions against Negro physicians as staff members in public hospitals; and (2) the establishment or development of model hospital units in key centers of Negro population in the country.

This may mean new hospital developments or the assistance and enlargement of existing hospitals. These centers, in addition to providing hospital and out-patient facilities for the adequate care of the sick, would serve as a kind of demonstration of what can be done for other communities. Each such center could duplicate the splendid work of the John A. Andrew Memorial Hospital for postgraduate opportunities. Last year more than 125 Negro physicians eagerly participated in the annual clinical course at this Tuskegee hospital. The John A. Andrew Clinical Society is now of national importance.

In order, however, to assure success and avoid the pitfalls which have accounted for the failure of so many Negro hospitals, these centers will require (1) active participation of the intelligent lay Negro public, (2) properly trained hospital administrators possessing business acumen and special hospital training, and (3) active participation by the competent and sympathetic white profession in actual staff responsibilities.

In the successful prosecution of this program, or of any program, one must enlist the sympatheic interest and support of every element in the community. To this end let us not be blind to some factors of transcending importance which must be approached with tact and diplomacy although with frankness and justice.

The assistance of the broadminded, sympathetic white profession in actual staff responsibilities is not only highly desirable, but, in the present stage of professional development of Negroes, except in a few cities where Negro physicians have enjoyed unusual clinical opportunities, it is absolutely necessary.

While in the past, a certain pride might have been justified in pointing to any hospital, no matter how ill equipped or inadequately fitted to meet the health needs of a community, as an example of the Negro's effort to help himself—to build his own—there is to-day no justifiable excuse for such a state of affairs. If approached on the broad basis of mutual help, of competent service, and of unselfish interest, benighted indeed is that community which cannot develop a method of approach to this problem which will redound to the benefit of the whole community.

I fervently believe that the next decade will furnish a more striking advance toward racial amity through the medium of health and hospital efforts than through any other channel. Such co-operation, however, must be in a frank, honest, and straightforward manner. Every effort should be made to remove the distrust and suspicion which many Negroes now have about a great many worth while interracial endeavors. A feeling is now entertained that some men are in positions of influence in such projects solely on account of their color, oftentimes with either sympathy or competence lacking. There should be no place for suspicion and distrust, which often are bred through lack of understanding and lack of frankness.

The general apathy of the intelligent Negro lay public toward the support of hospitals through voluntary gifts can be converted into an attitude of enthusiastic co-operation by the proper approach. In achieving this desirable end, the first and most important way lies through the approval of such hospital projects by the prominent and leading public-spirited Negro physicians. The minister is the traditional leader of his people. He has earned that position by reason of the influence of the Negro church, which to-day is the most important institution among Negroes. The Negro minister has been able to erect imposing church structures out of the pittances of Negro members under the promise of a life of ease and contentment in the world to come. Negroes have missed so much of the good things of this world, one can readily understand their willingness to expect unusual rewards in the world to come. As important as that is, the Negro physician and the Negro business man must strike the balance and see that much of that spiritual fervor finds practical application in meeting the conditions which actually confront their people in this world. The older physician whose influence is respected in the community should be utilized to the fullest in developing the community support, while the material, except in unusual cases, for developing competent staff members must be supplied by the younger group. This younger group, steadily growing in numbers and trained to-day under excellent conditions in modern medical education, is restless for a chance to develop further and properly, as is its right. During the past five years, 2,644 Negro students have been enrolled and 586 have been given degrees. Of these, 2,193 were enrolled in two Negro medical schools and 475 have graduated from them. On an average during the last five years there have been each year 529 Negro medical students enrolled and 117 graduated.

Thus both groups should be led to contribute that which they are best able to contribute for the benefit of the whole community. The organized Negro medical profession, through the National Medical Association and the National Hospital Association, now commands the respect of the Negro public. It should be thus strengthened and assisted into more substantial development. In the present state of organized medicine as a whole, time and effort might profitably be spent in assisting such a valuable co-worker as the National Medical Association.

The grateful patient will contribute to hospital support as far as he is able, the public-spirited citizen will contribute as his interest dictates, but the substantial contributors will be drawn from the ranks of persons who can be taught, in addition to its humanitarian appeal, the valuable contribution an adequate hospital can make to the economic, moral, and social progress of a community both by its direct service to the sick and by its educational value, which will ultimately touch the life of every citizen.

In cities with a large concentration of Negroes, the solution of this problem as it affects the Negro who is able to pay for his hospital care and who deserves the right to choose his own physician, and as it affects the whole problem of continued education through full staff opportunities and postgraduate opportunities under sympathetic and competent auspices, seems to lie for the present in the establishment or development of model hospital units to serve this particular need. One must realize that, as Dr. M. L. Harris, in "Negro Mortality Rates in Chicago," aptly states, "No effort to decrease the death and sickness rate of Negroes can be successful in the face of an opposed or apathetic public opinion. The Negro himself must realize that it is his problem and that to its solution he must bring every force within him and every factor subject to his control. His home, his lodge, his church, his business organization, must take a positive stand and an active interest."

When so-called Negro hospitals attain the same degree of excellence in facilities and professional treatment as other hospitals, I am confident that many of our difficulties will be solved. I am reminded of the splendid Freedmen's Hospital, the teaching institution of the Howard University School of Medicine in Washington, D. C. Its ambulance service covers the entire District of Columbia. For many years it has been the favored hospital for all emergency cases by police officers serving the district where it is located. The day has come when, as the Rosenwald Fund Report rightly says: "The Negro himself is taking increasing responsibility for his own advancement. As he is being accepted not as a group apart but simply as one race in a nation made up of many races, he is also accepting the obligations that go with American citizenship. The leaders of the race are demanding not only that he be not discriminated against but also that he be given no special favors. They insist that high standards be applied to members of this race and that they be judged rigorously by these standards. The old statements, 'that's doing well for a Negro' or 'that is a pretty good colored school,' should no longer be used to condone mediocrity, if this group of the population is to come up to proper American standards."

The Health of Black Folk

BACK in the dark ages when Frederick Hoffman published his "Race Traits and Tendencies" of the American Negro everything was nicely settled by science. The Negro was going to die out, and that not because he was poor and ignorant but simply because he was a Negro. Statistics proved it! Today, however, we have changed all that, and as Dr. Louis Dublin, statistician of the Metropolitan Life and student of health says:

"The pessimism which prevailed thirty and more years ago with regard to his future is now no longer even remotely justified. The doleful prophecies of those who saw the race problem solved through his extinction have been absolutely discredited by recent events. A race which lives in many areas under what are still rather primitive conditions of sanitation is today enjoying an expectation of life of about forty-six years, which is equal to that of white Americans only thirty years ago. In comparison with a death rate of 35 to 40 per 1,000 in Reconstruction days, the Negro mortality is now only about 17 per 1,000—a death rate about the same as the rate for a number of European countries before the World War."

The Negro death rate is not accurately known because of our incomplete vital data. According to official reports, there was in 1927, 17.3 annual deaths per thousand. While this may be called a normal death rate for persons in the economic and social position of Negroes, nevertheless, it is not by any means satisfactory. Compared, for instance, with the average of the nation, the Negro death rate is nearly two-thirds higher than that of the whites, and while the average white man at birth may expect to live fifty-four years, the average colored man can only expect at present to live forty years. What is the cause of this?

Five diseases (tuberculosis, cancer, heart disease, cerebral hemorrhage, pneumonia) together with fatal accidents, account for two-thirds of the mortality of Negroes. Other causes in which the death rate of Negroes is approximately double that of whites, are typhoid fever, whooping cough, bronchitis and puerperal difficulties. Our influenza death rate is two and a half times higher, while certain other causes like acute nephritis, typhoid fever, malaria, pellagra and homicides run from three to eleven times higher.

The most serious disease among Negroes is tuberculosis. In 1920 the rate was 202 per 100,000 as compared with 85.7 for whites. Pneumonia came second with 145.9 as compared with 97.1 for whites, while acute nephritis and Bright's disease came fourth with 104.3 for Negroes, 28.0 for whites. In 1925 the importance of organic diseases of the heart was revealed as a leading cause of death. Following this, in numerical order of seriousness, were tuberculosis of the respiratory system, pneumonia, external causes (excluding suicide and homicide), congenital malformations and diseases of early infancy, cerebral hemorrhage and softening, and cancer. These eight diseases were responsible for over 58 per cent of Negro deaths.

The susceptibility of Negroes to tuberculosis; the fact that over 50% of them are infected when they grow up, and also the fact that the disease is not hereditary as we used to think, shows not any lack of "racial" resistance, but the result among people who are poor and live in poor surroundings, with bad air and bad habits, dirt, lack of proper food, who sleep in crowded, unventilated rooms and wear improper and insufficient clothing. These are the causes of tuberculosis and pneumonia among us.

Every year, 35,000 Negroes die from tuberculosis in this country and at all times, 440,000 Negroes are ill with the disease. The disease is one of young persons; our exceptional rates come between the ages of 20-45 and our highest at the age of 25. One thing alone encourages us and that is that Negro mortality from tuberculosis has been declining rapidly in the last fifteen years. It was 463 per hundred thousand in 1910 and 239 in 1921. In New York City, 1910-1921, it dropped from 617 to 299.

Venereal diseases take a great toll from Negroes through sickness and death. This is not because of any greater amount of sexual immorality but because of the false shame which prevents infected persons from seeking or receiving the proper treatment. Among the better class whites, the facts are studiously concealed, which makes Negro rates appear higher.

Syphilis is a large factor in the Negro death rate, not only in itself but for the degenerative diseases which it superinduces. Here again there are ridiculous exaggerations of the amount of syphilis among Negroes, ranging from 3.2% to 75%. As a matter of fact, it is probably about 1½ times the rate for the whites, which is quite bad enough, even when we remember that the white rate is artificially lowered.

Cancer has apparently increased among both whites and Negroes, chiefly because diagnosis is better today than formerly.

Deaths and sickness from pregnancy and child birth are unfavorable for colored folks, and organic heart disease has a largely increased death rate for Negroes.

The death of children is a distressing cause of our high death rate. It is greater today than for whites in practically every registration area. Measles, scarlet fever and diphtheria are more serious for whites than for Negroes; whooping cough, convulsions and syphilis are higher for Negroes. In 1925, the Negro infant mortality rate was 110.8 and per thousand, while it was 68.3 for whites. Even at this, the Negro death rate has been greatly reduced, being 261 in 1910. There are, on the other hand, a number of diseases beside those mentioned where the Negro death rate is smaller, as, for instance, in erysipelas, some forms of cancer, diabetes, infantile paralysis, and perhaps recovery from wounds and major surgical operations, and in diseases of the nervous system. Negro teeth are probably better.

Life

By WENDELL PHILLIPS LAYTON

A SIP of earth's unstable ways,
Then death's cold dart,
Then what?

Making of Man

By WENDELL PHILLIPS LAYTON

GOD first made earth.
Then stood beside a silent stream
And by His image cast shaped man.

The Consumptive

By LANGSTON HUGHES

ALL day in the sun
That he loved so
He sat,
Feeling life go.

All night in bed
Waiting for sleep
He lay,
Feeling death creep—

Steady—like fire
From a slow spark,
Choking his breath
And burning the dark.

Souvenir

By MARCUS B. CHRISTIAN

ONLY one kiss to me
Out of the night;
Lips fluttering to free
Heart-cries in flight;
Hold me, dear, close to thee —
Teach me delight.

Molten words, spoken low,
Close to mine ear;
Soft laughter, broken so
Soon by a tear;
Love's only token —O!
Heart-souvenir.

Reaching the Negro Community[*]

M. O. BOUSFIELD, M.D.

*First Vice-President and Medical Director, Supreme Liberty Life Insurance
Company, Chicago, Ill.*

THE Negro furnishes one-tenth of the population of the United States, and as such his health problems should be important to public health workers. Three-quarters of these 12 million Negroes still live in southern states and the majority of them in rural areas where there are most often inadequate medical facilities for either white or black.

About 1915 there began the migration of Negroes from the rural areas and small towns to industrial centers. The importance of this shift of colored people is shown in the following changes in the 10 cities now having the largest Negro population:

	1910	1930
New York City	91,709	327,706
Chicago, Ill.	44,103	233,903
Philadelphia, Pa.	84,459	219,599
Baltimore, Md.	84,749	142,106
Washington, D. C.	94,446	132,068
New Orleans, La.	89,262	129,632
Detroit, Mich.	5,741	120,066
Birmingham, Ala.	52,505	99,077
Memphis, Tenn.	52,441	96,550
St. Louis, Mo.	43,960	93,580

Such a large and rapid movement, of a group of the population, into new living and working conditions, into crowded, segregated areas of bad housing, left a marked impression on the vital statistics of the people, from which they are now showing signs of recovery.

In the typical industrial city the Negro quarter is along the railroad, as in New Haven, Conn., or along the banks of some dirty stream as in Akron, Ohio. Again, it is in some abandoned section which is being gradually converted from residence to business, as in South Philadelphia. Occasionally, to be sure, a whole great city area, as on the south side of Chicago, or Harlem in New York City, is occupied by Negroes, but such cases are exceptional. The Hill District of Pittsburgh and the East Side in Cincinnati are rather typical instances of conditions to which Negroes are subject. Bound in, as they are, by natural or social barriers, with little opportunity for expansion, overcrowding is a certain result.

Negroes are for the most part unskilled or semi-skilled, low-paid workers, living in houses two or three generations old, which, in a recent survey, are reported to be on an average of only 16 per cent in good repair. The converted kitchenette apartment, now so prevalent in some Negro neighborhoods, in which a home built for one family, becomes the home of many families, constitutes a physical hazard of first importance, with reference to congestion, sanitary conditions, health and morals. There is lack of sunshine, fresh air, cleanliness, play space and normal recreation. There is nearly always a prevalence of influences which tend to destroy.

This concentration of Negroes in compact, segregated areas has generally had the disadvantage, in most cities,

---

[*] Read before the Public Health Education Section of the American Public Health Association at the Sixty-second Annual Meeting in Indianapolis, Ind., October 10, 1933.

of allowing to exist a great disparity of health effort between Negro and white communities. Health departments, always without sufficient funds, or personnel, to do the whole job, have concentrated their efforts in white areas where the best showing could be made before influential people, forgetting the social-educational philosophy of Professor John Dewey which says in effect that what the best and wisest wants for himself, that must the community want for all. Health officers should be interested in finding out what exists in the community for the less fortunate; put that information before the public; and secure action favorable to the elimination of these conditions. It is not popular to spend money on Negro health and the Negro is quite unable to finance his own needs. This, coupled with racial prejudice, accounts for the generally demoralized condition of health efforts in colored neighborhoods. This applies equally to official and voluntary agencies.

Many hospitals and clinics refuse to treat colored patients and it is only with great difficulty that even tax supported medical facilities are made available for Negroes, especially in the South. This keeps the average Negro from knowing very much about the use of medical facilities for the treatment or prevention of disease. Having no place to send the Negro for medical care it is easily assumed that there is small need to carry on an active and continuous health educational campaign. This very segregation also makes it relatively easy to correct the situation, because it affords an opportunity for concentrated efforts in health work. It becomes apparent that there is a sociological problem as a part of the health picture, and that a program planned for educating colored people must also be planned for white people to show them that in maintaining their social responsibilities and self-preservation, they must include for the Negro, not merely health education, but participation in medical facilities.

The health officer has an opportunity to do a double duty here. He may not only attack community health conditions, but he may assist in the broader aspects of race relationships. Contemplating such a double program he is likely to hesitate, but he need not, for all the elements of solution, including interracial organizations will be found to assist him.

A little preparation in the psychology of the Negro community will help. The Negro press is a good place to start. It is a large and powerful influence among colored people. There are several national Negro news distributing agencies, one of which has over 100 correspondent Negro newspapers. Interested health officers may gain enough of this preliminary information from either the local Negro press, to be found in almost every community, or by subscribing for one of the Negro weekly newspapers with a national circulation, such as *The Chicago Defender, The Pittsburgh Courier, The New York Amsterdam News, The Baltimore Afro American, The Norfolk Journal and Guide,* or others. *The Crisis* is the monthly organ of The National Association for the Advancement of Colored People. *Opportunity* is a similar monthly publication of The National Urban League. Both of these are published in New York City. All of these publications will reflect Negro opinion.

It may be necessary to write letters, or publish articles. If the word " Negro " is to be used, spell it with a capital N. Negro is a proper noun, and as such should be capitalized as much as Caucasian, Nordic, Asiatic, Indian, or the names of other races.

Negroes have waged an unceasing, and generally successful campaign, with the leading newspapers of the country for this recognition. Colored or black is the correlative of white and does not demand this treatment.

It is well in speech making to make no reference to the race question. Leave out former experiences with colored people, forego any expression of your own lack of prejudice and omit the "darky" story in dialect. Make your talk as you would in any other neighborhood, illustrating it if possible with statistics especially related to the Negro. In every community certain amenities and certain standards arise to plague the uninitiated, and somehow these few points have gained fame among colored people as being the common errors of white speakers. These points may seem unimportant to you, but the fact that they are important to the Negro should be sufficient to cause you to give them consideration.

Having got this far, let us proceed to look for a contact point within the community itself. The Negro community is not unorganized. There will be leaders and pseudo-leaders. There will also be the usual proportion of fools, objectors, politicians, ambitious self-seekers and obstructionists. In this you will unfortunately recognize a normal condition for any community. But there will also be intelligent, earnest, unselfish, racial-minded leadership too. Naturally, it is important to make the right contact. Begin with your Council of Social Agencies which will very likely be able to point out a trained social worker of color who will be an invaluable guide. A list of the available agencies for your assistance will always run into a score or so in number. Last year in Chicago we had about 75 coöperating organizations during our observance of National Negro Health

Week. Some of the principal agencies follow.

A Negro medical society which often is made up of the physicians, dentists and pharmacists, combined into one organization. If there is a colored hospital in the community it will of course be of inestimable help. There is great interest in the development of these colored hospitals and, with their out patient, and often social service departments, they are invaluable, especially in follow-up work after a campaign involving physical examinations or treatment. In addition, the following agencies should be sought:

The Colored Press
Colored Public Health Workers, including nurses
Negro Health Week organization
Social Service organizations with qualified, trained, experienced workers in charge, such as,
1. The Urban League
2. The Young Men's Christian Association
3. The Young Women's Christian Association
4. The Community Center
5. Phyllis Wheatley Homes
Negro Business League
Negro Life Insurance Companies with their managers and agents
Churches and Church organizations
Interracial Commission
Fraternal groups
Women's clubs
Study clubs
Political organizations
Neighborhood clubs
Industrial workers' groups
Social clubs
Schools
Parent teacher associations
Boy Scouts
Girl Reserves
Barbers
Beauty shop operators
The neighborhood movie house

These agencies are very much like those to be found in any community and may be used in the same way.

Pioneer work in health education among Negroes has already been done by the National Negro Health Movement, now under the supervision of the U. S. Public Health Service. This organization was founded by Booker T. Washington in 1915, and has developed from an early emphasis on clean-up activities, until today, in the various communities, according to their resources and leadership, it has assumed every phase of health conservation including pageants, keeping-fit methods, athletic contests, periodic health examinations and clinics for treatment. A *Health Week Bulletin* is issued and there is an annual poster contest. This annual observance is usually held in the spring at about the same time as the Early Diagnosis Campaign of the National Tuberculosis Association.

The importance of this movement lies in the fact that it has stimulated and kept alive the interest of colored people in health education. The following figures show the communities participating:

Year	Communities Participated
1925	139
1926	326
1927	405
1928	428
1929	464
1930	505

The National Negro Health Week celebration has been an effort coming from within the Negro community itself, financed from within the community, in most instances, and its direction and leadership emanating from the Negro group. Almost always it has the coöperation of the official and volunteer agencies. Of necessity it is often an indifferent job, while again often a very excellent piece of work is done. Official agencies, taking the lead in similar efforts, having improved methods of organization and greater resources could do the job infinitely better, and should.

In Chicago this work has been done in the name of a Health Council, un-

der the leadership of the Cook County Physicians Association, The Lincoln Dental Society, the Wabash Avenue Y.M.C.A. (which are colored organizations), and coöperating agencies. It is always well to get the medical men in early, and taking the lead. The secretary of the Y.M.C.A. is the active executive who pushes the work. A full-time social worker is almost imperative under the circumstances, if his organization will release him for several weeks in order that he may give the time to the immense amount of organization work preliminary to the campaign. Headquarters are maintained at the Y.M.C.A.

A thorough organization is set up with as many committees, and as many people contacted, as possible. This is done, not on the basis that all of them are going to work, but for its advertising value. The actual planning is kept in a small executive committee. Speakers are sent to churches, schools, and other public meetings several weeks in advance of the active campaign. Agents of the colored life insurance companies are called together in a mass meeting and interested in the work. They distribute pamphlets, posters and window cards advertising the meetings and the health examination clinic. They are given appointment cards for examinations to distribute on their debits, and turn these in in advance of the opening of the drive. During the 2 weeks of the campaign an effort is made to reach every church, school, and social gathering with a speaker or motion picture.

The campaign centers about a clinic for periodic health examinations at the Y.M.C.A. Motion pictures on health subjects are kept going for the waiting patients and a fine exhibit of educational posters and mechanical apparatus helps to hold their interest. The Municipal Tuberculosis Sanitarium erects a model fresh air school room and a

123

model sleeping porch. We use at least 6 examining rooms. Local surgical houses contribute tables, scales, test tubes, sterilizers and what-not for examination purposes. The dental equipment houses contribute 2 dental chairs and equipment for dental examinations. Many national agencies supply literature for distribution. Publicity is given by the white and colored press. In our most successful campaign in 1931, by stimulating the Health Department to examine one high school largely attended by colored students, we were able to count 3,375 babies, children, and adults who had been examined during this drive.

The management of the clinic may be of some interest. Mornings are given over to babies, afternoons to women, and evenings to men. The medical and dental societies adopt schedules for their members who volunteer their services. Each adult visits the clinic twice. On his first visit the patient's history is taken by nurses who give their services. Charts furnished by the American Medical Association are used. A specimen of urine and a blood Wassermann are taken from every applicant for examination. Provident Hospital and the Health Department take care of the laboratory work. These reports are assembled and the patient returns in a week, is examined, and advised according to his physical and laboratory findings. No treatment is given.

Another variant of this, but not so successful, was tried this year, when a complete roster of the medical and dental societies was distributed advising that during the 2 weeks of the campaign these examinations would be given free in any of the members' offices.

The advice given these patients is simple but thorough. They are told of the importance of physical examinations, that they should be repeated each year, that doctors are equipped to make these examinations in their offices, and where impairments are found efforts are made to see that they are corrected.

The matter of awards in such educational work is important. For a number of years we gave cups and medals for the best teeth, the healthiest boy or girl, etc. A far more successful method is a certificate for every person examined. For a time we considered grading them A, B, or C, according to some loose standard of physical fitness. This was decided against and rather impressive certificates were made up like stock certificates and a gold seal placed on them. They are signed by the chairman and secretary of the Health Council and the presidents of the medical and dental societies. One year the Health Commissioner signed them, too. The certificates merely read, " This certifies that John Doe has been examined in the 1933 health examination clinic, thereby showing an interest in his physical condition, and further, he agrees to have such an examination annually. This is a real contribution to racial development."

It is surprising the amount of pride which is taken in these certificates. They are distributed at a final mass meeting and they serve the added purpose of making this meeting a success. Two nurses in white uniforms present them with all the formality of a graduation exercise. They are made out individually and rolled and placed impressively on the stage on two tables and the individuals' names are read out as they come forward. There is an attempt to give dignity and seriousness to this ceremony.

In planning a campaign among colored people you may well make your main objectives tuberculosis, for which the rate is from 2 to 6 times as high as for white; syphilis, for which there is also a high rate, and maternal and infant mortality, the rates for which are about 2½ times as high as for white mothers and babies.

In so far as the work done by official agencies among Negroes is concerned, the health department of the city of Detroit perhaps has been as successful as any.

In Detroit, the care of the Negro sick has been made largely the responsibility of the Negro doctor, under the direction of the city Health Department. But Detroit has an excellent Health Council in the matter of organization. So have Cleveland, Rochester, and Boston. No city, operating with a health council, surveying its field in preparation for a program, can conscientiously neglect as large a group as makes up the Negro community, ergo, form a health council, if not for the whole city, at least for the Negro community.

The foregoing should make it apparent that there are within the Negro community about the same elements for health educational efforts as are to be found in other communities. It is important to stress this point for two reasons. First, because it dispels any idea that different methods are necessary, and lets us see the problem as being one of similar design and unity. This is very important. Secondly, it also demonstrates that no new or different agencies are necessary to deal with the problem but, instead, it needs merely a broadening of the usual program to include the Negro. Perhaps one of the greatest hindrances to public health work among Negroes is the gradually failing notion that the Negro is biologically different. Often he is thought to be so different, indeed, that the public health worker just stands back and asks the question " What shall I do for the Negro? " and does nothing.

It has well been pointed out that while it might be very interesting to prove that there is a biological difference between whites and Negroes, one could really do nothing about it and it would likely have no effect upon control measures.

The whole problem involves several thousand state, county and municipal health departments. The best way to begin, is to begin. The best answer to the question of what shall I do for Negroes, is to ask the question " What have you done? " It is inconceivable, under any other circumstances, than those associated with race prejudice, that health officers can so complacently review, year after year, the unfavorable vital statistical reports of one-tenth of the population and make no special effort to correct it. In the meantime a magnificent chance for fame stands unaccepted. There is no greater opportunity for brilliant achievement, along all lines of public health work, than exists today in Negro communities. Public opinion can and should be changed. There is a moral responsibility, not being assumed even for the white population, when the black people are neglected. The great voluntary agencies need to stimulate interest in the interracial approach necessary. This is no more impossible, nor any less humanitarian, than the change of public opinion they have wrought in their various specialized fields.

Experienced public health workers attempting to visualize conditions and programs for a colored community should go back to what was accepted as being good 20 years ago and make that the starting point.

It should be realized that the Negro community today has a death rate comparable to that of the white rate of 20 years ago. Even this lagging behind is a great gain over the Negro rate of 30 years ago. Inevitably some effects of the nation-wide improvements in health conditions, though few were specifically directed toward the Negro, have ameliorated his plight. Similarly, an improved Negro community health will lower the white rate further.

There is evident today a greater willingness than this country has ever known to experiment in social changes, under the inspired leadership of President Franklin Delano Roosevelt. The national administration stands emphatically for equality of wages, under the NRA, regardless of race, or color, despite the widespread inequalities heretofore responsible for so much of the low economic standing of the Negro which in turn contributed to low health standards. This has a certain appositiveness for the most desirable health conditions, and unless health officers plan a New Deal of equality of facilities, they must expect to be charged with plain stupidity.

Participation in these experimentations gives the greatest possible returns to the individuals so fortunately endowed as to be able to take part in the trends of the times. Such effort expended upon the Negro will come back in the form of his creative contributions to American life and in his better citizenship.

Health Problems of the Negro

By LOUIS T. WRIGHT, M.D., F.A.C.S.

THE health of the colored citizen is closely related to his economic and social condition. It is needless to say that the problems arising in this field have been many and difficult. It seems worthwhile to sketch briefly some aspects of this situation, in the hope that it may prove of interest and value. Such knotty complex social problems require constant correction of maladjustments in the social outlook of all of us. The basis for their solution is to be found in the principle of identical social justice for all, and it can be effected by awakening the public conscience.

A few years ago, just before the depression, the question of the health of the Negro was a subject of study, intensively pursued, by some foundations and individuals throughout the country. Most of these studies purported to show one thing, namely, that the methods and measures necessary to cut down the mortality and morbidity rates among colored people, were different from those that had proved successful in reducing these rates for other peoples. Although all this is patently silly nonsense, these studies have proved to be a troublesome obstacle to the sound solution of our health problems.

These racial surveys of Negro professional life and activities went on to show that the colored doctor and nurse were slightly different from other doctors and nurses and that they therefore needed peculiar set-ups suited to their own unique needs. And too, all arrangements to meet the purported needs did not come from within the Negro race but were superimposed from without by many well-meaning, sincere social experts. These social-planners, represent a very small group of honest, conscientious and cultured persons, who in spite of their good intentions have a contracted social viewpoint as far as colored people are concerned. No appeal to reason seems to help them adjust their attitude so that it may be consonant with the aims of the colored profession group in particular, and colored people in general. This is to be regretted. Simple justice was denied the Negro doctor and nurse in spirit and in fact, and that is the situation today as regards equality of opportunity for training and practice.

A hospital program and a health program for colored Americans grew out of these surveys, based upon the false idea that colored patients needed separate institutions and that physicians and nurses needed a special kind of training. Then we learned that that there should be "a colored hospital for every colored community throughout the country," and that nothing could be more fitting or desirable. Utopia was at hand. Colored medical societies at this time, sincere in belief that they were doing a genuine service to their people, quickly and eagerly endorsed these ideas. That an extra-racial operating agency had initiated and would control the proposed projects was lost

DR. LOUIS T. WRIGHT

sight of; nor were the dangers of social experiments of this kind thoroughly understood or appreciated. It seemed a new era for the better health of colored people and for larger and better opportunities for professional training.

Many of us were aware of the fact that the surveys of our health problems in some instances were inaccurate; in other instances the conclusions drawn from them were wrong; and in still other instances the uses to which they were put were harmful to our best interests. They had fixed in everyone's mind that we were, as a racial group, incapable of proposing and developing a health program and a hospital program of the best type. In increasing numbers colored applicants for the study of medicine were refused admission to Northern medical schools and hospital opportunities were denied our physicians in practically every city. The Negro physician and nurse wanted the same chance for training as anyone else, but everything seemed so permanently hopeless that they were willing to accept in theory and in fact segregated hospitals for patients and tacitly endorsed separate training in the field of medicine. They were honestly convinced in their belief that under the circumstances this was the best course to pursue.

The idea of segregated hospitals reached its highest development in Chicago, where the Provident Hospital under an arrangement with Chicago University became a hospital unit for the training of colored medical students in clinical work. This scheme is now in operation, because the colored physician and the colored citizens naively believed the golden promises of the efficiency social experts who promoted it. The results have been as follows: (a) Colored applicants for the study of medicine at the medical school of Northwestern University are not now admitted, and, as I understood it, the same restriction prevails in the Rush Medical College of Chicago University; and it is only in Loyola Medical School, that colored medical students receive their clinical training in the same institutions that their white class mates receive their instruction; (b) An increase in race prejudice, as evidenced by the strike of white high school students against having colored students attend the same high school; (c) A diminished income to the colored physician from private practice; (d) A lessened opportunity for employment and increased economic exploitation of the colored man in the realm of skilled and unskilled labor. It is indeed unfortunate that a university as large as the University of Chicago should participate in a morally wrong and intellectually dishonest arrangement, because of color prejudice alone, that outrages justice and debases the the physicians of both races that carry out its subtly degrading purposes. In October 1934, however, a group of courageous and intelligent Negro members of the profession in Chicago refused to sell their birthright for a mess of pottage. The resentment of the colored physicians against this un-American and dishonest plan is very bitter indeed. They now realize

that it is a moral and intellectual blight, and I am certain that they will withdraw from this unworthy and unholy type of professional enslavement in a relatively short period of time.

Four years ago, when Chicago was launching this tremendous experiment in segregation, there was a sharp division of opinion among the physicians of New York's Harlem over certain hospital problems. There was a growing dissatisfaction on the part of the leading physicians with existing local medical trends, and this resulted in the formal separation of the men into two groups. Thereafter those who were unwilling to accept inferior standards organized the Manhattan Medical Society.

Thus the Manhattan Medical Society came into being. It was evident that in order to maintain its own self-respect it had to fight the forces of racial intolerance and bigotry on every hand; in high places and in low places. It had to carry on its work against great handicaps; it has done this at great personal sacrifices on the part of its members, and with a splendid unselfishness of purpose. From its inception it took the position that the colored patient required the same care and skill to get well as any other patient, and that the colored doctor and nurse required exactly the same training as any other doctor or nurse if they were to be proficient, and that America needed more and better qualified doctors and nurses, irrespective of color, if its health was to be adequately protected.

In an open letter to Mr. Edwin R. Embree, President of the Julius Rosenwald Fund, the Manhattan Medical Society stated: "We maintain that a 'jim-crow' set-up per se produces a sense of servility, suppresses inspiration, and creates artificial and dishonest standards. We submit, that the Julius Rosenwald Fund has contributed in no small way to this unsatisfactory state of affairs. Colored medical students going to the same school as medical students of any other racial groups have rated in their school work on the average as the equal of any other medical mind, and on State Board examinations they average the same as members of any other racial group. We reiterate that what the Negro doctor needs is simple justice — no more, no less. He has no peculiar needs and therefore requires no special or unique arrangements....."

It was apparent that social justice and our professional training were closely tied up, the one with the

7

other, and that we could not approve of segregation in our professional training and refuse to approve of it in our public schools. This the Manhattan Medical Society found itself in complete agreement with the aims and work of the National Association for the Advancement of Colored People, and this has been mutually advantageous to both organizations and to the Negro race in its entirety. The National Association for the Advancement of Colored People, backed with its great power, the doctrine of equality of opportunity for the training of, and the practice by, the colored doctor and nurse; and it rendered a signal service to the profession when it sponsored the investigation of Harlem Hospital by the eminent committee of physicians and laymen under the Chairmanship of Dr. Walter L. Niles. On this committee were the former deans of Columbia University, Cornell University and New York University Medical Schools, and the President of the American Medical Association. The Committee concluded that all medical schools should open their doors to colored applicants for the study of medicine and recommended that opportunities for Negro internes should be enlarged and that there should be no discrimination at all against colored doctors in any tax-supported hospitals or medical schools. This is the first time that the leaders of the white medical profession have taken a stand in favor of opening wider the doors of Northern medical schools and municipal hospitals. This is indeed a great moral step forward.

Many have asked the question; "What can one do, when the barriers are so firmly fixed?" The answer is; "There is one thing that every real man or woman can do and that is to tell the plain unvarnished truth, whether immediately advantageous or not, and thus at least preserve our moral integrity." Sincere attempts to bring about better understandings between the two racial groups, coupled with hard work, conscientiously performed, are essentials for progress along the right lines. It is too obvious to say that disease draws no color line, but it seems less obvious at times that tax monies never show the color of the person paying them, which brings us to the question of the free and unhindered use of all tax-supported institutions by the colored doctor and nurse the same as any other citizen. There can be no legitimate excuse for this State or any of its sub-divisions, or any other State or any of its sub-divisions, to withhold any of its opportunities from any group of its citizens because of race or color, and no State should yield to the forces of intolerance by maintaining anything that smacks of "jim-crowism" whether it be nurses' training schools, hospitals, colleges or public schools; this is a stigma that we cannot and will not accept. Such set-ups are intrinsically dishonest in concept and design, and they debase the whites who are a party to them as much as they debase the colored. Oppression of weaker groups has always been a degrading factor in the lives of the oppressors—the beginning of their spiritual rot and decay.

In the book "Divine White Right," Trevor Bowen says: "From the national health point of view, Negro exclusion from hospitalization facilities is difficult to reconcile with any degree of even self-interested enlightenment. That it constitutes a grave challenge to responsible authorities at all times scarcely needs to be stated; and the challenge is even more forceful when the policies of church-controlled institutions contribute to these conditions. Where the exclusion exists in tax-supported institutions, the church-members on the tax rolls cannot well disclaim responsibility for their failure to carry into community affairs a realistic conception of social justice."

May I be permitted to take this opportunity to appeal to the members of the great Catholic Church in America to help us in the solution of this problem which is a challenge to the moral best in all of us.

8

CHAPTER XVI

PROBLEMS OF HEALTH SERVICE FOR NEGROES

MICHAEL M. DAVIS, PH.D.

Chairman, Committee on Research in Medical Economics, New York City

Is the care of Negro health a medical problem, an economic problem, or a race problem? If it is a mixture, in what proportions are its elements compounded?

As a medical problem, sickness and its care among Negroes are very much the same as the corresponding problem among whites. Some important diseases differ in relative frequency. But in the large, the medical problems of Negroes and of whites are different in emphasis, not in kind. Both groups need physicians, dentists, nurses, hospitals, clinics, medicines, and public health agencies.

THE ECONOMIC PROBLEM

I quote the following from a book written a few years ago by a professionally trained woman who, after studying carefully a certain area of the South, stated the following conclusions:

First, the economic level of the people ... is so low that they cannot provide for themselves even the minimum amount of medical, nursing and health care requisite for the protection of the individual or of the community.

Second, such people, except in unusual instances, are getting a negligible amount of health protection.

Third, the natural resources of the country in which these people live cannot in the immediate or near future be developed to such an extent as to raise the economic level to a point where they can provide adequate medical, nursing and health care for themselves.[1]

---

[1] Mary B. Willeford, *Income and Health in Remote Rural Areas.* New York: Frontier Nursing Service, 1932, p. 79.

Can any reader think of an area to which this statement would apply? If I heard it for the first time without knowing its source, I should certainly think of more than one rural community in which a large part of the population is colored. But Miss Willeford did not study a Negro section. Her report refers to a mountain area of Kentucky in which the Negro population is only one-fifth of one per cent.

One can find areas with almost wholly white population in Northern Michigan and Minnesota, in the Ozarks and elsewhere, to which her statement would apply just as much as it does to the Appalachian Mountain regions and just as well as it applies to many rural sections of the South in which a large part of the population is Negro.

This quotation illustrates the economic problem. The medical needs of people are determined by human physiology, whether the bodies are of the well-to-do or the poor. Measured by the incidence of the more serious diseases, the need is in fact somewhat larger among the poor. In the main, the medical needs of an area vary about in proportion to its population.

ECONOMIC STATUS AND MEDICAL CARE

But the medical facilities which an area possesses in the way of physicians, dentists, nurses and hospitals, and the amount of medical care which the people of different areas receive are found to differ rather in proportion to the wealth of the areas than merely to the number of their inhabitants. This is a striking, perhaps a tragic fact.

Let me mention a few facts to illustrate the relationships between income and medical care. In California there are more physicians in proportion to population than in any other state, but in 1934 a survey reported that more than one-third of the people whose family incomes were under $1,200 had no medical care whatever for a disabling sickness; whereas with people with more than $3,000 a year per family, only one-sixth went through a disabling illness without a physician's care.[2] There have been similar findings in a number of other studies, both during and before the depression. A group of studies made previous to 1930 and covering "over 24,000 persons of moderate or small incomes showed that 25 to 30 per cent of these people had gone through a disabling illness—not a minor one— without any care from a physician."[3]

Another way of illustrating the same point is by the number of visits from or to a physician which people in different income groups receive during the course of a year. Two studies, one national, the other in California, showed that families with incomes of under $1,200 received about two calls from or to a physician per person per year. As income increases, the number of physicians' calls becomes steadily larger until, with family incomes of $10,000 and over, there are about five physicians' calls per person per year. The latter figure is just about what Dr. Roger I. Lee and his associates in their book, *The Fundamentals of Good Medical Care,*[4] estimate to be needed by people in general.

Still another illustration of health contrasts among different economic groups is drawn from a study of mortality in Cincinnati in 1930.[5] In this investigation figures by local census tracts were utilized and these tracts could be classified according to the economic status of the population, based on rentals. Infant mortality in the "low" economic areas was 94 deaths per 1,000 live births; in the "medium" areas, 46.8; in the "high" areas, 34.5. Similar contrasts have been brought out in a number of other studies, especially those of the federal Children's Bureau.[6] Cincinnati statistics include figures for both whites and Negroes. In the "low" economic areas, the white figure of infant deaths during the first year per thousand live births was 76.5; the Negro, 139.3. In the "medium" areas, the figures for white and Negro respectively were 44.9 and 77.3. In the "high" economic areas, the white figure was 34.7 and Negro 30.3. These figures substantiate the effect of economic conditions on infant mortality and also suggest that economic rather than race influences account for the differences between the white and the colored group.

[2] Margaret C. Klem, *Medical Care and Costs in California Families in Relation to Economic Status,* San Francisco: State Relief Administration of California, 1935, p. 22.
[3] Michael M. Davis, *Paying Your Sickness Bills.* Chicago: University of Chicago Press, 1931, p. 54, Table V.

[4] Committee on the Costs of Medical Care, No. 22, *The Fundamentals of Good Medical Care* by Roger I. Lee and Lewis Webster Jones, University of Chicago Press, 1933; *The Incidence of Illness and the Receipt and Costs of Medical Care among Representative Families,* by Falk, Klem and Sinai, p. 124.
[5] Floyd P. Allen, *A Study of Mortality by Census Tracts in the City of Cincinnati, Ohio, for the year, 1930.* Cincinnati: Public Health Federation (Health Division, Community Chest), 1932, pp. 9 and 59.
[6] Children's Bureau, U.S. Department of Labor, *Causal Factors in Infant Mortality,* No. 142, Washington, D.C.

In another section of the same study, the tuberculosis mortality rates per 100,000 population, white and Negro, are shown according to classified census tracts. Table I brings out the main facts:

TABLE I

TUBERCULOSIS MORTALITY RATES PER 100,000 POPULATION OF CINCINNATI, WHITE AND NEGRO, ACCORDING TO ECONOMIC STATUS, 1930

	Low	Medium	High
Whites	22.0	11.5	10.0
Negroes	116.0	53.5	17.0

It will be noted that between the "high" areas and the "low" the differences in mortality rates for whites are only a little over 100 per cent, whereas for the Negro they are nearly 700 per cent.

MEDICAL CARE AMONG NEGROES

Most of the sickness surveys conducted in recent years have not included Negro populations. There is only a little direct information as to the medical care which Negroes secure and as to their expenditures for sickness. Figures reported by the health department of one large Southern state are to the effect that in 1929 one in every six Negroes who died in that state went through his last illness without any medical attendance and that in 1934 the proportion had risen to 23 per cent. The proportions among the whites were about one-third of these in each year.

Last October the magazine *Fortune*[7] published an account of a survey en-

titled "Doctors, Dentists and Dollars." A field staff working for the magazine had canvassed what is claimed to be a representative though small sample of the American population and the people were asked how much money they had spent during the past year for doctors, dentists, and hospital bills. These returns were classified according to the economic status of the family. All through the tables, the Negro appears as spending less money for medical care than the lowest white economic group. Forty-one per cent of the Negroes had spent nothing during the preceding year for doctors and hospital bills, whereas among the "poor" group of whites only 28 per cent had spent nothing. Sixty-nine per cent of the Negroes had spent nothing for dental care, whereas the figure among the "poor" group among the whites was only 42 per cent.

Low income is correlated with less medical care; and this is in spite of the fact which all of us recognize, that most physicians are willing to give their services in case of need, even if the patient cannot pay. Paying-power depends upon the manner in which sickness bills are paid, as well as on the amount of the bill in relation to the annual income. Systematic budgeting for sickness in advance and disbursing a fixed weekly or monthly amount throughout a year is easier than payment of an equivalent annual total all at once. Lodges or "sickness benefit clubs," a form of voluntary sickness insurance which utilizes this principle, appear to be common among Negroes, at least in cities. A study recently made in New Orleans under the direction of Professor

7 *Fortune*, October, 1936, pp. 221–222 and 224. Some of the figures cited here did not appear in the magazine but were kindly furnished by one of the editorial staff. For the interpretations in the text the writer is responsible.

Charles S. Johnson[8] showed that there was extensive participation in such clubs but that the financial status of these organizations was frequently unstable if not unsound and that the medical services which they supplied to members were generally unsatisfactory. Experience shows that any successful use of the insurance principle for meeting the costs of sickness must have a broad industrial or community basis.

That low income is generally associated with insufficient medical care is the heart of the economic problem for both Negroes and whites. The difference between the economic problem of the Negro and the white with respect to medical care is simply one of degree. By and large, Negroes average a lower economic status than whites. The economic problem of medical care for the Negro is the same as the whites' problem, only the lines are drawn in darker colors and with heavier strokes.

RACE RELATIONS

Race accentuates the economic problem. Color restricts the Negro's access to many medical facilities and services, even in those instances when he could pay for them, or when they could be given to a sick person for whom the race difference did not enter. So the race problem complicates and increases the economic problem of medical care which many Negroes face along with other poor people. In the North most Negroes live in cities where there are numerous physicians and hospitals and where race is of secondary significance as a barrier to securing these services. In the South race presents definitive barriers to the use of certain services particularly in institutions; and the medical care of the Negro in the South has the further characteristic that it is largely a problem of rural areas. The bulk of Southern Negroes are rural. Physicians, dentists, hospitals, and nurses are not distributed geographically in proportion to population. They are distributed, in the main, in proportion to the wealth of the population. The larger cities of the United States have only about 550 people for each physician. The country districts on the average have nearly 1,300 people per doctor. A study published by the American Medical Association in 1935,[9] following earlier studies of Professor Raymond Pearl and others, showed that the number of physicians in proportion to population varies among the 3,000 counties of the United States in rather close ratio to the spendable income of the people in these counties. The distribution of hospitals is even more highly concentrated in the cities and in sections of larger economic resources. The great majority of rural areas have no organized health departments.

Because the Southern states are largely rural and because, taken as a whole, they are poorer than most other sections of our country, they have fewer physicians in proportion to population and fewer hospital beds. In the Southern states, there is one physician to every 1,000 people, as compared with nearly 750 for the

[8] Harry J. Walker, "Negro Benevolent Societies in New Orleans—A Study of Their Structure, Function and Membership." Fisk University, 1936. (Unpublished.)

[9] R. G. Leland, *Distribution of Physicians in the United States.* Chicago: Bureau of Medical Economics, American Medical Association, 1935, pp. 7–10.

United States as a whole and about 600 for some of the wealthier states. But in Southern communities with less than 5,000 people, there are about 1,500 people to one physician, and in rural areas where the population is largely Negro, the supply of physicians is still lower. A majority of these Southern rural counties have no hospitals and when hospitals are present or are accessible in neighboring communities, few if any beds are open to the Negro.

The medical care of the rural Negro requires, it is obvious, that facilities must be available in the way of physicians and hospitals. But it also requires that the Negro patients themselves must be able to pay for the use of these facilities or that somebody else must pay for them. Provide the personnel and facilities which are now lacking and pay for them! Is the answer just as simple as that?

THE FOUR-FOLD PROBLEM

Even if ten-dollar bills were as plentiful as thorns on a blackberry bush, the answer wouldn't be as simple as that. There may be a doctor around the corner and a hospital within a mile, and both might be ready to give their services free. But the sick man may not seek the doctor and he may be afraid of the hospital. There is a problem of demand as well as of facilities and of payment. The problem is not only what the Negro needs and what he can pay for himself. It is also what the Negro wants and what he will use. The problem is one of education as well as facilities and finances. The total problem is thus four-fold: *medical, economic, racial*, and *educational*.

Effective health education of the Negro requires the participation of the Negro himself. Not only must the educational program be sympathetically conceived and wisely executed, but Negro physicians, Negro nurses, and Negro lay organizations must play a part in designing and executing it. By health education I do not mean only what is taught about hygiene and sanitation by health departments and by schools. I include also the development of understanding and attitudes which will promote the intelligent care of sickness and the intelligent use of physicians and hospitals.

HEALTH EDUCATION

Health education always faces the risk of being "preaching without practice." Personal hygiene involves habits which adults are very slow to change and the same is true of the ideas and attitudes held concerning physicians, hospitals and the care of sickness in general. Yet with adults, much may be accomplished through health education, provided motivation to action exists. Adults will generally have little motive to alter their ideas or habits unless the information and advice which they receive relates directly to diseases or conditions which cause pain or fear for themselves or their children.

With children in schools and with young people in colleges, other approaches may be effective. Classroom instruction in health matters, however, must be connected with activity and experience. This is particularly true of young persons in colleges and normal schools, where academic instruction concerning health is of little value unless it is accompanied (1) by personal health service through a well-organized plan of health examinations and medical care for the student body; and (2) by observation of a well-organized plan of public health work and medical care for children in a practice school wherein the future teachers participate.

Negro Physicians

What has the Negro group possessed in the way of physicians and nurses of its own people and of hospitals run for or by its own people? The handicaps imposed by poverty and by race have made the path of the Negro physician difficult. A study by Dr. Julian H. Lewis[10] of Chicago reported that in 1935 there were nearly 4,000 Negro physicians in the United States. The Negroes have about one-quarter as many Negro physicians in proportion to their number as the whites have of white physicians. The Negro physicians have found it necessary to concentrate in the cities, even more than have the white, and Negro physicians have gone more to Northern than to Southern cities. Four Northern states—New York, Illinois, Pennsylvania and Ohio—contain about 2,000,000 Negroes and 900 Negro physicians, whereas in 4 Southern states—Georgia, Mississippi, Alabama, and North Carolina there are altogether 4,000,-000 Negroes but only about 450 Negro physicians. Forty per cent of all Negro physicians are in ten Northern states which have only 18 per cent of the Negro population. This concentration undoubtedly results from the economic necessity of the Negro physician to work among people who have enough money to pay him. Very few Negro physicians can possibly make a living from practice for fees among Negroes in most rural sections of the South. Despite the great need for more and better dental care, there is little use in encouraging additions to the present small number of Negro dentists until better economic opportunities for dental practice among Negroes can be assured.

There are barely a hundred Negro physicians graduated from medical schools each year, the majority coming from Meharry Medical School in Nashville and Howard University Medical School in Washington, the remainder from various Northern schools. There is no doubt that the Negro physician has been improving in status in most Northern and in some Southern cities, as the education, opportunities, and economic status of the Negro group have advanced in these communities. But this is not true in Southern rural areas.

Hospitals

Hospitals are important not only as places furnishing medical care but also as agencies for the education of physicians and nurses and for the continuous professional improvement of the physicians who use their facilities. Substantial improvement has been made in this respect during the last ten years, largely as a result of the efforts of some Negro physicians themselves and of such agencies as the Julius Rosenwald Fund, the General Education Board, and the Duke Endowment. Whereas in 1930, there

---

10 Julian H. Lewis, "Number and Geographic Location of Negro Physicians in the United States," *Journal of the American Medical Association*, 104: 1272–3, Ap (6) 1935.

were only ten hospitals approved by the American Medical Association as good enough for the training of internes, today there are sixteen such hospitals.[11] Several have been enlarged and much improved during this period so that the number of good interneships now available to Negro physicians is, for the first time, somewhat in excess of the supply of young physicians. A majority of these first-rank Negro hospitals, though not a majority of the Negro beds, are in the South.

During the same period, there has been some improvement in the opportunities for the training of Negro nurses, but for Negro nurses in private duty the problem is to find positions which will be sufficiently remunerative to justify full professional training. In the public health field, the situation is much better than in private nursing. The interest of the United States Public Health Service and of a number of Southern state health officers has drawn into public health work in the South an increasing number of Negro nurses. Eight years ago there were less than a dozen Negro nurses employed in the whole South. Today there are probably more than twelve times that number. Opportunities for the training of Negro public health nurses are increasing. Only a fraction of the need has been met, but a good beginning has been made.

We cannot consider hospital care without its economic basis. It is costly. So costly, that nearly all hospitals for mental disease or tuberculosis have to be supported at government expense for both white and colored patients. Even in general hospitals, half of all cases throughout the United States are cared for without charge either in governmental or in voluntary institutions. Low paying power makes it necessary that the major part of hospital provision for Negroes be free or at very low cost.[12] The experience of the Julius Rosenwald Fund with a number of hospitals especially for Negroes has made it clear that a hospital exclusively for Negroes cannot be maintained unless it receives very substantial payments from other sources than its own patients. Such hospitals will require substantial grants from charitable organizations, foundations, or from government funds, or else these hospitals must be wholly maintained by taxes like Harlem Hospital in New York or the Negro unit of the General Hospital of the City of St. Louis.

HOSPITAL PROBLEMS

Hospitals for Negroes and hospital care for Negroes are two quite different things. Most general hospital care for Negroes, in both the South and the North must be in hospitals which will also receive whites. In the South, the colored provisions are in separate sections. In addition, a very limited number of hospitals especially for Negroes are required, in carefully selected localities; and for these hos-

---

[11] Julius Rosenwald Fund, *Negro Hospitals*, A compilation of available statistics, 1931, p. 46.

[12] In 1930 in addition to some 25 well-established Negro hospitals, there were nearly a hundred small hospitals managed by and for Negroes. A survey made at that time by the American Medical Association reported that most of these small places were inadequate, and many were definitely undesirable. The majority of these small Negro hospitals represented the effort of Negro physicians in various cities to have some hospital facilities through which they could care for private patients. The number of such small and unsatisfactory Negro hospitals has probably diminished on account of the depression, although no review has been made since 1930. See *Negro Hospitals, op. cit.*, Appendix II, p. 51.

pitals, the educational interest in the training of Negro physicians, nurses, and other Negro personnel should be the primary consideration. At the present time there are 15 or 20 such hospitals—Flint-Goodridge in New Orleans, Provident in Chicago, Mercy in Philadelphia, Lincoln Hospital in Durham, Harlem Hospital in New York—to name only a few. Such hospitals must be supported largely as educational enterprises. They will not only educate the small number of Negro physicians, nurses, and administrators whom they touch directly, but will stimulate many others indirectly and will be agencies from which many Negroes will learn to demand better medical facilities and to utilize them more intelligently.

Experience has shown that the administration of such hospitals presents not only the problems common to all medical institutions, but also unusual difficulties of financing and of race relations, particularly within the medical staff. The administration of every hospital involves delicate relations among the physicians who utilize or are interested in the institution and between physicians and the governing authorities. When these administrative problems are complicated by actual or by factitious race issues, the administration of the hospital may be seriously handicapped.

Public Health Services

Miss Willeford said of certain white areas that they cannot pay for the medical facilities they need out of their own local resources. A fortiori the same is true of rural Negro areas. For rural areas, general state funds must supplement local funds if adequate public health services and facilities for medical care are to be available; and in some instances, federal funds must be drawn upon to supplement state resources. The organization of public health departments in rural areas which have had none up to the present time is now proceeding under the stimulus of federal appropriations made in the Social Security Act of 1935. For the rural Negro, the establishment of well-organized local health departments is the first step towards providing the elements of modern medicine.

In the cities, both North and South, organized health departments almost invariably exist and the problems of both whites and Negroes are (a) adequate financing of these departments and (b) allocation of their activities in such a way that public health work will be concentrated on those problems and in those areas in which the need is greatest. While definite information is difficult to secure, it seems probable that the proportion of health department energies and funds which has been devoted to Negro areas has been less than the demonstrable needs of these areas would require. This is particularly true in relation to certain diseases which are of major public health significance for both races and particularly for the Negro. The outstanding examples are syphilis and tuberculosis.

Syphilis

We have little reliable information regarding the exact prevalence of syphilis in the United States. The knowledge we do possess indicates a higher rate among Negroes than whites. These rates, however, vary within wide limits. During 1929–31, syphilis control demonstrations were undertaken in six Southern rural areas by the United States Public Health Service in cooperation with the Julius Rosenwald Fund. One county in each of six states was selected. The ratio of syphilis cases to population was 8.9 per cent in one of these counties and ran up to 39.8 per cent in another. The average of the six counties was about 20 per cent. Dr. Taliaferro Clark of the United States Public Health Service makes the following important comment on the divergent rates in these counties: "The prevalence rates found in the different areas indicate that the higher rate for Negroes than for the whites revealed by these demonstrations and the one-day census studies, is not due to inherent racial susceptibility and can probably be accounted for on the grounds of differences in their respective social and economic status."[13] Dr. Clark also reports that "Treatment facilities were found to be quite generally inadequate for both races in practically all of the communities studied."[14]

The work done in these six counties was not only a study. It was also a demonstration of methods of controlling syphilis, perhaps the first systematic undertaking of this kind in rural areas in the United States. The depression came along just as the demonstrations were reaching their conclusion and it was impossible for local or state health departments or the Federal Service, to secure funds for carrying on syphilis control work. The leadership of Dr. Parran is now stirring the whole country to a recognition of the gravity of the problem of syphilis. It is time that syphilis-control programs in Southern rural areas be taken up effectively. The methods demonstrated in the 1929–31 experiments were comparatively inexpensive. They will bring economic benefits by improving working power and will achieve priceless human results in better life opportunities for men, women, and children.

Tuberculosis

Tuberculosis death-rates among Negroes are generally from 4 to 6 times those found among whites. Tuberculosis now appears as the first or second most frequent cause of deaths among Negroes, a position which this disease formerly occupied in the general population. It has sunk to the sixth or seventh as a cause of death among whites, but it remains a major danger to the Negro. Negro health programs should focus a great deal of attention upon tuberculosis. Control requires sympathetic but persistent case-finding; it involves education; it demands adequate nutrition; it will necessitate training physicians, and in addition travelling clinics or other diagnostic facilities for children and adults. There is some danger that we focus too much attention on the single issue of providing hospital beds for colored tuberculosis cases. This is important. But do not let us forget that tuberculosis beds will not take us far without other features which are also essential to the control of the disease.

Since Negro patients in the South are cared for in independent institutions or separate sections of institu-

---

[13] Taliaferro, Clark, *The Control of Syphilis in Southern Rural Areas*, Julius Rosenwald Fund, 1932, p. 53.
[14] *Ibid.*

tions, the provision of beds for Negroes has to be considered separately. Thus in eight Southern states from which recent estimates were secured, the number of white deaths from tuberculosis was 7,317; of Negro deaths from the same cause 8,066. These were the actual number of deaths in 1934, so that the death rate for the Negro, considering the size of the colored population, was approximately four times the corresponding figure for the whites. Sanatorium beds for whites in these states numbered 7,553, or somewhat more than one bed per death, whereas the number of tuberculosis beds for Negro patients was only 1,442, or less than one-fifth bed per death. The average cost of constructing and equipping a sanatorium bed in the South would be about $2,000. Adding 2,500 beds for Negro patients in the South would bring the ratio of beds to deaths up to about one-half and would cost about five million dollars. Even then there would be only one-half Negro bed per death!

The number of tuberculosis beds which should be built in any locality must be determined after study of the probable utilization of the facilities as well as of theoretical needs. The financial resources, the customs, and attitudes of the public and of the physicians of the region must be considered, as well as morbidity and mortality rates. Advances in medical technique, moreover, may influence greatly the amount of hospitalization required. Insofar as pneumo-thorax, for example, proves to be successful as a means of tuberculosis therapy and becomes capable of wide application, the number of hospital beds needed for a given total of tuberculosis cases might be reduced appreciably. Finally, the extent to which tuberculosis cases can be adequately diagnosed and treated in existing beds in general hospitals needs careful investigation in each locality before programs are undertaken which expand special institutions for tuberculosis. But the shortage of Negro beds is so great that without question large additions are imperative.

A bill has been introduced into Congress appropriating $5,000,000 from Federal funds to be distributed by the United States Public Health Service among states which meet certain conditions as to funds which they will provide for tuberculosis beds. Provision is made for maintenance as well as for construction. The National Tuberculosis Association, it is stated, has officially endorsed the principles of this bill. Such a measure should be of interest to all sections of the country and to all groups of the population.

STUDIES NEEDED

The Negro's problems of medical care should receive much further study. We should have more information about the facilities furnished for or by Negroes; about the services available and the services used; and about costs in relation to ability to pay. It would be well if the administrative and financial problems of some of the best Negro hospitals were systematically studied and the history of their development analyzed, as a guide for those who are undertaking or considering similar enterprises. The sickness survey covering over three-quarters of a million families, made last year by the United States Public Health Service and now in process of tabulation, is likely to furnish more information about the prevalence of various types of illness among both Negroes and whites than we have ever had before. Certainly additional facts are greatly needed on morbidity and mortality by age, sex, and economic groups among Negroes, and concerning the effects on health of low income, poor housing and unsatisfactory diet in rural and in urban areas. In the larger cities, studies by small districts should be pursued, such as have been made in Cleveland, New York and Cincinnati. The budget studies recently conducted by the federal Bureau of Labor Statistics in cities and by the Bureau of Home Economics in rural areas should, when the figures are available, give substantial information concerning the financial problems of the Negro with respect to medical care. It would be well to make further studies on the possibilities of increasing the purchasing power of Negro groups through co-operative methods of paying for medical service. It would be wholesome if studies were made in several communities, North and South, regarding the services made available by local health departments to Negroes for the prevention of infant mortality, the control of tuberculosis, the diagnosis and treatment of syphilis, and other public-health functions. The public should know how far these services and the expenditures for them correspond to the needs of this population, in comparison with services and expenditures in other areas of the same community.

CONCLUSIONS

1. The medical care of the Negro involves medical, economic, race and educational aspects.

2. From the standpoint of the diseases involved and the facilities required, the medical problems of the Negro are in general similar to those of whites, differing in emphasis because of the varying frequency of certain diseases among the two groups.

3. The Negro's economic problem of medical care is similar to that of other groups with low income, but is more severe for the Negro than for any other important section of our population.

4. In the cities, the problem of medical care is largely the utilization of existing personnel and facilities. In the rural areas, medical personnel and facilities are generally insufficient as well as their utilization.

5. Race relations in the South accentuate the economic problem of the Negro by limiting his access to existing medical facilities and services.

6. The utilization of medical facilities and services is also limited by the educational as well as by the economic status of the people concerned.

7. The expansion of organized public health departments is the most immediately practicable means of improving the health of the Negro, particularly in the rural areas; and would be a step in the direction of improving facilities for care in sickness.

8. Most Southern rural areas cannot support modern public health services, much less adequate medical and hospital care, out of their own resources. Funds must be drawn from

state or federal sources as well as from the locality, according to the principles already established in the Social Security Law; but larger state and federal funds are required than the present law calls forth.

9. Well-trained Negro physicians and Negro public health nurses are essential for improving the medical care of the Negro and as educational measures for the whole group.

10. The problems of syphilis and of tuberculosis need especial and vigorous attack.

11. In planning the work of public health departments and of voluntary health agencies, the primary obligation is to study all of the areas and the population groups involved, in order to ascertain the health problems which are especially important among each; and then to distribute the available effort and money among those areas and in behalf of those groups in proportion to the need. If this policy is carried out, a considerably larger amount of health service and medical care will be made available for the Negro.

12. It is the long-standing tradition of the medical profession that the needs and not the resources of the patient should be the measure of the service which he ought to receive. This fundamental principle should guide the development of medical facilities and of public health work for the Negro. It will also be remembered that in the field of health, the disease problems of any one section of society affect the interests of all.

CHAPTER II

THE PROBLEM OF NEGRO HEALTH AS REVEALED BY VITAL STATISTICS*

Louis I. Dublin, Ph.D.

Third Vice-President and Statistician, Metropolitan Life Insurance Company, New York City

The facts on Negro health are of the greatest interest to workers in the health field for a variety of reasons. Negroes constitute close to one-tenth of the total population of the country. They are a racial group, with very definite health problems that call for solution. Health is basic to the general welfare of the Negro as it is to no other race. An improvement in Negro health, to the point where it would compare favorably with that of the white race, would at one stroke wipe out many disabilities from which the race suffers, improve its economic status and stimulate its native abilities as would no other single improvement. These are the social implications of the facts of Negro health. There is, however, another and very interesting aspect of this discussion, namely, the health of the Negro as a racial problem. The Negro in America has clearly been outside of his normal environment. Just as it has proved difficult for white men to live in the tropics, so have Negroes struggled to adapt themselves to the rigors of our Northern country with its variety of parasitic organisms to which they have had little or no immunity. An opportunity is thus afforded to study the relative susceptibilities and immunities of the Negro to disease as well as the gradual adaptation of these people to their new environment.

Such facts as we have with regard to the health of the Negro, we are compelled to get largely by indirection. But this is equally true for the white as for the colored race. As a nation, we keep only partial records, as yet, of the diseases and disabilities from which individuals suffer. We must resort, therefore, to the facts of mortality, as these are made available to us by the publications of official statistical and health agencies, and more recently by the life insurance companies. At this time, my chief reliance will be on the materials which have been collected for twenty-five years by the Metropolitan Life Insurance Company, which now insures the lives of close to two million Negroes. Fortunately, this coverage is almost country-wide and embraces men, women, and children of all ages and engaged in all occupations. The only serious limitation in this material is that the business is conducted, very largely, in the urban areas. The conditions which prevail in the rural South, where a large proportion of the Negroes still live, are therefore not closely reflected by the insurance experience. Nevertheless, I believe that the picture which I shall draw will be fairly representative of the conditions which prevail among Negroes in the United States.

---

* Based on an article originally published in *The Annals* of the American Academy of Political and Social Science, November, 1928. Revised with the latest available statistics.

EXCESS OF DEATH RATE

Taking the country at large, or rather the Registration States, for the latest census year, namely, 1930, the standardized death rate of white persons was 9.9 per 1,000 of population; that of the colored was 18.0. This means that the colored death rate was 82 per cent higher than the white. This is, in general, the situation at the present time. If we limit ourselves to the rural part of the Registration States, the excess of the Negro over the white mortality is 81 per cent; in the cities of the Registration States the rate for Negroes is 95 per cent higher. There is, therefore, a difference between the mortality of urban and rural Negroes. In view of the fact, however, that the tendency of the Negro population has been definitely away from the farm and toward the city, it is all the more important that we consider the facts for urban Negroes. These facts, fortunately, we have available in considerable profusion.

It is important to determine whether the excess of the colored death rate over that for the white holds true in each sex and for all age periods. The accompanying table contains the very latest data available (that is, for the year 1935), and presents the comparative standardized death rates for more than fourteen million white persons and nearly two million Negroes insured in the Industrial Department of the Metropolitan Life Insurance Company. It brings the following differences into clear relief. At every age period, from infancy to old age, and for each sex, the death rate for colored persons is in excess of that for whites. In every age group the excess is more pronounced for females than for males. Colored infants of each sex suffer from death rates approximately 80 per cent above those of the whites. From five years of age up to adolescence, the margin is 54 per cent excess for males and 63 per cent for females. The most pronounced differences, however, are found between 15 and 25 years, where the death rate for colored boys and young men runs nearly two and a half times that for the whites, and where the mortality among colored girls is more than three times that for young white women. From early adult life to "middle age" (25 to 44 years) the comparison remains extremely unfavorable to the colored. Between 45 and 64 years, the adverse margins for the colored men are not so large as in the earlier age groups. However, the death rate for colored women is 64 per cent above that for white women. In old age, that is, 65 to 74 years, the excess mortality for colored males and females is much reduced, being only 17 and 23 per cent, respectively.

These higher death rates necessarily mean curtailed longevity. This is true, especially because one of the important items in the excess mortality of Negroes is their high infant death rate. The death of a colored infant cuts off, at one stroke, 48 years of life, and when there is a heavy infant mortality, the life expectation is very seriously affected. The latest reliable figures relating to the general population for the period 1929–1931 show a life expectation at birth of 47.52 years for colored males and of 49.53 for colored females, as compared with 59.31 years and 62.83 years, respectively, for white persons.

OUTSTANDING DISEASES

The higher mortality and shorter expectation of life of the Negro result, very largely, from their high death rate from a number of conditions. Tuberculosis is an outstanding cause of death among Negroes. In 1930, we computed the loss in life expectation for colored persons caused by the ravages of this disease. We found that nephritis for 1.34 years to the male and 1.12 years to the female.

In 1935, organic heart disease was the leading cause of death among the colored Industrial policyholders of the Metropolitan Life Insurance Company. Their death rate was 208.1 per 100,000, or a little more than one and a half times that for the whites.

Tuberculosis followed very closely

DEATH RATES PER 100,000 FROM ALL CAUSES
EXPERIENCE OF METROPOLITAN LIFE INSURANCE COMPANY,
INDUSTRIAL WEEKLY PREMIUM-PAYING BUSINESS, 1935

Age	Males			Females		
	White	Negro	Per cent Negro of White	White	Negro	Per cent Negro of White
Ages 1 to 74*	838.6	1,273.9	152%	617.7	1,090.9	177%
Under 1	2,144.7	3,725.7	174	1,638.6	3,019.6	184
1 to 4	353.1	532.6	151	323.2	520.5	161
5 to 14	152.8	234.8	154	121.2	197.9	163
15 to 24	223.9	540.4	241	183.0	595.5	325
25 to 44	552.6	1,143.8	207	400.6	941.1	235
45 to 64	2,203.4	2,972.7	135	1,487.9	2,442.8	164
65 to 74	6,620.3	7,717.7	117	5,280.3	6,499.4	123

* Standardized on "Standard Million," England and Wales, 1901.

if the mortality from tuberculosis among colored persons could be entirely eliminated, every Negro male baby, at birth, would have 2.79 years added to his expectation of life, and every girl baby would have an addition of 2.85 years. Let the male baby survive to reach the age of 32 and we find that tuberculosis still reduces his tenure of life by 1.47 years. It shortens the life of the Negro woman of the same age .29 years. Cancer cuts the life span of colored males, at birth, four-tenths of a year, and that of colored females .91 of a year. Heart disease is responsible for 2.32 years loss of life to the Negro male, and for 2.64 years to the female; and chronic

with a rate of 152.4, or more than three times that for the whites. Third in numerical importance was pneumonia, with a rate of 104.3, double that for the whites. Both chronic nephritis and cerebral hemorrhage, another "degenerative disease," take double the toll of life among the Negroes that they do among whites. These five diseases, together with fatal accidents, which also run higher for the colored, account for 60 per cent of the Negro mortality. The death rate of Negroes, in 1935, from whooping cough was nearly two and one half times that for whites, and from puerperal conditions it was nearly 75 per cent higher. Their influenza death rate was more than double. Certain other causes like typhoid fever, malaria, pellagra and homicides run from two and a half to eight times higher than for white persons.

The record of improvement for conditions arising from pregnancy and childbirth is not as favorable for colored females as for whites. Among white women insured in the Metropolitan's Industrial Department, the death rate from these causes showed a decline of 57 per cent between 1911 and 1935. With our insured colored women, the rate declined 40 per cent.

No comment on the health status of the Negro would be complete which did not take into account the ravages of syphilis. This disease is a significant factor in the high Negro death rate. In fact, syphilis and its sequelae account very largely for the great excess of the Negro death rate today over that for the whites. Among the latter, the general trend for syphilis has been downward during the last two decades. Among the colored, the picture is a very different one. For colored males, the upward trend, since the year 1919, has been very marked, and among females, the rates for 1934 and 1935 were as high as those prevailing twenty-five years ago. Since the World War, state and municipal health departments, the United States Public Health Service and the American Social Hygiene Association have cooperated in putting before the public the best measures for the prevention and treatment of syphilis. These agencies have been successful in a limited degree in checking the mortality among the whites, but syphilis is actually taking a greater toll of Negro lives than it did in pre-war years. It is obvious that the movement for the control of venereal disease must concentrate more attention on the Negro population.

DECLINE IN DEATH RATE

After evaluating all of the relatively unfavorable items we have noted above, the fact still stands out that a remarkable decline in the mortality of the American Negro has taken place in a little less than two decades. In 1911, the standardized mortality rate of the colored Industrial policyholders of the Metropolitan was 18.5 per 1,000. In 1935, the death rate of these insured Negroes had declined to 11.8, which represents a drop of 36 per cent in this period. There would have been almost ten thousand more deaths of colored policyholders than actually occurred, in 1935, if the 1911 death rate had prevailed. This marked decline is due, for the most part, to improvements in the death rates from tuberculosis, pneumonia, malaria, typhoid fever, diphtheria, diarrhea and enteritis, and pellagra. A number of factors are clearly at work which are operating favorably on the life and health of our Negro population. Particularly noteworthy has been the great development of health activities in the South and Southwest. The betterment has been a broad one, affecting virtually all areas, with scarcely a state (in which there is a significant Negro population) failing to show a decided decline in the total death rate. While it is true that the mortality among Negroes is still high, reflecting marked deficiencies in the health provisions for them, we cannot but conclude that the public health movement is making a favorable impress upon our colored population.

The following graph shows the course of the death rate among both colored and white policyholders in the Metropolitan since 1911.

The general tendency of the lines of mortality, it will be observed, is very much the same for both colored and white. Both races show significant improvement. The greatest gains were

46.97 years, an increase of almost 6 years, or 14 per cent. The expectancy of Negro females at age 10 was 41.30 years in 1911–1912 as compared with 49.38 in 1935. This is a gain of 8 years, or 20 per cent, which is a better record than the increase of 7 years, or 14 per cent for insured white females. There can be no mistake in the conclusion that the last twenty-five years

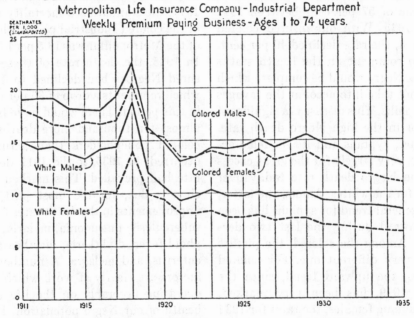

DEATHRATES OF WHITE AND COLORED PERSONS
Metropolitan Life Insurance Company - Industrial Department
Weekly Premium Paying Business - Ages 1 to 74 years.

made immediately after the influenza epidemic, that is, from 1918 to 1921. After 1921 the death rate among the colored showed a rising tendency, especially among the males. Beginning with 1930, however, an improvement was again registered for both sexes.

The general improvement in the death rate is, of course, reflected in the figures for expectation of life. In the two years 1911–1912 the expected life span for Metropolitan colored male policyholders at age 10 was 41.32 years; in 1935, the expectation was

have seen a pronounced improvement in the health situation of the colored people; and this, in spite of the fact that these years included the periods of the war, of the influenza epidemic, and of the recent economic depression, as well as an immense migration to Northern cities, often undertaken under the most unfavorable conditions.

FUTURE INDICATIONS

What are the indications for the future? In the first place, the pessimism concerning the Negro which prevailed in many places a few decades ago is no longer justified. The Negro in America, far from being destined for extinction, is steadily lowering his death rate and adding to his life span. The appalling mortality of the reconstruction period following the Civil War, with its death rate of 35 to 40 per 1,000 had been cut to about 15, in 1934. This is no higher than prevailed in a number of European countries before the World War. The Negro is getting a share, if not his full portion, of the benefits of sanitation and public health work in this country. His expectation of life in 1930 was the same as that of the white man about thirty years earlier. The male Negro in the general population who lives to reach the age of 50 has a life expectation within $3\frac{1}{2}$ years of that of the white man—and the Negro woman of the same age has about $4\frac{1}{2}$ years less of life expectation than the white woman. Our figures prove that the Negro race is physically well organized, and with improving environment will continue to increase its life expectancy.

I consider the outlook for the future of the Negro as very hopeful, provided environment improves and the race shares in the progress which communities are making in public health and personal hygiene. It should be possible, for example, to add fully two years to the expectation of life through intensification of public health work, whereby tuberculosis and infant mortality can be reduced by 25 per cent.

RACIAL IMMUNITY

We have an opportunity to consider, also, another phase of Negro health, namely, the question of sus-ceptibility and immunity to certain diseases. We have already given the main facts as to higher or lower death rates for white and colored persons. Shall we interpret these differences as reflecting, in any degree, racial immunity or susceptibility to the diseases in question?

I do not believe that there is such a thing as *absolute* racial immunity to any disease. But color, doubtless, does exert more or less influence over the prevalence of, and the death rate from many diseases. Just how much of this influence is due to racial immunity or susceptibility, and how much to racial customs, economic status and environment, is difficult if not impossible to determine. The factor of the "crossing" of the white and Negro bloods also beclouds the issue—since the mulatto, the octoroon, etc., have both white and Negro blood, although they are classified as "colored."

The Negro death rates for practically all diseases in which care and sanitation are of paramount importance are much higher than among the whites. It is probable that their higher death rate is due more than anything else to ignorance, poverty and lack of proper medical care. Pulmonary tuberculosis, typhoid fever, pellagra, malaria, and puerperal conditions are examples of such diseases in which the mortality rates are much affected by unfavorable or insanitary environment—or by low economic status—and all of them have higher death rates among Negroes.

Army investigators[1] state that the nervous system of Negroes shows

[1] Lieutenant-Colonel A. G. Love, M.C., U.S.A.; and Major C. B. Davenport, Sanitary Corps, U.S.A., "A Comparison of White and Colored Troops in Respect to Incidence of Disease," *Proceedings* of the National Academy of Sciences, Vol. 5, No. 3.

fewer cases of instability than that of the whites. Only about one-third as many cases, per 1,000 examined, of neurasthenia and "constitutional psychopathic state" was found in Negro troops as in the white. There were fewer eye and ear defects, and only half as many cases of functional cardiac disturbances of nervous origin. There was less diabetes and gallbladder infection and fewer cases of urinary calculus. The skin of the Negro was found to be more resistant to micro-organisms than that of the whites. Only one-third as many acute abscesses and infections of the connective tissues of the skin, and only one-quarter as many boils were found; there was much less dermatitis arising from traumatism. Venomous bites and stings were found to have less effect on the Negro, who has a thicker, tougher, more active and more highly pigmented skin than the white man; and this is doubtless both a mechanical and a chemical protection against micro-organisms which are responsible for certain diseases.

During the World War, the medical examinations of white and colored troops seemed to indicate that the Negro possessed a certain degree of immunity to diabetes. Within the last ten years, however, there have been important developments both in the treatment of this disease and in the mortality statistics for it. In the general population, and more especially in the rural sections, the diabetes death rate has always run much higher among the whites than for the Negroes. This still holds true for the population, in general. But among nearly two million Negroes insured by the Metropolitan Life Insurance Company, the diabetes death rate in very recent years has been going up rapidly and now equals that of the white policyholders. It should be borne in mind that these insured Negroes live, almost altogether, in the cities. The fact that the standardized diabetes death rate among them is now about equal to that of the whites may be due, in part, to their failure to obtain the benefit of the insulin treatment to the same extent as do the whites. Whether or not this be the case, the evidence is that there is little or no racial immunity among the Negroes to diabetes; for, even if the more or less carefree rural Negro is more immune than the white man, it now appears that in urban surroundings the Negro is subject to much sickness and high mortality from this disease.

DISEASE COMPARISONS

It is much more common to find Negroes than Anglo-Saxons who, at 20 to 30 years, have teeth that show no sign of decay, even though they have had very indifferent care. Negro teeth are naturally resistant to the organism of caries. There is, undoubtedly, less prevalence of diphtheria, scarlet fever and German measles among colored children than among whites, and there seems to be no doubt whatever that colored people are less apt to be attacked by the organism of acute anterior poliomyelitis. The best evidence is that measles is not so common in Negroes as in other races; but once attacked by this disease, the Negro has less resistance than the white child—and the same is true for diphtheria. The Negro child is more susceptible and less resistant to whooping cough than the white. The Negro attack-rate is much higher up to five years of age, where the disease is most common, most contagious and most fatal. The whooping cough death rate for Negroes is higher for all age groups where there is a significant mortality; and the Negro case-fatality rate is also higher.

Cancer of the skin is another condition in which the Negro death rate is relatively low. This holds true year after year; and it is very probable that the pigmentation in the Negro contains some protective element against skin cancers.

The death rate from cancer of the breast runs slightly higher among Negro women than among whites; and the former also sustain a higher mortality rate from rectal and anal cancers, although in other parts of the intestinal tract the opposite is true.

Erysipelas is one of the few diseases which shows a much lower death rate among Negroes. Their mortality from this disease, in fact, is only about two-thirds that for the whites. A very important difference, in favor of the Negro, also obtains for anemia.

There is good evidence that Negroes have extraordinary power to survive both wounds and major surgical operations and that, once convalescent, they are less liable to the reactions of fever and other complications.[2] With wounds there is less suppuration. Mental defects among Negroes oftener take the form of idiocy, and cases of acute mania run sooner into imbecility. The Negro, by and large, is of a more cheerful and carefree temperament than the white man. The rural Negro seldom commits suicide, but this cannot be said of the urban colored man. In our most recent Metropolitan Life Insurance Company experience, the Negro suicide rate is nearly two-thirds as high as the white.

I doubt whether we really know just what part of the higher mortality of the Negro is attributable to racial susceptibility and what part to the effects of racial customs and environmental conditions.

---

[2] Odum, Howard W., "Studies in History, Economics and Public Law," Faculty of Political Science, Columbia University, Vol. XXXVII, No. 3.

CHAPTER IV

THE PRINCIPAL CAUSES OF DEATH AMONG NEGROES:
A GENERAL COMPARATIVE STATEMENT*

S. J. HOLMES, PH.D.

Professor of Zoology, The University of California

INTRODUCTION

Barring the effects of migration into or out of the country, the relative rates of increase of whites and Negroes in the United States will obviously depend upon which race has the greater surplus of births over deaths. Ever since we have had reliable birth statistics the Negro birth rate has been higher than that of the whites and will probably continue to be so for many years. On the other hand, the mortality of the Negroes has been so much greater than that of the whites that the surplus of births over deaths has been to the advantage of the white race. Partly as a result of the restriction of immigration from Europe, the differences in the rates of natural increase of whites and Negroes have become reduced. When proper allowances are made for the influence of age composition in the two races, the present rates of natural increase are shown to be not far apart. In the near future, at least, the biological prospects of the Negroes in the United States will depend largely on the trend of mortality.

For many years birth rates and death rates have been falling in both whites and blacks. Since about 1890 the decline of both rates has been roughly parallel in the two races. In the reduction of both mortality and fertility in the Negroes we are dealing with a phenomenon of lag. But from the nature of the case the mortality of the whites cannot long continue to fall as it has done in the past, and it will fall much more slowly as the natural span of life is approached. There is no reason to doubt that the Negro may continue to make gains in life expectancy long after these have practically ceased in the whites. What will happen in the meantime to the birth rates of the two races we can only conjecture. There seems to be no clearly marked tendency for the present disparity in birth rates to be reduced, nor is there much to indicate that it will grow less in the future, at least for a considerable time to come.

If one would estimate the rôle of mortality in the future increase of the American Negroes, he would gain little by simply studying the trend of the general death rate. What is especially desirable to know in such an inquiry are the chief causes of Negro death and the reasons why these causes take so heavy a toll of life. Some of the older writers on Negro mortality were persuaded that the Negro is a "constitutionally inferior" type of human being and naturally prone to succumb to many diseases to a greater extent than his white competitors. In view of the many anthropological differences between Negroes and whites one might expect, *a priori*, that the races would differ in their reactions to

*Additional data on the topics covered in this article may be found in a volume by the writer on *The Negro's Struggle for Survival* which is being published by the University of California Press.

many diseases. Different degrees of immunity to infections are shown by many varieties of animals which are more closely related than Negroes and whites. A demonstration of such differences in reaction is much more difficult in human beings, however, than in the lower animals and plants which can be subjected to controlled experimentation. It is not often that Negroes and whites live under conditions that are so nearly alike that it is safe

high rank. Under slavery tuberculosis was probably less prevalent among Negroes than it was soon after the Civil War. The demoralization resulting from suddenly throwing over more than four million slaves on their own resources, combined with the miserable conditions under which so many of them were forced to live, led to a rapid increase of mortality from tuberculosis and from most other diseases. Probably the highest Negro

TABLE I

DEATH RATES PER 100,000 WHITE AND COLORED POPULATION OF BALTIMORE, MD., 1876–1920

| | Pulmonary Tuberculosis | | | | |
Years	White	Colored	Years	White	Colored
1876–80	299	633	1901–05	189	488
1881–85	279	667	1906–10	179	498
1886–90	239	552	1911–15	148	444
1891–95	199	485		129*	
1896–00	174	440	1916–20	150	406
	All Forms of Tuberculosis				
Years	White	Colored	Years	White	Colored
1901–05	215	559	1911–15	173	529
1906–10	203	562		150*	
			1916–20	172	487

* Inclusive of five years average of pulmonary deaths in sanatoria.

to attribute all of their differences in disease incidence to constitutional causes, especially since environmental factors include such influences as education and previous exposure to infections, as well as present habits, and such direct influences as food, climate, housing, and medical care. For this reason differences in mortality which some ascribe to racial factors are claimed by others as due to environment, and in most cases there is no very conclusive way of deciding the issue.

TUBERCULOSIS

Among the diseases affecting the Negro, tuberculosis has always held a

mortality from tuberculosis occurred sometime in the '80s. One of the best records of the trend of mortality from this disease is afforded by the statistics of Baltimore compiled by Dr. Howard. These data, corrected for deaths of residents outside the city, are shown in Table I.

The trend of tuberculosis mortality in Washington, D.C. is similar to that of Baltimore, the highest Negro rate occurring in the period 1885–1889.

Since 1920 the decline of mortality from tuberculosis has been decided, though relatively less rapid than in the whites. In order to obtain abundant data for a constant area I have calculated the mortality from tuberculosis in the white and colored population of the Registration states of 1920 from 1920 to 1929, inclusive, after making allowances for an undercount of 150,000 in 1920, as estimated by the Bureau of the Census. The trend is shown in Table II.

Further valuable information is furnished by the mortality data of the

period show a tuberculosis rate eight times greater than that of the white girls." After middle age the difference in the tuberculosis death rates of the two races is not nearly so great. According to Dublin, "More than five years could be added to the life span of the colored people if tuberculosis were brought under control."

It is probable that the same factors

TABLE II
DEATHS AND DEATH RATES PER 100,000 FROM TUBERCULOSIS OF THE WHITE AND
COLORED POPULATIONS IN THE REGISTRATION STATES OF 1920
(1920–1929)

| Year | White | | Colored | |
	Number	Rate	Number	Rate
1920	78,479	99.38	18,887	258.52
1921	68,179	84.97	17,560	236.07
1922	68,157	83.61	17,327	228.86
1923	67,684	81.76	17,017	220.90
1924	65,335	77.73	17,720	226.13
1925	63,169	74.03	18,004	225.93
1926	63,740	73.61	18,426	227.44
1927	59,507	67.72	17,799	216.17
1928	59,393	66.63	17,944	214.47
1929	57,249	63.32	17,417	204.93

insured wage earners of the Metropolitan Life Insurance Company. In 1911 the mortality from tuberculosis per 100,000 policy holders was 230.8 for white males, 165.4 for white females, 422.2 for colored males, and 415.0 for colored females. In 1930 the rates had fallen to 68.0 for white males, 57.1 for white females, 223.8 for colored males, and 213.0 for colored females. The marked differences between the whites and the colored in the relation of mortality from tuberculosis to age is strikingly shown by the statistics of the same company. In ages 10–14, according to Dublin, the "tuberculosis death rate among colored boys is eleven times as high as it is among white boys of the same ages. Colored girls of the same age

which have reduced the death rate from tuberculosis and changed the character of the disease in the white race are operative also among the Negroes. The Senegalese troups inducted into the French army during the World War suffered severely from tuberculosis and not infrequently died from this disease in a few months or even weeks after exposure. In the colored troops from the United States the disease assumed more of the slow chronic character commonly found in the whites. Apparently the American Negro is gradually becoming immunized directly or indirectly to this prevalent malady. The extent to which he may be permanently handicapped as a result of his racial inheritance is a difficult problem. His lung capacity is distinctly less than that of the whites, as is shown by the measurements taken during the Civil War and the investigations of Smillie and Augustine and of Roberts and Crabtree on large and comparable samples of whites and Negroes in the South. How far the Negro's so-called "tropical lung" may predispose him to tuberculosis is uncertain, although it may well be a factor. But whatever the natural susceptibility of the Negroes may be, it is probable that in the future they will suffer relatively much less from tuberculosis than they have in the past.

PNEUMONIA

Another chief cause of Negro mortality is the acute respiratory infections, especially the pneumonias. The statistics on mortality from pneumonia are eminently unsatisfactory, owing to changing fashions of diagnosis. Since pneumonia is responsible for the fatal termination of several other infections, such as influenza, measles, and whooping cough, the proportion of deaths ascribed to the initial disease and the final cause of death has been subject to much variation. In general, the mortality rate for the colored population has been over 50 per cent higher than that of the whites. It is a striking fact that the disparity of the pneumonia rates of the two races is very much greater in cities than in rural areas. In general, urban life is relatively more fatal to Negroes than to whites, but the Negro mortality rate from pneumonia is increased relatively much more than mortality from other causes.

Mortality from pneumonia, as for most other diseases, has gradually declined, although at a rather slow rate, and the decline has been rather less rapid in Negroes than in whites. In the extensive experience of the Metropolitan Life Insurance Company since the period 1911–16, while the pneumonia mortality had been falling in the white insured wage earners, it had actually been rising somewhat in the colored wage earners. The U.S. mortality statistics show a slow decline in the pneumonia death rate of the colored population during the last few years.

While the Negro has a relatively high death rate from all the respiratory infections, he seems to be especially prone to succumb to lobar pneumonia. Since bronchial pneumonia is more prevalent in earlier years, whereas lobar pneumonia is especially common in advanced age groups, the difference in age composition of the two races would explain in part the relation mentioned, but it cannot be the sole cause. The matter of racial susceptibility is, of course, complicated by the fact that the unfavorable status of the Negro has the effect of enhancing the death rate from respiratory infections, as from most other diseases. In fact, the influence of environment, including under this category the previous history of the individual, is much greater for respiratory diseases than for most other maladies. In order to secure data somewhat less influenced by extraneous factors than those derived from the general population, I have compiled the statistics on the admission rates and death rates from respiratory infections in the U.S. Army during the World War. The data shown in Table III bring out some rather striking facts. They include only the cases appearing after the recruits had been inducted into the Army after having passed the physical tests of fitness for military service.

While it cannot be assumed that environmental factors surrounding the white and colored troops were precisely the same either in Europe or in the United States, they are doubtless much more nearly alike than in the general population. Nevertheless, differences in the mortality rates of the two races are even greater than in the general population, even in cities. Es-

a notorious fact that our data on case mortality are miserably inadequate, and there is relatively little available for pneumonia aside from the Army data. Dr. F. B. Kelly, who has reported on 6,500 cases of lobar pneumonia in Cook County Hospital, Chicago, states that "From 1917–24 the case fatality was 39.2 per cent for 3,749 white males, 34.9 per cent for 818 white females, 30.6 per cent for 1,876 colored males, and 31.7 per cent for 388 colored females. The case fatality for the two races was about the same up to the 40th-year-and-over group, above which the Negro

TABLE III

PERCENTAGE OF DEATHS TO CASES RESPIRATORY DISEASES IN THE
AMERICAN ARMY, 1917–1919

	Influenza		Broncho-Pneumonia		Lobar Pneumonia	
	W	C	W	C	W	C
U.S. Army in U.S.	3.1	4.0	25.8	23.0	19.8	19.4
U.S. Army in Europe	3.3	3.4	27.1	19.9	26.8	18.8
Total U.S. Army	3.1	3.8	26.5	22.0	22.2	19.3

pecially noteworthy are the remarkable differences in mortality from lobar pneumonia, both in the United States and in Europe. This high mortality is due largely to the relatively high admission rate of the colored troops. When we calculate the ratio of deaths to cases the rather surprising fact appears that after the colored soldiers once contracted pneumonia the chance of recovery was not greatly different from that of the white soldiers. Evidently the different mortality rates of the two races are not the result of differences in care received during illness. This factor may be of importance in the general population, but it is difficult to secure conclusive information on this point. It is

had the greater resistance." The human material coming into a large urban hospital may, of course, be selected somewhat differently in the two races. In the endeavor to secure additional information on the case fatality of pneumonia in relation to race I have written to several physicians associated with large hospitals in the Southern States but without obtaining many conclusive data. Dr. J. H. Musser, who has kindly supplied statistics from the Charity Hospital of New Orleans of much the same kind as those of Dr. Kelly, states that although Negroes are very apt to contract pneumonia, "we have never considered that after the Negro has developed pneumonia he is more likely to die than the white man." Dr. J. Ritter has furnished data from Miami, Florida showing a case mortality from pneumonia of 52.0 per cent in 202 whites, and 52.9 per cent among 170 blacks.

In interpreting the significance of the mortality and morbidity statistics on pneumonia it should be pointed out that these present a marked contrast to those of tuberculosis. The death rates from these two great scourges of our colored population are greatly increased by unfavorable surroundings. So far as initial infections with tuberculosis are concerned, several studies on the proportion of Negro and white children of various age groups have shown that most Negroes, as well as whites, especially in urban areas, give a positive tuberculin reaction. Negroes are much more apt to develop severe cases of tuberculosis later in life and their case fatality rate is much higher than among the whites. Among the Negroes, as well as the whites, the great majority become infected with tuberculosis, but of those infected a larger proportion of Negroes develop severe cases. In pneumonia, so far as our data indicate—and they are not as complete as could be desired— a much larger proportion of Negroes become infected, but of those infected the proportion of cases that prove fatal is at least not much higher than in the whites.

One cannot be safe in drawing conclusions in regard to the influence of racial heredity in causing these differences of reaction without taking into consideration the effect of gradually acquired immunity built up by overcoming minimal infections during early life. The Army experience dur-

ing the World War showed that city-bred recruits, although less husky than those from rural areas, were less prone to come down with many infections, such as measles, mumps, etc., than recruits from the country. One might surmise, therefore, that Negro soldiers drawn largely from the rural South, were less protected against various infections which often lead to pneumonia, if not against the initial infection with the latter disease. This surmise receives a measure of support from the fate of the Senegalese troops recruited for the French army. With little previous exposure to either tuberculosis or pneumonia in their native land, these troops suffered severely from both these maladies and large numbers of them died. But after their first baptism of fire their mortality rate from these diseases was not particularly high. How Negroes and whites would respond to respiratory infections if they lived under the same environmental conditions and were subjected to the same exposure to infection from early infancy we cannot tell.

Under present conditions there are two, and not improbably three, important factors involved in the differential mortality of Negroes and whites from respiratory diseases: (1) external factors, such as food, climate, care, etc.; (2) previous immunization due to contact with infective germs; and (3) racial heredity. Whether the third factor is operative or not, differential mortality from tuberculosis and acute respiratory infections will have much to do with determining the vital prospects of the American Negro. These diseases are much more severe in the North than in the South.

They constitute very important factors in determining whether or not Negroes can thrive permanently in the Northern states. As I have pointed out in a previous paper, deaths among Negroes have exceeded births in the Northern states until less than two decades ago, and the recent excess of births over deaths in the North is due to the exceptionally favorable age distribution of Northern Negroes. The Negro population of the North is mainly urban and largely for this reason its natural increase is not sufficient for permanent maintenance. But the destructive effect of cities of the South is even greater than those of the North, and this despite their greatly reduced Negro mortality from respiratory infections. Should the American Negro acquire as much resistance as the whites to the pneumonias and the maladies of which they form the sequelae, urban life, both North and South, will not prove nearly so severe a handicap to the Negro as it has in the past.

HEART DISEASE

Negroes are especially prone to diseases of the circulatory system. Mortality from heart disease among Negroes has on the average been running about 50 per cent higher than among the whites, notwithstanding the fact that the higher age composition of the whites would favor an increased death rate from this cause. A recent summary of twenty years' experience of the Metropolitan Life Insurance Company with diseases of the circulatory system shows that the colored policy holders suffer from a much higher death rate than the whites from organic diseases of the heart and the frequently associated disorders of arteriosclerosis, cerebral hemorrhage, and chronic nephritis. According to Dublin, "it is especially among the colored patients that syphilitic heart disease is prevalent; in this group it accounts for about a third of the cases." Davidson and Thoroughman, as a result of their studies, find over 25 per cent of positive Wassermanns in Negro heart cases and conclude that "syphilitic heart disease causes the greatest amount of disability next to the arteriosclerotic group." The adjusted death rates of Negroes from nephritis have often been twice as great as in whites, and the much higher mortality rate is found from early childhood to advanced ages.

VENEREAL DISEASES

Unquestionably a very important influence in the relatively high mortality of American Negroes is the prevalence of syphilitic infection. Estimates of the extent to which this disease is distributed in the general population, both white and colored, are very discordant. The most extensive typical random sample of this disease is afforded by the soldiers recruited for the World War. In this examination only the more obvious cases were detected, but the data are important for the purpose of comparing the prevalence of the disease in the two races. The admission rates for the entire army in the United States and in Europe were 12.65 per thousand for the whites and 64.99 for the colored. Deaths ascribed to syphilis in the Army were .02 per thousand for the whites and .18 per thousand for the colored. The extensive data on mortality from syphilis compiled by the Metropolitan Life Insurance Company between 1911 and 1920 showed the following rates per 100,000 policy holders: white males, 16.4; white females, 7.1; colored males, 46.1; colored females, 25.7.

Much information concerning the prevalence of syphilis in our colored population has been brought to light as the result of several surveys carried on by the U.S. Public Health Service. In an investigation by Carley and Winger on 7,228 rural Negroes in Mississippi the planters rounded up all their Negro employes, and tests were applied to all over nine years of age. A positive reaction was given by 19.3 per cent of the males and 18.0 per cent of the females, the maximum number occurring between the ages 20 and 29. No clinical cases were included and all the subjects examined were apparently well. The results may well justify the conclusions of the authors that "from a public health and economic point of view syphilis is probably the major public health problem among the rural Mississippi Negroes today." Several surveys in other localities have yielded similar results. Doubtless the prevalence of syphilis is an important factor in the high proportion of abortions and stillbirths in our Negro population and in the high rate for early infant mortality. It is also an important factor in the high Negro mortality from nephritis, heart disease, cerebral hemorrhage, and various other maladies. Directly and indirectly syphilis is a powerful influence in checking the natural increase of our colored population.

Another check on Negro fertility is gonococcus infection, which is es-

pecially prevalent and not improbably is largely responsible for the rather high proportion of childless marriages. If by any miracle venereal infections could be completely eradicated our Negro population would respond by a decided reduction of mortality and a very marked increase of the birth rate.

SCARLET FEVER, MEASLES, DIPHTHERIA

Although Negroes succumb more frequently than whites from most causes of death, there are several diseases to which they are relatively immune. Scarlet fever has long been recognized as relatively uncommon in the Negro race. From the earliest data down to the present time mortality from scarlet fever has been three or more times as high in whites as in Negroes. The experience of the Metropolitan Life Insurance Company (1911–16) showed the following rates per 100,000 for all persons over one year of age: white males, 10.6; white females, 8.6; colored males, 2.5; colored females, 2.2. The admission rate for scarlet fever during the World War was nearly nine times as high for white as for colored troops, and the death rate precisely nine times as high.

The mortality from measles, although complicated by the fact that deaths ascribed to this cause are so frequently due to pneumonia to which the Negro is peculiarly susceptible, has been rather higher in the whites than in the Negroes. Up to 1900 the censuses showed a somewhat higher mortality rate for this disease in the colored population. One cannot be entirely certain that the Negroes are coming to be more immune to measles, although the trend of the statistics seems to support this conclusion. Both the admission rate and the mortality rate for measles in the U.S. Army in the World War were about 50 per cent higher for white than for colored troops. The relatively low death rate of Negroes from measles is the more significant because the factors of care and other environmental factors which are so important in this disease would tend to cause a relatively high Negro death rate.

A much more decided difference in relation to race is shown by diphtheria. Year after year, in practically every city and state, the death rate from diphtheria, with remarkable consistency, is significantly lower in the colored than in the white population. The same racial difference was found in deaths assigned to the croup of former days. The differences occur in every age group after the first year up to the ages in which the cases become too few in number to be statistically significant, but in deaths under one year of age there is an equally consistent disparity in favor of the whites. Apparently the susceptibility of the two races to diphtheria is not due to their natural immunity, as revealed by the Schick test, for the studies of Doull, Fales, Bull, Wright, and others have shown that the percentages of positive reactions to this test are not greatly different in white and colored children. In diphtheria, perhaps even more than in measles and scarlet fever, the advantages of superior status and education are in favor of the whites, especially since the chances of recovery are so dependent upon promptness of treatment with anti-toxin in the early stages of this disease.

SKIN INFECTIONS

The Negro is commonly considered to be relatively resistant to infections caused by streptococci, a fact which probably accounts for his relative immunity to scarlet fever. The racial differences in mortality from erysipelas are very striking. The disease is peculiarly fatal in early infancy when infection often occurs through the umbilicus soon after birth. A comparison of the infant mortality statistics under one year from 1914 to 1923 shows that 7,498 white and 284 colored children died of this disease. Infant deaths from other causes were in the ratio of 1 colored to 7.45 whites, but those from erysipelas were 1 colored to over 30.33 whites. The mortality rate becomes reduced in later childhood, but it rises rather sharply in the old age groups. A very striking contrast is presented in the infant death rate from tetanus. Like erysipelas, tetanus often gains access through the umbilicus in early infancy, and both diseases would tend to be more readily contracted in the unsanitary conditions which so often surround the Negro child. Hence the fact that tetanus mortality is very much higher in Negro than in white infants, while the mortality from erysipelas is precisely the reverse, is a strong indication that the Negro has a natural immunity to the latter disease.

For most diseases of the skin the comparative immunity of the Negro is quite marked. The skin of the Negro differs from that of the white man not only in its pigmentation but also in its dermal and connective tissue elements and sweat glands. The peculiar tendency of the Negro skin to form keloid ridges and tumors and its different response to syphilitic infection point to differences in the physiological reactions of the skin in the two races. The mortality statistics of the Metropolitan Life Insurance Company show every year a consistently lower death rate in the colored than in the white races for most cutaneous affections. Many skin diseases rarely lead to fatal results, but most of them attack the whites more readily than the Negroes, as is

TABLE IV

ADMISSION RATES FOR SKIN DISEASES PER 1,000 WHITE AND COLORED TROOPS IN THE U.S. ARMY, APRIL, 1917–DECEMBER 31, 1919

	White	Colored
Carbuncle	.59	.13
Furuncle	5.44	1.59
Abscess	4.17	3.15
Cellulitis	3.46	1.62
Defects of Nails	2.21	.64
Eczema	1.06	.50
Herpes	.80	1.03
Scabies	8.29	2.37
Psoriasis	.40	.09
Impetigo	.71	.21
Other diseases	5.03	4.17

quite clearly shown by the experience of the U.S. Army in the World War. The admission rates of white and colored troops for a number of skin affections are shown in Table IV.

In their reactions to hookworm, a not unimportant cause of depleted vitality and death in the Southern states, especially until recent years, the Negroes, as several studies have shown, are less heavily infested and suffer much less from the infestations which they harbor than the whites.

CANCER

If we interpret the statistics at their face value we must conclude that the Negroes are relatively free from cancer, but cancer statistics are notoriously deceptive. The age composition of the white population favors a higher cancer mortality because there are relatively more whites in older age groups, in which cancer is especially prevalent. It is easy, however, to make allowances for this circumstance by splitting up the population into five-year age groups and comparing the mortality rates of the two races in each group. I have recently made a comparison of cancer mortality in the white and colored population of a large part of the United States. (See Table V.) In order to avoid certain sources of error while obtaining an abundance of statistical data, I chose a constant area, the Registration states of 1920, and have compared the cancer mortality of the white and colored population in each group for each year of the decade 1920 to 1929, inclusive. Mortality rates for the several age groups were also calculated for cancers of different organ systems. In every year from 1920 to 1929 the mortality from cancer was nearly twice as high in the white as in the colored population. Year by year there was a steady and marked increase in cancer mortality of the whites and a somewhat greater, though a little less regular, increase in the colored population. If we break up our populations into five-year age groups we find a similar trend in every group, both white and colored, in which the rates are based on a large number of cases. When we compare the cancer mortality of the white and colored within the limits of the several age groups, however, we find some curious facts. Among which it is between two and three times as great as in colored males. Cancer mortality in colored females greatly exceeds that of white females

TABLE V
Deaths and Death Rates from Total Cancer per 100,000, 1920-29 Inclusive, in the Registration States of 1920

Ages		Number Whites	Number Colored	Rates Whites	Rates Colored
20–24	M	1,691	173	4.76	4.69
	F	1,554	307	4.21	7.45
25–29	M	2,509	234	7.19	6.83
	F	3,612	805	10.28	21.71
30–34	M	4,002	387	12.09	13.48
	F	8,191	1,407	25.46	48.26
35–39	M	7,933	705	23.97	22.60
	F	17,471	2,709	56.47	93.57
40–44	M	13,529	1,237	47.52	51.37
	F	29,020	3,670	109.48	171.62
45–49	M	21,723	1,681	84.48	71.67
	F	40,465	4,338	174.23	246.76
50–54	M	33,345	2,185	153.88	121.73
	F	51,167	4,126	257.56	317.47
55–59	M	44,282	2,006	262.77	181.19
	F	56,546	3,245	360.46	415.40
60–64	M	55,267	1,919	399.93	221.93
	F	61,459	2,961	473.28	451.64
65–69	M	59,582	1,613	606.23	285.78
	F	60,960	2,192	642.88	483.16
70–74	M	52,898	1,237	791.24	351.22
	F	52,385	1,601	785.76	496.69
75–79	M	38,032	756	993.09	377.54
	F	38,783	991	957.44	523.83
80–84	M	19,373	376	1,130.93	380.64
	F	22,285	608	1,105.77	550.72
85–89	M	7,368	201	1,187.86	469.29
	F	9,743	330	1,208.73	666.93

males up to age 45 cancer mortality in the whites is not markedly greater, if not a little less, than in the colored. After this age cancer mortality in the white male becomes increasingly higher than in the colored as we advance to the older age groups, in the age groups from 20 up to about age 60, after which the mortality of white females becomes increasingly preponderant up to the advanced ages, when it is about double the rate for colored females. This sex difference in the two races is largely due to cancer of the female genital organs, which in colored females is more frequent than in white females in all age groups from 20 to 85. Uterine cancer stands out as a striking exception to the general rule that mortality from all kinds of cancer is higher in the white than in the colored population. One reason for this may be the greater neglect of uterine traumas associated with childbirth. The tendency of fibroid growths to develop in Negroes, the so-called "fibroid diathesis," whatever may be its cause, may be an additional factor in the high death rate from conditions diagnosed as cancer of the uterus. If we remove the cases of cancer of the breast and female genital organs from the total number of cases of cancer mortality of both white and colored females and calculate the age specific mortality rates of the two groups, we find that in the older age groups the mortality rates for white females exceed those for colored females, but in the earlier age groups the relation is reversed.

This fact is illustrative of a general and peculiar difference in the racial trend of cancer mortality with advancing age. I have calculated the age specific mortality rates from various types of cancer in the two races and found that whatever type of cancer we are dealing with the mortality rates in the two races are not far apart, or are even higher in the colored than in the whites in the early age groups. But they come to be very much higher in whites in advanced age groups. Even in cancer of the skin, in which the differences in advanced ages are enormous, there is little difference up to about middle age.

One cannot reasonably explain the different age trends of cancer mortality in the two races as due to differences in diagnosis, because there seems to be no valid reason for supposing that diagnosis is much more accurate for young Negroes than for old ones. The evidence seems to support the view that the difference is largely a peculiarity of race.

If one should ask how cancer mortality affects the struggle for numerical supremacy between whites and blacks the answer which seems immediately to suggest itself would probably be wrong. Since our statistics indicate that the general mortality rate from cancer is relatively high in whites, one would naturally infer that its racial incidence would favor the vital prospects of the colored population. But quite aside from the fact that the number of deaths ascribed to cancer in the colored population is probably too small, the deaths occurring in the reproductive period of life are relatively more numerous in the colored than in the whites. Over four-fifths of the deaths from cancer occur after the usual reproductive period is passed. From the standpoint of the biological struggle for existence it matters relatively little what becomes of people after they no longer contribute to the natural increase of their kind. Our statistics show that for the age periods in which the birth rate is relatively high cancer mortality is somewhat greater in the colored than in the white population. With greater accuracy of diagnosis of the true causes of death, the preponderance of cancer mortality in younger members of the colored population would probably be considerably increased. Moreover, a very important factor in the situation is the marked prevalence of uterine cancer in colored females. This circumstance would naturally affect the birth rate of the colored population more than that of the whites. Hence the cancer mortality that is really effective in the long run in its influence on the survival rates of the two races is probably exercising its most destructive effect on the colored, and hence the Negro population of the United States.

HOMICIDE

To the racially destructive influences affecting our Negro population one must add deaths from violence, and especially homicide. In the Negro the rate for homicide has been from five to eight times as high as in the white population. In the experience of the Metropolitan Life Insurance Company (1911–16) the homicide rate for Negro males from 15 to 35 years of age was about ten times that of white males; for this age period "homicide ranked third as a cause of death, being exceeded only by the figures for tuberculosis and the acute respiratory diseases." The homicide rate in colored females is about one-fourth as high as in colored males and about four times as high as in white females of the same age limits. As a factor affecting the death rate of the colored population, especially in the reproductive period, homicide plays a not unimportant rôle.

INFANT MORTALITY

One important cause of the high mortality of Negroes is their high death rate in infancy, and, to a less extent, in early childhood. Infant mortality has been greatly reduced from the appallingly high rates prevailing in the '80s and '90s and it is now not far from the white rate of about twenty years ago. The high infant mortality rate of Negroes is largely the result of environmental factors, although Negro infants are favored by a lower death rate from certain causes, such as erysipelas, congenital malformations, and injuries at birth. A reduction of infant and child mortality contributes largely to the biological increase of a people, because in a few years it leads to an increase of individuals in the reproductive period. This is especially true of the Negroes, because they are propagated relatively more than the whites from young mothers. The reduction of mortality rates is more readily accomplished in the younger than in the older periods of life, and it is in the earlier years that the greatest gains have been effected. If the death rate of Negroes continues to decline we may expect that the mortality of young Negroes will be reduced relatively more than that of young whites.

GENERAL SUMMARY AND CONCLUSIONS

The most effective factors in checking the natural increase of the Negro population are not necessarily the diseases which cause the highest death rate; they are the diseases which kill people before the close of the reproductive period. From the standpoint of biological survival the most formidable enemies of the Negro are tuberculosis, the respiratory infections, venereal diseases, uterine cancer, the intestinal disorders of infancy, and puerperal fever. Although cardiac affections, chronic nephritis and cerebral hemorrhage claim many Negroes before age 45, their devastations are mainly confined to people who have passed this milestone of their career.

If diseases act as selective agents affecting the survival rates of different races, their fatality must depend to a certain extent upon inherited racial peculiarities. If a high mortality is the direct result of an anthropological character, such as a relatively small lung capacity, the differential death rate thus produced will remain a permanent handicap, however greatly the mortality from this cause may be reduced. It seems not unlikely that the Negro suffers from some handicaps of this kind; but, on the other hand, he is favored by some partial immunities which will probably constitute a valuable permanent asset. That the Negro is "constitutionally inferior" to the whites, as was formerly asserted by some writers, is a conclusion devoid of adequate foundation. With the possible exception of his greater proneness to tuberculosis and the acute respiratory infections, he is, on the whole, probably a better animal than the white man, But granting that the higher mortality of the Negro from most diseases is due to an unfavorable economic and educational status, these diseases are nevertheless selective as a result of inherited racial peculiarities. In human beings natural selection often works in devious and indirect ways. The relationship between black skin or kinky hair and a reduced span of life may be very indirect and may involve the factors of inadequate education and the handicaps of poverty. But these and other social factors affect the Negro unfavorably because he happens to possess the anthropological features which cause him to be recognized and treated as a Negro. A disease may act as a selective agent on the basis of color or other racial characteristic quite regardless of the fact that these characteristics may not have the slightest direct influence upon the disease. It will so act as long as environmental conditions render the disease more fatal to one race than to another. The operation of natural selection depends upon differences in genetic constitution, but the relation of these to mortality may be very indirect, and may involve the cooperation of influences of the social environment. Doubtless the American Negroes will be subject to the adverse selective action of diseases for many years to come, although their handicaps from this cause may gradually be reduced.